To: Athena
(my student!)

6 Nov '9

Every life is a journey.
I hope you find this
portion of mine interesting.

Sincerely,

Robert M. Fletcher

AN AIRMAN'S JOURNEY
From 1947 Enlistment through 1972 Retirement

Always A New Adventure

Robert M. Fletcher, Sr.

Fort Benning, Georgia • Lackland, San Antonio, Texas • Randolph, San Antonio, Texas • Goodfellow, San Angelo, Texas • Las Vegas, Nevada • Robins, Warner Robins, Georgia • Camp Stoneman, California • Johnson, Japan • Korea • Germany • University of Georgia, (AFROTC) • Tyndall, Panama City, Florida • Tinker, Oklahoma City, Oklahoma • Oklahoma A&M, Stillwater, Oklahoma • Pinecastle, Orlando, Florida • McCoy, Orlando, Florida • Naha, Okinawa, Japan • Grand Forks, North Dakota • Shemya, Alaska • Ramstein, Germany • Simmons, Fort Bragg, North Carolina • Pope, Fayetteville, North Carolina • Tanson Knut–Vietnam • Eglin, Florida

Strategic Book Publishing and Rights Co.

Strategic Book Publishing and Rights Co
USA | Singapore

ISBN: 978-1-63135-400-7

Designed by PeggyAnn Rupp
Dedicated Book Services (www.netdbs.com)

When I think of a life "well done" I think of you.
I love you dad.

Robert M. Fletcher, Jr

Publisher's Note:

As the CEO and owner of a mid-sized publishing company, when my father said, "Son, I've written my memoirs", I shuddered, knowing what was next. At the same time, I knew I had to deliver before his 85th birthday, so the race was on.

It's been an incredibly fun project and quite a family connector. I am pleased beyond belief at how this memoir looks and feels. I would like to give a special and sincere thanks to Leslie for patiently typing 200 pages of handwritten text (see the next page) and Peggy Rupp and DBS for their caring design and quality execution of "a bunch of pictures and some text".

It has been my sincere personal pleasure to publish *"Always a New Adventure"*. And now, I have to go create his business cards and press release and set up some book signings because he wants to get out there and sell it. Go Dad, go!

Robert Fletcher, Jr.

Publisher
Boca Raton, Florida
May 2015

PAT CAME DOWN FROM ATLANTA FOR MY GRADUATION AND COMMISSIONING. ONCE AGAIN I HELD UP MY HAND AND SWORE TO PROTECT THE CONSTITUTION AND MY COUNTRY. IT WAS ONE OF THE PROUDEST MOMENTS OF MY LIFE WHEN PAT PINNED ON MY SHINEY NEW SECOND LIEUTENANT'S BARS. I WAS NOW AN OFFICER IN THE UNITED STATES AIR FORCE!

I NOTICED A LARGE GROUP OF NCO'S HANGING AROUND DURING OUR COMMISSIONING CEREMONIES. IT WAS A TRADITION THAT A NEW OFFICER HAD TO GIVE ONE DOLLAR TO THE FIRST ENLISTED PERSON TO SALUTE HIM. I KNEW ABOUT THIS AND HAD MY DOLLAR READY. THAT WAS A PROUD MOMENT TOO.

TABLE OF CONTENTS

CHAPTER

ENLISTMENT

JULY 10, 1947

▶ **HIGH SCHOOL GRADUATION**
MAY 1947

▶ **FORT BENNING**
GEORGIA

▶ **LACKLAND AIR FORCE BASE**
SAN ANTONIO, TEXAS

▶ **RANDOLPH AIR FORCE BASE**
SAN ANTONIO, TEXAS

▶ **FORT SAM HOUSTON**
SAN ANTONIO, TEXAS

S pring of 1947. I was 17 on May 5, 1947. I graduated from high school that month. This was in Fitzgerald, Georgia, a small South Georgia town of approximately 6,000.

Fitzgerald was a farming community. The only large businesses were a garment factory and a cotton mill where cloth was made. During my junior and senior years of high school, I was in a quandary about a career choice and what kind of work I wanted to do. I had done a paper route, delivered groceries on a bicycle, picked cotton, shook peanuts, worked in a fertilizer plant and tobacco markets, peddled door-to-door chickens, vegetables and eggs, sold fishing worms and lots of other things. I was always trying to make money, for my family was not well-off and there were twelve of us. From the age of 12 I bought my own clothes. In Fitzgerald I could only look forward to working in a grocery store or a filling station.

For Years, all kids graduated after 11 years of school. Elementary school was 7 years and high school 4 years. High school had 16 credits, 4 each year, all "hard core". There were 2 recesses each day and you went home for lunch or brought a "brown bag". There were no buses if you lived inside the city limits. The principal and one secretary ran the entire school. There was no guidance department or school nurse. Discipline was not a problem. There were no frills or optional courses. All extra-curricular activities, such as football, band, etc., had to be done after school. There was only one coach. He taught class full-time and coached football, baseball, etc., after school.

After WWII there were so many veterans returning and jobs were scarce, so it was decided to add the

COLLETTE McDOWELL
CARRIED IN MY
BILLFOLD IN BASIC

MY "HOME"

6348

DEC 47

Pvt. Robert M. Fletcher
14264605
Squadron BM8 Flight 2159
Lackland Air Base
San Antonio, Texas

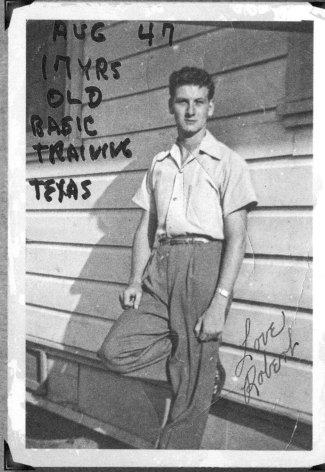

AUG 47
17 YRS
OLD
BASIC
TRAINING
TEXAS

love
Bobok

12th grade to keep students off the job market for a year. Then they added physical education (P.E.) and other "frill" classes. If I had told my father I had P.E. at school, he would have died laughing. He made sure I had plenty of exercise at home.

In the news at the time there was discussion of reinstating the draft or requiring every male to take military training. It was called "UMT" (Universal Military Training). I never considered college. I never knew anyone who went to college except a few rich kids at school.

I had five brothers in WWII. I was a teenager most of WWII, so I was well acquainted with the military. Since it seemed I would be drafted anyway, I decided to enlist. I talked it over with my Dad and Grandfather. Both said, "Get a job you don't get shot at. Stay and get a pension. We have worked hard all our lives and have nothing!" Good advice! I'm glad I listened to my elders.

I didn't like Navy uniforms, and I certainly didn't want to carry a rifle on foot in the Army. So, I decided I would enlist in the Army Air Corps and be a pharmacist. I hitchhiked to Tifton, Georgia, about 30 miles away. The recruiter gave me a battery of tests. You needed a score of 70 to enlist. I had a score of 120 which was enough to get me into any tech school in the military. I barely passed the weight requirement. I ate a lot of bananas weighing and came in at 129 pounds. I must have been pretty skinny! My parents had to sign a lot of papers because of my age.

A week later I had to report back to the recruiter. I gave all my stuff away; I had received mostly clothes for graduation; packed a small bag and hitchhiked back to Tifton.

My Mom gave me $5.00! OFF TO FACE THE WORLD AT 17 WITH $5.00! The recruiter put me on a Greyhound bus to Ft. Benning, Georgia. My older brother, Louie, had been a paratrooper at Ft. Benning during WWII.

Ft. Benning is a huge base. The old original base consisted of 3 or 4 huge groups of barracks. I think they called them "quadrangles". They were built in the 30's with several stories and built with bricks and steel. Imposing structures still in use today. Each quadrangle would house a division of men, approximately 20,000.

Most of one of the barracks was used for processing men in and out of the Army. We were in many long, long lines. At times, my "in" processing line would be next to the "out" processing line. I'll never forget those guys yelling at us, "You'll be sorry!"

I experienced for the first time standing naked in a long line of naked men!

The enlistment for regular Army was for 2 years; 3 years for the Army Air Corps. I was unaware that the Air Force was becoming an independent command that very month.

I was sworn in July 10, 1947. I was given my first serial number. You gave up being an individual and became a number. I was RA14264605. The "RA" stood for "Regular Army". The "14" stood for southeast U.S. I was to have 4 more serial numbers in my career.

The swearing-in is scary. You hold up your arm and repeat a lot of statements. Some said you would lay down your life for your country if necessary. Once you said "I will", your butt belonged to sergeants and the Army!

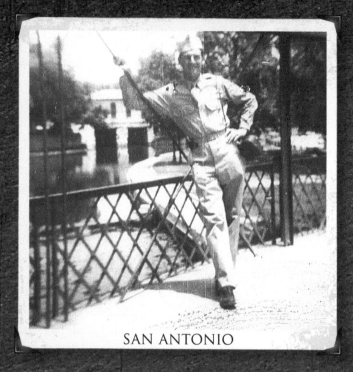

SAN ANTONIO

We were put on a train to San Antonio, Texas. That train had a coal burning engine, no air conditioning, and all the windows stayed open. Everything was covered in ash and soot, including us.

I had $3.00 in my billfold. When I went to the toilet it fell out of my pocked onto the seat. When I returned, my $3.00 was gone. Now I was completely broke!

We arrived at the train station in San Antonio late at night and bussed south of town to Lackland Air Force Base. We began our "in" processing the next day. I was assigned to squadron BM3, Flight 2132. The "BM" stood for "Basic Military". We stood in long lines for clothing, shoes, khaki towels, uniforms, field packs, etc. We spent several hours getting medical checkups. Nude lines again! While getting dental exams, several of us were pulled aside and put in a room. "Why", we wondered. The dentist came in and told us to line up and he was going to pull all our wisdom teeth! Just like that! No warning, no questions! I had two wisdom teeth that had not even come through yet. He cut them out anyway! We got so many shots at one time, we were all sick the rest of that day.

At the time, all the buildings on the base were the old WWII wooden types. At the time, there were so many troops, some were billeted in tar paper shacks on a bluff overlooking adjoining Kelly Air Force Base.

At Kelly there were WWII P-51's fighters parked as far as you could see. They were taking out their engines and smashing the rest for scrap! Such a beautiful plane. Practically worth its weight in gold now!

On pass we had to wear our uniform. Also, the River Walk and large sections of downtown were "off limits" to us. San Antonio was a rough town in those days.

After a few weeks at Lackland, it was announced that we would not get 4 years of college on the WWII G.I. Bill as we had been promised at enlistment. But, we would be eligible for one year. Because of this anyone so desiring could be discharged from the military. Some actually left! They had had enough of basic training! This G.I. Bill thing would affect my career a few years later. We were also promised medical care for life. This would affect my life many years later.

At the time the base was segregated. The black airmen were in one section of the base. We used to go over and watch them march. They were permitted to march differently from us. Their style of marching was very entertaining. Later, in Korea, there would be integration. There had been a race riot at Lackland in 1946. Black and white airmen met on the parade field at night and there was a brawl for several hours. It was a hush-hush event.

We were assigned 60 men to a barracks. This was called a "flight". I was in Flight 2132. After a few weeks into basic, I was put in the hospital for 2 or 3 days. I can't remember why. I was assigned to another flight, 2159. 2132 was a great flight, all southerners. Southern guys took to military training much better than the "Yankees". They could out-march, out-shoot, what have you, the Yankees. 2159 was a mixture. We were never a "good" flight 'cause the Yankees were constantly screwing up.

The barracks were two-story buildings, 30 men up and 30 men down. The D.I. (Drill Instructor) had a small private room. The building was heated by a coal burning furnace. There was no air conditioning. South Texas was hot in July and August.

There was a shower room, no stalls, a room with sinks and mirrors, a toilet room with no stalls. There is no privacy in basic training. I only had to shave once a week.

You learned quickly what happens to a barracks' thief. He was thrown into the shower room, scrubbed with a G.I. brush and soap, and beaten up badly. An excellent deterrent!

The walls were unfinished. Just 2X4 studs and the side planks. There was a 3-foot rod where we hung our uniforms in the open (no closets or wall lockers). The bunks (I won't call them beds) were double-deckers. There was a foot locker to hold your underwear, socks, brass, and personal items. It could be kept locked except during formal inspections. You had one pair of brogans (high top shoes) and one dress pair of shoes. These were kept on the floor under your bed, highly polished.

Every item you had and every man's in the open bay had to be placed exactly alike and exactly the same way. Your bunk had to be made up just right. The D.I. would flip a quarter on it. If it didn't bounce, he would tear off the sheets and blanket and order you to make it up again.

The D.I. checked your bunk and area every morning. An officer would conduct a formal inspection every Saturday morning. You wore your dress khakis, belt buckle, brass polished, shoes shined, etc. The D.I. would yell "'Ten Shun" when the inspecting officer entered the door. Standing by our bunks, we would snap to attention and hold this position as long as he was in the bay. He wore white gloves. He stood

ME - K.P.!

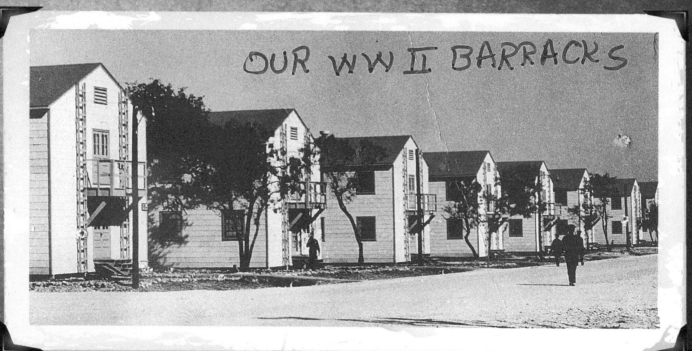

OUR WW II BARRACKS

SKINNY
G.I. JOE

FLIGHTS

GAINED
30 LBS

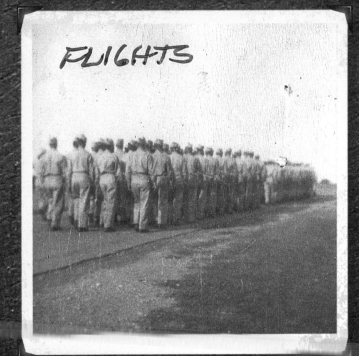

FLIGHTS

in front of you, looked you over good, checked your footlocker, wiped a few places with his white gloved hand, maybe ask you a question, and then proceed down the aisle to the next man. The latrine (toilet) had to shine. If you failed an inspection, there was hell to pay. You would get 8 hours of close order drill Saturday and Sunday.

Every Friday night, we had what was called a "G.I. Party". We scrubbed the entire barracks. The wooden floor had been scrubbed so much it was bleached blond.

The D.I. would come into the bay blowing his whistle loudly, every morning at 4 A.M. Rush, rush, rush! Toilet, dressing, making bunks, etc. Then we fell into formation on the road by 5 A.M. and marched in formation to the mess (dining) hall. There we stood in formation with other flights until our turn to enter. Rush, rush, rush! Only 30 minutes to eat. As you finished and exited, you formed into formation again, then marched back to the barracks.

You learned to hate that mess hall! When you went through the serving line, you had to be careful about what you accepted on your steel tray as some of the food was impossible to eat. When you finished and handed in your tray it had to be empty. There was a guard there to ensure it was. We learned to stuff unwanted food into our boots and pockets.

At least once a week, we were assigned to the mess hall as a "K.P." (kitchen police). Any veteran will tell you this is the worst duty in the military. On the day you had to get up at 3 A.M. and march to the mess hall. You were lucky if you returned by 8 P.M. You sat like condemned prisoners waiting for your job assignment for the day. The best job was "garbage cans". You were outside and not harassed too much. You had to keep the cans orderly and polished. Pretty bad were potato and onion peeling. This is what you did all day! You put the potatoes in a machine to get most of the skin off, and then cut out all of the eyes by hand. We soon learned if you leave the potatoes in the machine long enough the eyes would be gone too. Of course, the potato would be decreased to the size of a golf ball. We got into trouble a lot because of this trick. The onions had to be hand-peeled. There were a lot of tears. Everyone passing loved to say, "What's the matter? You homesick"?

The worst job was "pots and pans". There were two or three sinks full of soapy water. Steam pipes came down into the sinks so that the water would be near boiling. You were surrounded by mountains of greasy pots and pans. You never caught up. By the end of the day your hands were raw.

Some guys helped the cooks prepare the food. Some cracked crates and crates of eggs. In one incident, one airman bet another he wouldn't immerse his head totally in a large can of raw eggs. He did and he was caught. He had to spend 4 hours at "parade rest" on top of a huge stove with his head up a vent pipe. The stove wasn't on but there was a lot of smoke and smells going up that vent pipe. The eggs were cooked and served! I didn't eat any that morning!

Once a week we pulled guard duty. Four-hour shifts all night. All you had to do was walk through the barracks areas and try to stay awake. You had a billyclub, a helmet and a cartridge belt. It was boring. I looked at Collette's picture a lot, composed a song to her.

One night this animal kept running across the road in front of me. I thought to myself, "Just for fun,

I'm going to chase it". I saw it again and took off after it. It ran 'round and 'round me, and then… "P-U" (putrid)!! It was a Texas polecat and he doused me good! I had never seen one before and didn't know what it was!

On guard duty, if you have a problem, you yell out "corporal of the guard". This is relayed by other guards until it reaches the office of the sergeant in charge of the guard detail. This I did and I was relieved from my post. The smell was so bad it was wafting through the barracks and I could hear airmen waking up and complaining of the smell. I undressed outside my barracks and went into the shower and scrubbed myself with a G.I. soap (a powerful concoction used to scrub showers and toilets). My uniform had to be thrown away. Never chase a polecat!

I was always an early riser thanks to my dad. I would get up in the morning before the D.I. woke up everyone and leisurely go to the latrine, get dressed, make my bunk, and then observe the bedlam that took place after the whistle blew.

I only got into trouble one time. I was on the upper floor of the barracks. We were timed on "falling-out" of the barracks and assembling in formation on the road. The guys on the upper floor had a harder time getting out on time. There was a small porch out front and a wooden fire escape ladder to the ground below. To get downstairs quickly, we were shimming down the ladder instead of using the stairs. The D.I. caught us one morning. For punishment, I had to scrub the stairs with a toothbrush.

There were two other types of common punishment: an airman had to dig a hole with his pack shovel, 4 ft. X 4 ft. X 4 ft., in that hard Texas ground. The D.I. would actually take a tape measure and measure the

hole. Then he would flip a cigarette butt into the hole. Then he would tell the airman to fill the hole. The surface had to look good and be patted down so that you couldn't tell that a hole had been there. Then the D.I. would tell the airman to dig the hole again, find the butt and refill the hole. This was an all day job.

Another punishment was during close order drill. For someone who screwed up, the D.I. would say, "See that tree on the horizon? Run to it and get a leaf and bring it to me. You have ____ seconds or _____ minutes to accomplish this". The poor guy may have to do it over and over again to get back in the allotted time. One day we spent so much time on the drill field that we couldn't relieve ourselves. During a break, the men dug little holes and urinated in them. A D.I. came upon the rows of little pee mounds, found my flight and gave us hell! We had 4 hours of extra drill that afternoon!

Our day usually consisted of 2-4 hours of physical exercise, running, push-ups, side-straddled hops, etc. We had 2-4 hours of close-order drill. We attended a lot of classes on military history, etiquette, how to salute, how to report to commanders, etc.

I overheard two recruits talking about how much they hated basic training.

One: "I'm fed up with this place. I'm thinking of taking off and going AWOL (Absent Without Official Leave)."

The other: "Are you crazy? Look how flat the land is out there! They can see you for two days!"

I overheard a D. I. (Drill Instructor) talking to his flight. The flight consisted mostly of Yankees with Polish, German, Italian, and other European names. He seemed a southern red-neck type and was struggling to pronounce the names as he called the roll. Finally he called out the name "Williams". "Williams! Williams!" he blurted out, "My God, an American!"

NOTE: The graphic details in this section may not be suitable for some readers.

In the late 40's and early 50's the military really had a thing about VD. Any time spent in a hospital because of VD (Venereal Disease) was considered "bad time". (Hospital time from sunburn was also considered "bad time".) This was added to be served at the end of your enlistment.

In every "orderly room" (squadron office where Commander and First Sergeant stayed) there was a box near the door with "prophylactic kits" in it. This small package consisted of a condom, sterile wipes, and a small vial of substance that was injected into the penis. To go on pass you had to sign for one of these.

In basic training we were shown numerous horrible movies showing what VD had done to numerous soldiers. These movies were so graphic that many recruits ran outside to vomit.

"SHORT ARM" INSPECTIONS

This type of inspection was practiced from my entering the service until I was shipped to Japan in early 1950. Next to standing in long lines of naked men for medical examinations, this was the most degrading event I ever experienced.

You were awakened without warning usually between 1-4 a.m. All the barracks were "open bays". There were no private rooms. Your bunks, wall lockers, and footlockers were lined up in open bays.

You had about six feet either side of you to the next guy. No one slept in pajamas. Everyone slept in OD's (Olive drab, a dark green color.) issued shorts and undershirts.

You were sound asleep. Suddenly the lights came on, a whistle blew, and the First Sergeant yelled, "Up! And at attention!" You had to jump off your bunk and come to "attention" at the foot of your bunk next to the aisle.

There would be a Medical Officer with the First Sergeant. He would proceed down the row of men, stand before you and order "milk it down". You can imagine what you had to do. He would look at your privates intently, say "at ease" and proceed to the next man. You had to stand there till he inspected every man. When he had finished, the First Sergeant would turn out the lights and yell "as you were". This was a terrible experience. I never knew of one man being removed because the Medical Officer believed he was infected.

Often in some of the films, there was a recurring theme that the soldier thought his prostitute was "such a nice girl". This became a prominent expression among the troops: "she was such a nice girl."

In Japan and Korea there was a ward full of VD patients in every hospital. On the ship I was in coming back there was a hospital ward where VD cases were confined. Upon our landing in San Francisco, these men were immediately bussed over to Fizsimmons Army Hospital. Some had types of VD totally unknown.

In the latrines on Johnson AB there were a lot of curvy bent pipes over the urinals. Everyone swore they got that way by airmen with VD painfully trying to urinate.

During our briefings at Yerba Buena Island there wasa VD lecture. We had three day passes to San Francisco. We were told abou the section of town known for prostitution. It was really funny . . . When the guys were showering and dressing most said that section of town was where they were going.

A few years later the military ceased their "horror" VD program. The program never worked. It never slowed the VD rate.

I loved close-order drill. The flight (60 men) soon learned to act as one unit. You had four "squads" headed by a squad leader.

One man stood out front and was called the "right guide". Finding your correct position was called "dressing down". The squad leader, far right, stood behind the right guide exactly one arm's length. The next squad leader stood one arm's length to the left, etc. The next rank of 4 stood one arm's length behind the squad leaders, etc. to the rear. When the entire flight did a "left face", the right guide smartly moved to the front rank.

The right guide had a lot of responsibility. Just any man couldn't do it. You had to march in a straight line. There is no one in front of you. I was picked because I could do the job well. What I did was pick an object on the pavement ahead of me, or a distant sign, post or tree, concentrate on it and go by line of sight straight toward it.

Being part of a 60-man group, acting as one, was quite thrilling to me. We sang as we marched. The D.I. would count cadence in a sing-song voice. At times we encountered other flights at intersections.

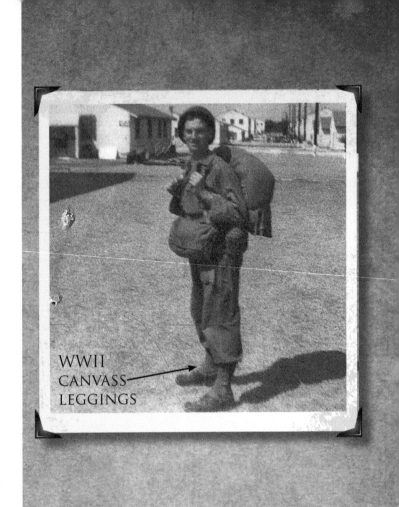

WWII CANVASS LEGGINGS

We would all sing loudly so as to drown out the other D.I.' s cadences. It was fun and I loved it.

Some Saturdays, we had a base parade involving 20,000 airmen. Now that was impressive! We would assemble at dawn. Then the flights would assemble into a squadron. Then the squadron would march across the base to the parade field.

In previous practices, the squadron had to practice turns as a unit. This was not easy to do. In a left turn the left most corner man marched in one spot and

BIVOUAC BASIC

G.I. JOE BASIC

MY DEAREST FLETCHER, OUR OWN BELOVED FLETCHER, PUL-LEEZE: TOMORROW IS SUNDAY, A DAY OF PEACE, FOR PEACE, TO BE LIVED IN PEACE AND QUIET! PLEASE, PUL-LEEZE DONT YUMP UP IN THE MORGEN AND SCREAM AND YELL. IT ONLY COMES ONCE A WEEK. LET US SLEEP ONE MORNUNG. I BEG OF YOU. HAVE MERCY. DONT WALK LIKE THE WALKING MAN! WALK LIKE A SPOOK! REMEMBER- SILENCE IS THE ELEMENT IN WHICH GREAT THINGS FORM THEMSELVES! AND JUST IN CASE YER DONT- REMEMBER: A KNIFE IN THE BACK IS BETTER THAN ONE UP THE ████! ↑

eensored

did a 90 degree turn to the left. Everyone to the right had to stay in a straight line by varying his speed. The last man on the right was practically running. The ranks left to right had to form straight lines. The squadrons were judged on these turns.

The squadrons passed by a reviewing stand in front of the commanding general and many high ranking officers. A large band played Souse marches. It was magnificent!

Now this was July in Texas, It was hot, hot, hot! Hours of standing in the sun with no water took its toll. You could see and hear Plop! Plop! Plop! Guys passing out (mostly Yankees). Medics with stretchers were busy carrying them off the parade ground. You couldn't help anyone. You never "broke ranks" no matter what.

We were required to take salt tablets every day. As a past time, you could hit the back of the airman in front of you on his fatigues and make a cloud of white powder that was produced by his sweating.

I loved the firing range. Southern boys make the best shooters. I grew up with rifles and hunting. Some of the Yankees had never fired a rifle. On the human silhouettes I'd ask the instructor if he wanted them all in the heart or head. That .30 caliber rifle was just like shooting a .22. The .45 caliber pistol was a different story. It was so loud we put cotton in our ears. It had a bad kick too. Some guys never learned to fire it. I got the hang of it quickly and was a good shot. We also fired an old WWII .45 caliber sub machine gun. It was terrible! You couldn't hit anything with it. It was later abandoned by all the services. It was called a "grease gun".

There was strict discipline on the firing range. Any infraction of the rules and you had to return to day one of basic training. If an airman with a rifle turned around or pointed it in any direction other than down range, the instructors would yell "hit the dirt". Everyone dropped prone on the ground immediately and he was hauled off!

We had many 10-mile night marches with full field packs. I loved them! I would take a couple of extra water canteens, sell the water for $2 each. Those crazy guys would drink all their water in the first couple of hours. I'd take apples, oranges, candy bars, etc., and sell them. Made some money that way. I also made money lending out money a few days before payday. I'd loan $10 and get $20 on payday.

I loved bivouacs. In the field pack was a half tent shelter. You joined it to another's and two men slept in the same tent. A G.I. blanket was also part of your pack. We would spend 3 or 4 days camping out.

The old WWII gas masks were a pain! It was heavy and bulky. It was the size of a woman's large purse and weighed about 3 pounds. It had to be carried with a strap hung from around your neck.

We had actual gas training once. We practiced putting it on after an outcry "gas"! We had to practice over and over till we could do it in a few seconds.

We were put in a concrete block enclosure. Tear gas was released. Then the order, "Gas, Don masks!" Some guys didn't make it! Choking, burning eyes! Then the door opened and everyone rushed outside! There was a lot of coughing and burning eyes! The importance of doing it right was certainly evident to us after that!

The services modernized these masks long ago. During the Arab Gulf wars the men carried very small canisters in a pouch on their belts.

At Lackland, at one of the main base entrances, was a huge American flag and a large open area. Squadrons would take turns doing a "Retreat" at this position. This was a large ceremony. A band would play the Star Spangled Banner, the flag would be lowered, and we stood at attention and held a salute till the music stopped. To me this was a very patriotic and meaningful event.

A bugle recording would play "lights out" at 10 p.m. and "taps" at 11 p.m. There was something deeply stirring about these pieces.

On Fort Sam Houston the Army had a bugle call several times a day. I learned to love them. Here are the ones most used:

1. First Call: wake up-rise and shine

2. Reveille: cannon fired, flag raised, assemble in formation in front of the barracks

G.I. JOE

BASIC

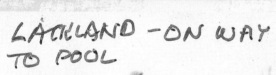

LACKLAND - ON WAY
TO POOL

COLLETTA

TX 1947

ME - BUDDY
OLD HOSPITAL
LACKLAND

OLD HOSPITAL
LACKLAND AFB
RICHARD SANGSTER
LIFELONG HOMETOWN
FRIEND

3. Mess Call: breakfast in "chow hall"

4. Mess Call: noon meal

5. Retreat: cannon fired, flag lowered

6. Tattoo: lights out in barracks

7. Taps: mournful, beautiful tune

On Fort Bragg a canon was fired every morning at 5 a.m. by the 82nd Airborne Division and woke up the entire base.

The Air Force never went in for bugle calls like the Army did. Even the Army has cut back. For years on USAF bases, only "retreat" was sounded. Everyone on the street turned toward the base flag, stood at attention and saluted. If you were in an auto, you stopped, got out, faced the direction of the flag, stood at attention, and saluted. This isn't done anymore. The bases are too large, there is too much traffic, and too many civilians on the base.

Something about bugle calls made you feel more a military person, set aside from civilians. You get the same feeling when saluting.

Taps is so beautiful. I want a bugle call of taps when I am buried. I don't want a rifle volley fired. I never cared for this. Maybe it's because I never fired a shot at anyone, and I was never fired at.

CATCH 22

In basic training you start to hear all the jokes and stories that have circulated around for centuries. Joseph Heller wrote a famous book "Catch 22" that was a best seller and was made into a popular movie. What he did was collect military jokes and stories from WWII, create a military unit with many characters and place them in WWII in Italy. This is a very funny book and movie. Even more so to anyone who was ever in the military. Starting in basic I heard a lot of the jokes and stories Heller put in his book. Here is an example:

A soldier (or airman) had had enough of basic training and was trying to get out of the military. G.I.'s who were were deemed "crazy" or "insane" would be discarged on a regulation called "Section 8". Here's what he did: He was in charge of the latrine detail for a very important barracks inspection by a high ranking general. He stood at attention near a row of commodes. He had placed a wad of peanut butter under the lip of a commode. When the general saw it he said, "What's this? Looks like sh_!" The soldier reaches down, takes the wad with his finger, and puts it in his mouth. "Tastes like sh_, too, General!" The story goes that he got his discharge. There were thousands of stories like this in the military.

There are a couple of expressions about the old way we were paid. One was: "The Eagle sh_s today." The other was: "Do you back up to the table to get your pay?" Here is some background on the origins of these expressions.

For years the military paid in cash. In Basic in 1947 and through most of the 50's payday was quite a day. There was no income tax and $1.00 was deducted from your pay for the "Old Soldiers' Home". It took so long to get paid it was like a holiday from regular duties.

The men assembled by flights and squadrons and lined up in an open outside area in front of a large table. A couple of M.P.'s (Military Police) stood behind an officer who sat at a table with stacks of bills and boxes of coins.

You approached the officer after your name was called. You stopped, came to attention, saluted, and said: "Sir, Private Robert M. Fletcher, RA 14264605, reporting for pay." He counted out your pay on the table. You signed a roster, picked up the money, put it in your pocket, saluted, did a smart "about face", and stepped aside for the next man. As you can see this was a lengthy process. It went on all day.

After getting paid, most of the men went to the BX or to their barracks and gambled at dice or poker the rest of the day.

I stood near the table and immediately collected money owed to me. I had loaned out $10 to several the few days before. Now I collected $20. This practice was later stopped by regulations.

Basic was the beginning of comradeship with your buddies. This is a feeling for your companions that is never felt anywhere like it is in the military. You think as a unit. You have a place, a position of importance and your life greatly depends on the other members of your unit. Anyone reading this would think I was crazy for loving basic training. I had played soldier all my life and to me, basic was like playing soldier. My Dad taught me to say "sir" to anyone older than I, so it was easy to use the word. Some old sergeants told me it wasn't necessary when I addressed them. My D.I. often told me I was the best military looking and acting airman he ever had.

After 14 weeks basic was coming to an end. Upon completion, we were automatically promoted to P. F. C. (Private First Class) and sewed one stripe on our sleeves. It was like the one the WWII soldier had. I was really proud of my first promotion.

All through basic I had stated that my preference for "tech school" was pharmacy. We were assembled to receive our tech school assignments and our next base. Very few guys got what they wanted! That's the way the military was in those days!

I got Medical Corpsman and Surgical Technical School. I was posted to Randolph Air Force Base just north of San Antonio. I was processed and put in "casual" status. This meant you were waiting for an assignment and pulled all sorts of crazy work assignments. It was at this point I learned a lot of ways to avoid bad work details.

I was soon bussed over to Ft. Sam Houston, also in San Antonio, to begin Medical Technician School. At Ft. Sam Houston everything was strictly "Army"!

I think it's time to start talking about the girls in my military career. I liked girls! And, when you're 17 and out in the world, you have a lot of hormones!

First, there was Mary Jo Cooper. She lived up the street while I was growing up. I think I was 3 years older than she. We were church friends at first but as she got older, we started liking each other. We were in and out of "sweethearts" for the next 8 years.

In the spring of 1946, I was 16. Mary Jo was 13 or 14. Her cousin, Colletta, was visiting her. Colletta was my age and we really fell for each other. She lived in Douglasville, Georgia, just west of Atlanta.

We didn't get to see much of each other. She returned home, and I was soon to enter the service and go to San Antonio. We started writing to each other most every day.

In basic, every airman wrote to his girlfriend. "Mail call" was quite an event in our lives. I kept Colletta's picture in my wallet. I looked at it often and even wrote a song for her.

"Our song" was "Blue Room", by Perry Como. I have it on a CD now and think of Colletta every time I play it. Also popular at the time was Perry Como's "I Wonder Who's Kissing Her Now?"

I started corresponding with Mary Jo also. Just friends. Near Christmas, 1947, I had 10 days leave. I took a Greyhound bus to Atlanta and Douglasville. I'll never forget that trip! The bus was packed. I had to sit on my suitcase in the middle of the aisle all the way. Colletta and I had a great visit. Her brother took me in his car to Fitzgerald.

Mary Jo and I also spent a lot of time with each other. Then and later, Colletta found out about us and her letters gradually stopped coming. Also, we didn't spend much time together, so she started dating other guys. So now, it was just Mary Jo and we were still just good friends.

Randolph in 1947 was the most beautiful base in the Air Force. As you entered the base, there was a mile-long boulevard. At the end of it was a beautiful bell tower covered with colored tiles. The housing and barracks were of Spanish architecture, built in the 30's with wide porches, verandas, red tile roofs and beautiful stone exteriors. The base was called "The West Point of the Air". It was scheduled to become the Air Force Academy, but politics caused the Academy to be built in Colorado. The base entry is no longer beautiful. It is barricaded and entry is in another area and heavily fortified. There were a few old WWII barracks left near the flight line. As a "casual" I was billeted in one of these. They have

since been torn down. I can still stand on the barren, grassy areas near the flight line and see, in my mind's eye, how it was in 1947.

At Randolph AFB at the time there were two famous West Point football players. One was Glenn Davis, the other, Doc Blanchard. Davis had dated the actress Elizabeth Taylor. They were called the "Touchdown Twins". Doc Blanchard won the Heisman Trophy in 1945, Davis in 1946.

Both Davis and Blanchard were in flight training school together at Randolph AFB while I was there. The cadets wore distinctive uniforms, and they were extremely sharp. We would go to their area and watch Davis and Blanchard as they marched. They were real celebrities.

THE DUFFLE BAG

At the end of basic training we were issued a "Duffle Bag". These bags have a long history. The first were made in Duffle, Belgium — hence the name.

It is a large cylindrical bag made of a canvas type material colored O.D. (olive drab - a dark army green). It has a drawstring type closure at the top with metal grommet holes. These could be locked with a regular padlock. Loaded it looks like a barrel about 40 inches high with a diameter of about 18 inches. At issue it had the airman's name and serial number stenciled on it. The bag has a sling like handle which makes it convienient to carry slung over the shoulder.

When an airman moved from one location to another this bag was the only luggage permitted to be carried by him. Thus everything an airman possessed had to fit in the bag, and he had to be able to carry it on his shoulder. It included his clothing and personal items.

So at the end of basic and upon transfer to Ft. Sam Houston Medical School, everything I owned fit into that bag.

The duffle bag became part of your life. You had no choice but to carry all of your military and personal clothing so there wasn't much room for other than essential personal items. When I was discharged six years later I still had that same bag. And everything I owned fit into it.

THE FOOT LOCKER

The "foot locker" was so named because it was usually located at the foot of a soldier's bed. The early ones, like the one I had in basic training, was a light plywood material painted O.D. It was about 18 inches high, 18 inches deep, and 36 inches long. There was always a small wall rack to hang your uniforms upon. Everything else had to fit in the foot locker. Except for inspections you were allowed to padlock the box.

An airman could not take the foot locker with him on transfers. However, NCO's were issued a permanent foot locker. It was constructed of a lightweight metal. It had his name, rank, and serial number stenciled on top. When he transferred he was allowed to ship the box at government expense.

The foot locker was part of your life. It allowed you to have a few more personal items than that put into your duffle bag.

When I became a staff sergeant I bought my own foot locker. It was of a lightweight aluminum construction. It was military approved. I kept that box after I was discharged. I had it in my college dorm room. I shipped it everywhere I went as a commissioned officer. Of course I changed the rank on it. I still have that foot locker.

I was bussed over to Ft. Sam Houston to enter training for Medical Corpsman. Ft. Sam Houston is a large Army base, active since the 1800's. The city of San Antonio has grown completely around it. It was and is the center for all Army medical services.

At Fort Sam Houston we had a "clothes swapping" event. At Lackland we were issued "fatigues" (work clothes) that were full one-piece mechanic coveralls left over from WWII. They were ok, but in the heat you couldn't take off the top.

The Army soldiers at Fort Sam Houston all had two-piece (jacket and pants). The pants had the large pockets on the sides. They are now called "cargo pants". For some reason they wanted our coveralls. I found a soldier my size and we swapped our fatigues. Taking the jacket off in the heat was great, and I liked the large side pockets: Still do to this day.

There is a row of old, beautiful Army officers' houses that are still in use today. There are plaques on them stating the famous officers who lived there: Generals Pershing, Bradly, Eisenhower, etc.

There was a large area of old WWII wooden buildings and barracks. This is where the school was located and where I was billeted. The area was fenced in and across from the fence was a large Mexican housing area. There were holes in the fence and guys were sneaking girls in and out.

I learned a lot about first aid, bandaging wounds, caring for wounded on the battlefield, how the medical service operated, etc. It was very interesting. We learned how to give shots and take blood. We practiced on each other! We also had to learn the Metric System of measurement.

Everything was strictly Army. We were having one day, by Army officers, a barracks and personal inspection. The major looked me over and really startled me when he asked, "Where do you get your uniforms tailored"? "They aren't, Sir, these are issue." For some reason all my issued uniforms always fit me perfectly.

I got into trouble once. For breakfast each morning, we stood a long time in the dark in formation. I saw my buddy in a line approaching me, so I smartly left my line and stepped in front of him. When we got to the door, a large hand grabbed my shoulder and jerked me out of line. A big burly Army sergeant said "Gotcha". I was put at the end of the line and told to report to the commander. That captain was a left over "kook" from WWII. He just gave me a detail of hauling dirt all day in a wheelbarrow.

The night before graduation there was a big party. The men were being assigned all over the world. I actually got on stage and sang "Far Away Places" (made hit parade by Jo Stafford and Perry Como).

Oh, yeah, we had to pull guard duty at Fort Sam Houston. It was scary. I usually had the motor pool, and I was warned that the Mexicans slipped in and stole gas and tires. I actually hid most of the time instead of walking my post. The sergeant of the guard rode in a jeep. When I knew he was coming I'd be walking my post.

All the WWII buildings are now gone. Like Randolph there are now just grassy knolls. I have walked those knolls and relived the memories of what went on there. Gone forever. Sad.

From Ft. Sam Houston I was bussed back to Randolph. Now I entered surgical technician school. I learned a lot about setting up and assisting doctors in surgery. It was an interesting course, but I wasn't too keen on being a surgical technician and working in surgery, and I never had to.

In those days, San Antonio was a dirty, rough and dangerous town. I was to be assigned there again from Korea in 1952. It had changed a lot and for the better. I have been back several times and it is now a beautiful, interesting city. The River Walk is now a wonderful place. My wife and I love the city.

I have revisited Lackland AFB many times. All the WWII wooden buildings are gone. My old mess hall, for some reason, is still there. It is used as an office building. One of the old chapels is still there. It houses a museum. The large parade field is covered in vintage aircraft. The drill field is covered in buildings. Very little is recognisable anymore.

Upon completion of Surgical Technician School, ten of us were assigned to a newly reopened air base, Goodfellow, in San Angelo, Texas. On to a new chapter in my Air Force career. And I get acquainted to west Texas.

FALL 1947 – 1949

▶ **GOODFELLOW AIR FORCE BASE**
SAN ANGELO, TEXAS

HOSPITAL

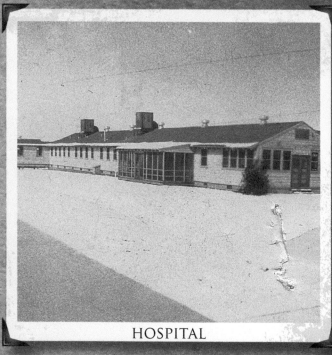

HOSPITAL

I had completed basic training at Lackland AFB. I completed medical corpsman training at Ft. Sam Houston and surgical technician training at Randolph AFB.

Now my first real assignment was to the hospital at Goodfellow AFB. I took a Greyhound bus from San Antonio to San Angelo. My first look at west Texas.

Goodfellow had been closed since the end of WWII. It was reopened as a basic pilot training base. The students would be flying a plane called the T-6 Texan. Previously, all pilot training took place at Randolph, but now the Air Force was independent of the Army and was expanding rapidly.

When Goodfellow was built there was plenty of flat land. The base was laid out and organized better than I have seen before or since. The buildings were all wooden WWII types. It was a very small base, and the hospital was small.

1. Commander (a Colonel) and surgeon
2. Administration/personnel
3. Eye clinic
4. X-Ray
5. Surgery
6. Registrar
7. Sick call/emergency
8. Wards
9. Veterinary
10. Medical supply

At Randolph, personnel had screwed up and sent 10 of us (surgical technicians) to that small hospital. The hospital administrator told us it was obvious 10 of us were not needed in surgery. "Can anyone

23

MY BUNK

VETERINARY

PAT
TORE
OFF
MARTHA

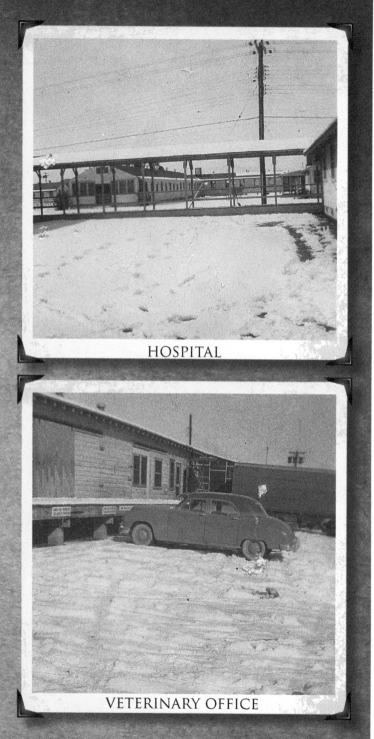

HOSPITAL

VETERINARY OFFICE

type?" I saw a chance to stay out of surgery… "Yes, sir", and raised my hand. Actually, I was a good typist. I could type 60 words a minute in high school. "Good, we need a morning report clerk. You're it." That sounded good to me!

In those days a "morning report clerk" was an important position. There were no computers. The morning report was done by every unit in the military. It was the instrument whereby the military knew how many men it had and where they were at all times. Any change in the duty status of an airman in the unit had to be recorded. On leave, on TDY (temporary duty elsewhere), change in job status, hospital stay, etc., had to be recorded daily seven days a week. The report had to be made in several copies, difficult to do on a typewriter. It had to be perfect. You had to use official abbreviations and there could be no strikeovers or erasures. I went to work early every morning and sometimes filled half a wastebasket with forms before I could get a perfect copy.

Once in a WWII movie called "Breakthrough" (about the "Battle of the Bulge" with Van Johnson), the men are a ragtag bunch walking in lines through the snow. A corporal (the morning report clerk) was going down the line asking if anyone knew what happened to Private _____. Finally a soldier responded, "I was with him. He received a direct hit by an artillary shell and was blown to bits!" The clerk blurted out, "Thank God! Now I can finish my morning report!" Well, it was a very somber moment in the movie, and I let out a laugh! All eyes were on me, and I was really embarrassed!

Becoming a clerk typist would change my enlisted career forever.

We didn't have a swimming pool on Goodfellow. About half a mile from the barracks area and near the north end of the runway was some sort of water reservoir. It had large wide concrete flat surfaces around it. It was great for lying in the sun and an occasional dip in the water to stay cool.

On the way to the reservoir was a large open area covered with only low tumble weeds. There were a lot of jack rabbits in the weeds, the first I ever saw. They stood about two feet high and had very long legs. They could really run fast. Now, I was always a fast runner myself. As a pastime I chased these jack rabbits. I could barely keep up with them. It must have been a sight: a crazy young airman and jackrabbits racing along the runway and leaping over tumbleweeds!

At Goodfellow all the airmen, except the medics, had been transferred from the US Army Air Corps to USAF. The Air Force had no medical department. We remained Army. We were named "SCARWAF" (Special Category Army with Air Force.) We did not change our brass on our uniforms. I was constantly "chewed out" by NCO's and officers for wearing the wrong brass on my uniform. They didn't know our situation.

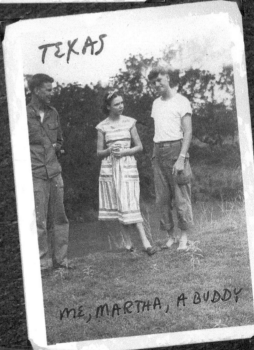

TEXAS

ME, MARTHA, A BUDDY

In late 1949 I was at Las Vegas AF Base. The Air Force formed a Medical Command. We were given a choice, Army or Air Force. Some of those idiots actually chose Army and were transferred.

TEXAS 48
MARTHA'S SISTER-
N-LAW

San Angelo was a beautiful city. It is on the edge of the west Texas "Badlands". There and to the east was good farming. There was good rainfall. To the west the land was only good for cattle and sheep. San Angelo was the sheep capital for all of the U.S.

A beautiful, clear river ran through the center. The base was only 2 miles from the town and city buses ran regularly to town. I had no car.

San Angelo is no longer a beautiful town. The base closed long ago. Downtown is deserted and full of closed businesses. Sad.

I joined the choir at the downtown First Baptist Church. I made a lot of friends there. We gathered at a member's house every Sunday night after church for a social. Here an older girl took an interest in me. I liked her too, but for some reason I wasn't supposed to have an affair with older girls. This happened several times in my career. I look back now and see how foolish I was! Why didn't I "go for it"?

There was a car full of us one night and she was sitting next to me. She said, "I bet you a nickel I can kiss you and you won't know it." Ok, so I bet. She put her arms around me and really planted a kiss on my lips! When I came up for air, I blurted out, "I knew you kissed me"! "Ok, she said, "here's your nickel." I've pulled that one a few times since and it really works.

We had several cute nurses who liked to flirt with me. I think they were playing with me because they were so much older than I was.

I have always loved to skate, and I was always very good at it. I could even skate backwards well. I started going to the local rink. I met Martha Dean there. Her folks would bring her over on Friday or Saturday from their home in Ballinger, about 30 miles away. She was only a junior in high school, but I was only 17. We hit it off, skated well together and looked for each other every weekend.

I soon met her parents and they invited me to come to their farm in Ballinger. I think they thought I was just a lonely G.I. kid far from home. Their oldest son had been in the Air Force too.

I loved the farm. It was about 3 miles out of town. Old, old farm house. No air conditioning existed, but in this part of Texas, the wind blew constantly. A large river ran through the farm. It stayed muddy. The only fish in it were catfish, but I enjoyed catching them. The family was good to me. Mrs. Dean would cook my favorite foods.

Mrs. Dean had a shop in downtown Ballinger. She made buttons and only buttons. It's amazing how much money she made doing only that. She was a cat lover and would pick up strays and take them to the farm. I really didn't care for all those cats. The front porch would be covered with them. You had to sneak up to the front screen door, open it suddenly and close it quickly. Behind, you would hear splat-splat-splat on the screen door as they flew against it trying to get in.

Martha was a majorette. She was good at it and eventually got a scholarship to a Texas university. Her family took me all over west Texas to her high

28

MRS DEAN
MARTHA'S MOM

PAT TORE
OFF
MARTHA

TEXAS.

DAD
"HUB"   MARTHA   MOM

Olenthus Wiley (Pete) Fletcher

19 YEARS OLD

KILLED IN ACTION IN
FRANCE, 24 JULY 1944
WWII INFANTRY

BROTHER'S BODY
RETURNED FROM FRANCE.
FUNERAL SERVICES
MAY 1948

school football games. I discovered what a "blue norther" was. They always kept a lot of blankets in the truck. When I asked "Why", they said, "You'll find out". Sure enough, at a ball game one evening it was announced, "A blue norther" is a hitting. Everyone ran to their vehicles to get their coats and blankets. I had never seen such a temperature drop! In 20 minutes the wind was howling and the temperature dropped 40 degrees!

Weather in west Texas was strange. For the first time in my life, I developed a nose bleed because the air was so dry. This happened to me again in Nevada and North Dakota. Also, I experienced my first dust storm. Out of west Texas came a wall of dust. It was like a heavy fog with visibility near zero. The dust was in your bed, your food, everything! This happened three times.

One day, Mrs. Dean startled me by saying, "Martha started letting you kiss her, didn't she?" I guess I was taken aback and replied, "Yes, how did you know?" She said, "She has never kissed a boy. She came to me and told me you were always trying to kiss her. She wanted to know what to do, so I told her, "Kiss him or lose him!" Now there is a wise mother! It was never anything heavy. Just two young teenagers falling in love for the first time.

Martha said to me, "When school starts, you can take me to the dances". "I don't know how to dance", I told her. She and her mom said, "What? We'll fix that!" So, they had an old phonograph, put on some records and taught me some basic two steps. They had three songs, "Underneath the Arches", Tree in the Meadow", and "My Happiness". I have copies of those songs and when I play them, I am back in those happy times. Her high school friends readily accepted me and I was really happy there.

Martha and her mom also made me shave under my arms. I had never done that. There was no deodorant in those days. You used baby or baking powder. Shaving really helped.

THE BEGINNING OF MY "FEAR OF FLYING"

The hospital at Goodfellow was a bee-hive of activity. The base was a "Basic Pilot Training Base" and the airplane was the T-6. The students had a lot of problems with this plane.

Several accidents occurred that made me feel I never wanted to fly, and I developed "a fear of flying".

In one a student pilot involved in a crash had a large cut across his face which also affected his eye. I happened to walk by when they were sewing up his face and eye. His eyeball was jerking so violently it seemed it would jump out of it's socket. It made me sick to my stomach.

In another accident, on an outlying practice landing field, the planes created so much dust the visibility was almost zero. The pilots couldn't see the other planes. One plane came up from behind on another. The propeller chewed the front plane to pieces from the tail to just behind the cockpit of the student pilot. Another foot and he would have been mincemeat! I saw him in the emergency room. He was shaking so violently they had to knock him out.

Flying can be dangerous!

RIVER THROUGH FARM, CATFISH
ONLY FISH, SAW RIVER FROZEN
OVER

I had to hitchhike back and forth to Ballinger. This got me into trouble once. There was a parade one morning and I barely got into the barracks to get dressed in time to "fall-out". I was in a hurry and forgot to change my civilian socks to G.I. brown. I "fell out" and got into the ranks. My commander took one look at me and yelled, "Fletcher, where did you get those god damned socks? Fall-out, stay put, and report to me after the parade!"

When I reported he said to me, "You want an article 15 or a courts martial?" Wow! I didn't know what to say. The first sergeant looked at me and said, "Take the article 15." This was really a mild form of punishment and wouldn't be entered into your permanent records. I got one more later in my enlisted career.

Sometime while I was at Goodfellow, I was notified that my brother, Pete's, remains were being returned from France. Pete (actual name – Olenthus Wiley) had been killed in action in France on July 23, 1944. He was only 19 at the time.

I got an emergency leave to attend his funeral in Fitzgerald, Georgia, my hometown. I got a "hop" in a C-47 that made a special stop for me at Turner AFB, Albany, Georgia, the nearest base to home. I hitchhiked to Fitzgerald. It was a full military funeral with rifles and echo taps. Sad, sad, sad. This was the last time all eleven of my family, plus my mom and dad, would be together at one time. I rode a Greyhound bus back to San Angelo.

For some reason I was assigned to part time duty in the veterinary office. It was fun. The TSGT (technical sergeant) in charge was a character. He illegally gave dogs shots and operated on them. One time he spayed one and had her entire insides strung up in the light. He couldn't find her ovaries. "Oh well", he said and stuffed everything back inside and sewed her up. He told the owners that everything went okay. Another time he cut the tails off a bunch of Doberman Pincher puppies. He didn't leave enough skin to cover the tail bones. He pulled and pulled over the entire puppies' bodies to get enough skin to sew over the bone nubs. Those were some tight-assed puppies!

We pulled inspections on all the meat and dairy products delivered to the base. We inspected all of the silverware and dishes in the mess hall. The TSGT told me not to accept any gifts from merchants downtown. It was amazing what they offered me, cases of coke, ice cream, candy, etc.

At Goodfellow I met the first person in my life who was a "hemophiliac". The poor guy had bandages on his face all the time from shaving with a blade. (No such thing as an electric razor those days.) I don't know why he was kept on active duty.

He had dual Mexican/American citizenship. He was from an aristocratic old Mexican family who had a long history of being ambassadors around the world. He said there was a lot of inter-marriage among his cousins.

Because he was born on an American ship in an American harbor he was an American citizen and was actually drafted into the US Military. When he got drafted he chose the US Army Air Corps.

We had a good thing going in the hospital to make money. The hospital was authorized to pay $25 to a blood donor for a pint of blood. We kept this a secret from the rest of the base. So we kept the information within the hospital, and we gave the blood. I tried several times to give blood, but I couldn't. My blood would clot in the needle or the tubes and they could never get a full pint.

I can't remember why, but I had this desire to get stationed closer to home. I was very happy with my job, the base, the city and with Martha and her family.

The new Air Force was expanding rapidly. Columbus AFB, Mississippi, was to reopen so I applied for transfer there. But Las Vegas AFB, Nevada, opened first and I received orders for a transfer there.

It was a sad and tearful goodbye to Martha and her family. Martha and I promised to write, be true, etc. as unexperienced and naïve young people do.

I came back to see them about a year later when I was reassigned from Las Vegas AFB to Robins AFB, Georgia. I drove my "A" model Ford nonstop from Vegas to Ballinger in 36 hours. Martha's dad helped me put a new set of rings in the engine. We all enjoyed the reunion, but it was not the same. Martha knew I had dated in Vegas.

We both knew I wouldn't be back, so we called it quits.

I have been back to Ballinger twice since then. Martha's mom and dad are dead. I visited their graves but Martha would not see me. The old farmhouse is still there, abandoned, and falling apart. So many beautiful memories.

I have been back to Goodfellow. All the buildings are gone. The runway is still there. There are some large brick USAF Security Service buildings nearby. The base has been mostly deactivated for a long time.

I caught a train to Las Vegas and experienced my first time in New Mexico and Arizona.

Off to a new adventure!

3

1949-1950

▶ LAS VEGAS AIR FORCE BASE
LAS VEGAS, NEVADA

HOSPITAL STAFF

DESERT

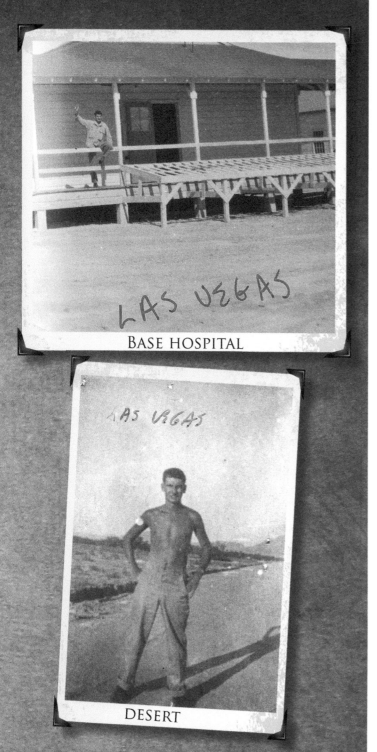

LAS VEGAS

BASE HOSPITAL

LAS VEGAS

DESERT

I was at Goodfellow AFB, San Angelo, Texas. Columbus AFB, MS, was to reopen so I volunteered to go there. But instead, Las Vegas AFB reopened first and I was transferred there.

I rode a train to Las Vegas. It was my first time in New Mexico and Arizona. There was snow on the ground all the way and it was beautiful. I saw my first mountains.

The train station in Las Vegas was at the end of Fremont Street. It has been replaced with a huge hotel.

There was only desert and sagebrush between North Las Vegas and the base. The base was all old WWII wooden buildings. There were heaps of sand dunes everywhere. Bulldozers had to clear the roads. We had to shovel sand out of the hospital buildings. There was no air conditioning. The new Air Force was really expanding. The base was to be used for advanced single engine pilot training, and the planes were WWII P-51's.

There was not one blade of grass or tree. Tumble weeds were everywhere. Las Vegas was not a large city then. All the action was on Fremont Street. The "strip" was a two-lane road with tumble weeds and sand everywhere. The casinos on the strip looked like large motels. The Gold Nugget on Fremont was the largest casino.

I couldn't gamble in the casinos. I tried, but I guess I looked too young. I'd go in the door and some huge gorilla looking guy would confront me. "You aren't 21 are you?" "No Sir, I was just leaving."

37

MY BARRACKS

THE BASE. ALL WWII BUILDINGS

BUCK
SGT
LAU VEGAS
1949-50

MY BUDDY
RAY SERGEANT

I became the morning report clerk again. Easy job. I was experienced. One day, a base letter came out that all recommendations for promotion had to be submitted by a certain date. I did personnel work. I was barely eligible for E-4, Buck Sergeant, 3 stripes. I told the officer in charge of promotions, "Look, I have to type all of these promotion recommendations. Can I put in one for me?" "Sure", he said. "Go ahead." It just so happened that everyone on base recommended was promoted. Wow! I was a sergeant, and only 18 years old! Boy, was I proud! I could answer the phone with, "This is Sergeant Fletcher"!

Just like Basic Pilot Training at Goodfellow, we had a lot of crashes at Las Vegas AFB. We had WWII P-51's and another plane called a P-81. The P-81 was where two P-51's were put together. It looked like a weird P-38 of WWII.

Out where "Area 51" is now we had a gunnery range. When the planes were out there practicing straffing and bombing we were required to have an ambulance parked near the practice field. Large targets were on the ground at the end of a large open field.

It was exciting to watch the bombing and straffing, so sometimes we would go out with the ambulance and watch the show. The P-81 had an empty cockpit, so to balance the weight, "real brave" airmen would volunteer to ride in the empty cockpit.

I went out one day and watched the show. The medics who went out the next day came back traumatized! A P-81, with pilot and volunteer airman, never pulled up and went straight into the target. The medics had to help pick up the pieces. I had to do this at a later time at another base.

In another accident a P-51 caught fire on landing. The pilot died. After the fire was extinguished two of our guys tried to lift the dead pilot out of the cockpit. He came in two at the waist as they lifted him up. Those were two traumatized medics! They never asked to go out to another wreck. We all felt the same way.

Our first major casualty after opening the hospital was one unlucky sergeant. The P-51 has a huge propeller and the plane lands at an angle tail first. When it gets level the propeller barely clears the ground. This P-51 tilted too far down and the blades broke off. This poor sergeant was walking in front of a hanger a quarter mile away. One propellers broken blade hit him and almost cut him in two.

A high school classmate of mine was a P-51 pilot at Las Vegas AFB. His P-51 caught fire and he had to bail out over the desert. He was not injured.

Airplanes are dangerous!

I also assisted the veterinarian technician. We made money boarding dogs. The base commander's wife left her dog with us one weekend. She told us, "Keep and eye on my dog. She is in heat, and I don't want any other dog to get near her." Well, Saturday morning when I went to feed her, she wasn't in her pen! Someone had left the gate open. I was really worried! I looked for that dog all over the base Saturday, and Sunday. I finally found her Sunday

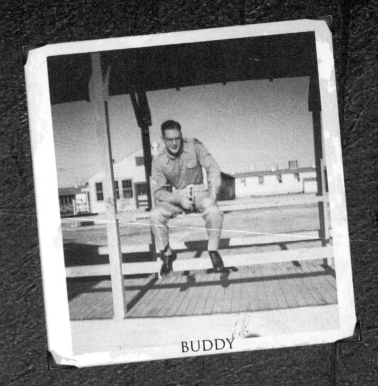

BUDDY

afternoon. Had she been violated? I had no idea. The commander's wife picked her up Monday morning. "Anything happen to my dog?" "Oh no mam, we kept her locked up all weekend." "Well, good, and thank you."

She never came back so I guess the dog hadn't been violated. Whew! I was really sweating that one out!

One Sunday morning I was awakened by a new man moving into the barracks. I heard someone say, "Your name is Fletcher? There's another Fletcher right there", pointing to me. I got up to meet him. His name was Bill Fletcher and his hometown was Moultrie, Georgia, about 40 miles south of

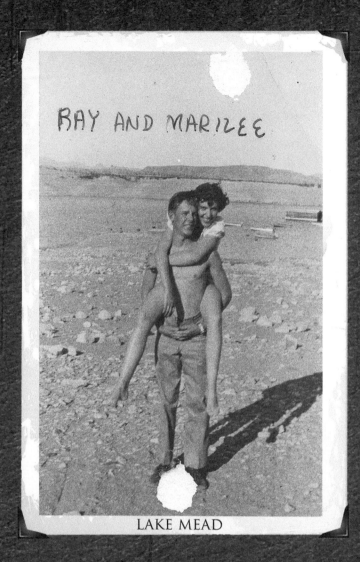

RAY AND MARILEE

LAKE MEAD

I was still regular army here even though the Air Force had been independent for almost two years. The problem was the Air Force had not formed a medical department. Finally, we were told it had been formed and we could transfer to the Air Force or be transferred to the Army. Some of my idiot buddies actually went back to the Army. I went from a "Buck Sergeant" to an "Airman First Class". What a let down!

I was on the medical unit's baseball and bowling teams. I was a good third baseman, and I had a respectable 182 average in bowling.

I started going to the Baptist Church in downtown Vegas. I joined the choir. In no time at all I had many friends.

In Las Vegas, the people really took a shine to me. Las Vegas had a lot of Mexicans. The teenage boys ran in gangs and were called "Chicanos". The local Caucasians didn't want their daughters to have anything to do with them. So, here I am, a southern boy from Georgia with a charming southern accent, who didn't curse or smoke, went to church, and treated adults with respect. All the families with daughters opened their to doors me.

Yes, there were girls!

I was still writing to Mary Jo in Georgia and Martha in Texas, but I needed someone to talk to – Ha! I was pretty fickle and a little bad…

One of the first girls I dated was Virginia. She was as pure and sweet as they come. She had had polio and wore a brace on one leg. We became very good friends. I was the first boy she had ever dated.

Fitzgerald. He was also a distant cousin of mine! We also had a guy from Tifton, Georgia, where I started my enlistment.

Bill had a new '48 sedan. He, Ray Sergeant and I took a great trip across Death Valley. Through Bishop and Lone Pine, through Yosemite National Park, to Reno, Carson City, and back to Vegas.

SATURDAY MORNING STAND-BY INSPECTON

THUNDERBIRD

It was just church, movies, etc. It was never real serious. I probably felt she was too innocent for me. Years later, while visiting my brother, Monte, in Vegas, I met her mom at church. We were happy to see each other. Monte said she asked about me often. Virginia never married and died in her mid-twenties. So Sad. She was a wonderful person.

I finally decided I needed a car. I bought a 1929 Ford Model-A, 2-door sedan for $200. I got my first driver's license there in Vegas. That Model-A had been in the desert all its life and was in great shape. I had a great time in that car. All the kids loved it. It had pull-down curtains which came in handy at the drive-in movies.

At church, I also met Ruby and Marilee. There was a large and very active downtown youth center. I would go there often. Headliners at the casinos would perform there, free on weekends. I remember Kay Star. Her big hits were "If You Love Me, Really Love me" and "Half of a Photograph". They could never classify her music as country, contemporary, pop, etc. She had huge hits in every category. I have copies of all her CD's. Whenever I play her music, I am back at that youth center dancing with Marilee and Ruby.

I took Marilee to the youth center one night and a buddy of mine, Ray Sergeant (he was a corporal), took Ruby. We partied together that night. Ray and Marilee fell for each other like a ton of bricks! Ruby and I liked each other too, so we wound up switching dates! Ray and Marilee got married right there in Vegas.

Ruby and I started dating heavily. Ruby and I had a lot of chemistry between us. I don't think I loved her. I think I was so young at the time I really didn't know what love was.

I was mean to Ruby. I would date other girls and then return to her. A song came out about that time called "Careless Hands", by Mel Torme. "I let my heart fall into careless hands", Ruby would sing it all the time. I guess she thought she was in love with me. I have a copy of that song, and when I play it, I think of Ruby and how mean I was to her.

My brother, Monte, married Ruby's sister, Dorothy, and years later, while visiting them, we went to see Ruby. She married an Air Force guy, had kids who were all grown, and was divorced. We had a cordial meeting, and I haven't seen her since.

This is a good time to tell about Monte and Dorothy. Years after I left Vegas, Monte was in the Navy and stationed in San Diego, California. He wrote and told me he was going up to Vegas. I told him how good the Ross Family (Ruby's) had been to me and to look them up. He did. Ruby's younger sister, Dorothy, had grown up. They fell in love, eventually married, and Monte stayed in Las Vegas. Boy, did I ever change his life!

The Ross's were a great family. Mrs. Ross liked to cook for me. For the first time in my life I ate mutton. Wasn't bad. They also ate a lot of rabbit, sold in the grocery stores. Mr. Ross worked on my Model-A. He was from Canada and had worked in many of the mines in the area. Mrs. Ross was one of the finest ladies I ever met.

On the train to Las Vegas, I met another airman going there. He told me he wouldn't be there long because he had a "compassionate" transfer to New Hampshire. He told me how his senator had gotten it for him. I still wanted to be stationed in the southeast, so I decided to try for this compassionate transfer. My Dad was old and sickly, so I got doctors' statements, sent them to Senator Walter George, a powerful senator who headed military affairs committees, and he approved my request.

I got a compassionate transfer to Robins Air Force Base in Warner Robins, Georgia, just south of Macon and 50 miles north of Fitzgerald.

Ruby really took it hard. She wanted to get married and go with me. No way!

On a Thursday evening, I packed up my Model-A, and headed toward Georgia. I said goodbye to Ruby, went by the church where all the kids were painting the church. Lots of tearful goodbyes.

I drove all Thursday night, all day Friday, Friday night and didn't stop till I reached Martha's house in Ballinger, Texas, Saturday. About 36 hours! I think I averaged 40 miles per hour. Martha and her family were happy to see me. It wasn't the same with Martha and me. She knew I had dated in Las Vegas and that I'd never return to this area, so we called it quits.

I drove to Shreveport, Louisiana and spent a day with my brother, Louie. Then… off on a 24 hour drive to Fitzgerald… and Mary Jo!

A new assignment and a new adventure… Robins AFB, Georgia.

LAS VEGAS AIR FORCE BASE
LAS VEGAS, NEVADA

ROBINS AIR FORCE BASE
WARNER ROBINS, GEORGIA

I DROVE MY MODEL-A FORD ALL THE WAY.

1949-1950

▶ ROBINS AIR FORCE BASE
   WARNER ROBINS, GEORGIA

▶ CAMP STONEMAN
   PITTSBURG, CALIFORNIA

▶ YERBA BUENA ISLAND
   SAN FRANCISCO BAY, CALIFORNIA

I received a "compassionate" transfer from Las Vegas AFB, to Robins AFB. I drove my Model-A Ford all the way. That was a sweet little car.

Warner Robins was a small village, old and run-down looking. It is a large and thriving city now. It sat across the highway from Robins AFB.

Robins was an Air Material base. It was huge with numerous large warehouses and hundreds of WWII planes stored there. Its main mission was to mothball and store WWII aircraft.

The base was about ten miles south of Macon, Georgia, and about 50 miles north of Fitzgerald, my hometown. After two years I finally got stationed near home.

The base hospital was small. It was built during WWII. All the wooden buildings were designed just like those at Goodfellow AFB and Las Vegas AFB.

I know the hospital staff and doctors were competent and professional, but I was concerned and worried about what went on at times.

A master sergeant was brought in one night after he had been in a car wreck. He was drunk and covered in blood. He was cursing loudly and thrashing about. He was so obnoxious I guess the doctors figured he had nothing seriously wrong with him. So they cleaned him up, sedated him and put him under observation till morning. Well, come morning, he was dead! It turned out he had several broken ribs. His lungs had been penetrated by the ribs and he bled to death! They didn't take any x-rays!

In another case a civilian was hit in the forehead by a gallon can of paint that fell from a high shelf. He

CAMP STONEMAN

PITTSBURG,
CALIFORNIA

had to be transported to a large hospital in Macon in one of our ambulances.

For some reason I was grabbed as the only loose body to accompany him in the ambulance.

The can had mashed his forehead in and he was bleeding profusely. It was an hour and a half ride to the hospital. He was lying on a stretcher. I had to cup his face and apply pressure with both my hands to stop some of the bleeding. That seemed to me a terrible procedure. Months later I saw this man. He was ok but he had a caved in forehead.

In another incident a dependent wife was given a routine tonsil operation. She bled to death during the night.

The hospital operations went like this. A full colonel was commander of the hospital. He was a surgeon of some type and rarely took part in any administrative procedures. The hospital was actually run by an "Operations Officer". He was usually a captain or major and had no medical degrees. The First Sergeant and his staff were directly under him. The personnel clerk (which I was) was under the First Sergeant.

At the Robins AFB hospital our commander was a full colonel. He was actually an eye surgeon. We had two captian surgeons that did all the rountine surgeries.

The colonel's office and waiting room was right in front of our orderly room. He was very unfriendly, unapproachable, and a reclusive man. He made me his driver. He had his own staff car, and when he needed to go somewhere the First Sergeant called on me to drive him. He also called me in one day

and taught me how to put drops in peoples' eyes. I didn't like doing this, but I certainly couldn't tell him that.

The colonel was strange. He asked for me all the time to help him and drive him places, but he never spoke to me. We had some long drives. He would tell me where to take him, climb into the back seat of the sedan and remain silent as though deep in thought. I could sense he liked me, but he never let me know it.

The hospital was torn down. It is now a housing area - strange, the same parking lot is still there.

I became the morning report clerk again. I was a "buck" sergeant, 3 stripes and probably made about $80 per month. Two civilian secretaries worked in the office with me. One was about 26, beautiful and single. Her name was Virginia. The other was a much older married woman. Virginia's desk faced mine. She liked me and we flirted quite a bit. In fact, my commander called me in one day, chewed me out, and told me to cool it with Virginia! I didn't date her. Now that I think back, I was crazy not to, but she was older and we couldn't date co-workers.

My first sergeant was a character. He was married to a distant cousin of mine from Vidalia, Georgia. He made a show of demanding my pass and tearing it up in front of people. I went along with it for I had a drawer full.

There were benefits of being assigned to a hospital. We had our own mess hall and there were always a few pretty nurses. I flirted with them, but there were strict rules about enlisted fraternizing with officers. Nurses didn't take their officer status seriously.

49

We took turns at lunchtime manning the emergency phone. One day, it was my turn and I received a call that a plane had crashed. I called the MOD (Medical Officer of the Day) and alerted him. He told me to get an ambulance and driver immediately. I couldn't find one. The MOD said, "Can you drive an ambulance?" "Yes, Sir!" "Then, you'll do, let's go!" We drove about 20 miles west of the base. A jet fighter overhead recognized us, wagged its wings, and headed west. We followed. Soon, we saw smoke. The plane had gone straight in near a church and at the edge of a cemetery. Thank goodness it hadn't blown up any tombstones or graves. It was a large hole about 20 to 30 feet wide with smoke pouring out of it and pieces of the plane strewn about. The doctor jumped out first while yelling, "Bring my bag!" Then he yelled, "No! Bring rubber bags!" I searched the ambulance. No rubber bags! "Sir, no rubber bags!" "Then bring the pillow cases", he said. So, I took two pillow cases to him. He was peering down into the hole. He said, "Do you want to use your hands or forceps?" Oh, oh! "For what?" I am getting all shook up! "Start picking up the pieces!" Wow, I am getting sick!

But, I took the forceps and started picking up pieces of flesh and putting them into a pillowcase. It was like pieces of beef lying around. That wasn't too bad. What was really bad is I found part of a hand with all of its fingers and his wedding ring intact. Also, the back of his helmet with part of his skull embedded in it. Also, part of his backbone was fused into his parachute. This was traumatic! I had never seen such a thing! I had seen many injuries from crashes at Goodfellow and Las Vegas but nothing compared to this.

We probably found about 40 pounds of the pilot. We had to take the full pillow cases back to the base and turn them in to the morgue. That night, the guys kept telling me that we had stew meat for supper.

I have never forgotten that experience. It was to be repeated again years later at another base.

After a few months at Robins, I traded my '29 Model-A Ford for a red '49 V-8 Ford. That car was hot! I loaned it to a friend one day. Later, in a conversation with someone, I was asked how fast it would go. "I don't know. I have never opened it up." My friend piped up, "I know. It will do 110!" So much for loaning a car to a friend! When I left Robins for Japan, he bought the car from me.

Girls! Yes, there were girls. I was going down to Fitzgerald every weekend. I was seeing Mary Jo but we weren't going steady.

My sister, Twilla, had a girlfriend who lived in the "cotton mill village". Books have been written about these places. It was a village of row houses next to a huge cotton mill. The mill owned the houses. It was on the outskirts of Fitzgerald. These people were considered low-class with low morals, and looked down upon by the people of Fitzgerald. This wasn't true but throughout the South, in those days, that's what people thought of them.

Twilla's friend had a daughter about my age. She was very pretty and a little wild. We had some great times together, swimming, dancing, drive-in movies, etc.

ENROUTE BY FERRY
FROM CAMP STONEMAN
TO YERBA BUENA ISLAND
IN SAN FRANCISCO BAY

BETTY
MACON
GEORGIA

CAMP STONEMAN,
PITTSBURG, CALIFORNIA

The cotton mill had two big bosses. One of them was Mary Jo's dad. He would tell Mary Jo he saw my car in the "village" and she would get angry and accuse me of "slumming" out there. Well, my girlfriend's mom must have heard something about the boss' daughter and me. I drove up one day and she was still standing on the porch. She gave me hell! She accused me of "slumming" and hurting her daughter. She told me to leave and never come back! I took it seriously, for I was scared of those people out there.

A couple of buddies and I started going to a large dance hall in Macon. It was rather country, square dancing, etc., but it was great fun. So we all had girlfriends. Mine was "Betty". We danced for hours on Friday and Saturday nights. I started really liking Betty and didn't go back to Fitzgerald to see Mary Jo.

One day a picture of Betty fell out of her billfold and when I picked it up to hand to her, I noticed her last name was different. "You've been married before", I exclaimed! "Why didn't you tell me?" She replied, "I knew how you felt about dating someone who had been married, so I couldn't bring myself to tell you." I did have a phobia about dating married women. I didn't want some jealous ex-husband gunning for me, so Betty and I broke up. I started going to Fitzgerald again and dating Mary Jo.

In 1949 the world was at peace. Things on military bases were slow and easy. I even went out for the base football team. I wasn't big enough to do anything spectacular but I got to play a few times. What was really interesting was that we had no blacks on the team. When we played a team that

did, our guys tried to kill the black players rather than pay attention to the game.

I started to work part-time in the office of the registrar. I liked this and decided to build my career here. On the career ladder for a registrar, I first had to possess the military occupation specialty (MOS) of "clerk typist". This was 1950. The North Koreans invaded South Korea on June 25th, and we were at war. There was a big buildup of U.S. forces in Japan. All of a sudden I get orders for reassignment to the USAF Security Service (USAFSS) at Johnson AB, Japan. My commander did everything he could to stop this. I was medical and only possessed the "clerk typist" MOS on my career ladder to being a registrar. But it was in vain. The order wasn't changed so this was the end of my medical career.

I took a 10-day leave and went home to Fitzgerald. I spent a lot of time with Mary Jo and we really "fell in love". Strange thing about all my relationships with Mary Jo... If I had never left home, I am sure we would have married, but fate dictated otherwise. More about Mary Jo in my future.

The last time I was with her before departing for Korea, I tore a $2 bill in half and gave her a half. "We will join these together the next time I see you and spend them together," I told her.

I carried that $2 bill in my billfold the entire tour in Korea. I looked at it often and thought how wonderful it will be if I survive and I can keep my promise to her.

I don't know why but I still have my half. I sometimes run across it in my things. It brings back a lot of precious memories of our time together.

I caught a Greyhound bus from Fitzgerald to San Francisco. Very few flew in those days. It was either bus or train. Four days and nights on a bus! But I was young… met a lot of interesting people, saw a lot of new country… Tallahassee, New Orleans, El Paso, Phoenix, Los Angeles and San Francisco. From San Francisco, I caught a bus to Camp Stoneman, an Army base about 50 miles northeast of San Francisco.

In those days everyone went overseas by ship. You reported to a base and there you waited until they could fill a troop ship. This was usually about two weeks. These bases were called "repo depots", or "staging areas", or "casual collection points". While you waited, they'd check your shot records and give you what was needed for your assignment area. I got a shot called "Japanese B" and it made me sick. Later it was declared useless. They put you on crappy work details. But you soon learned how to avoid the worst of these.

Eventually we were on our way. About 3000 of us would be put on the ship. We were put on a huge ferry and went down river to Yerba Buena Island. This island sits in the middle of the Oakland Bay Bridge which spans the San Francisco Bay.

There we boarded our ship. The Army was anxious to get supplies to Korea, so we had to carry some military gear which included a metal helmet, a full field pack, rifle and a gas mask. The gang plank was steep. I had my duffle bag on top of the field pack between my head and the pack. The rifle slung over my shoulder. I'm sure all of that weighed as much as I did. I don't see how I made it.

So, off to Japan and a new adventure!

Note: For some reason, I have no pictures of Robins AFB or Macon, Georgia. Only one of Betty.

YERBA BUENA ISLAND
SAN FRANCISCO BAY, CALIFORNIA

1950-1952

▶ EN ROUTE TO JAPAN
OCTOBER - THE CRUISE

PACIFIC OCEAN
1950

USNS HEINLEMAN

TROOPSHIP
3500 G.I.'s
23 MISERABLE DAYS!

ENROUTE JAPAN 1950

OKINAWA

North Korea invaded South Korea June 25, 1950. I was reassigned from Robins AFB, Georgia to Johnson AB, Japan. During October 1950, I was on my way via troopship. I boarded it in San Francisco.

The ship was the U.S.S. General Heinzleman. It was a tub! It had been used to haul refugees from Europe to the U.S., after WWII. It was unstable, and it rolled because all the lifeboats hung high up the sides. It had been retired but pressed into service again for the Korean War.

There were about 3000 of us on this ship. It was very crowded and the bunks were stacked six deep in the holds. Guys in the upper bunks had a lot of climbing to do to get into their bunks. The aisles were narrow and full of equipment. The air was stale and smelled terrible. You spent as much time as possible topside. It was crowded on the outside decks. You had to stand behind something out of the wind. If you didn't you might get splattered with vomit from so many leaning over the sides to vomit.

Someone advised me to take a lot of soda crackers with me, for they helped sea sickness. This actually worked. I never vomited but my stomach felt so sore I could hardly touch it. When you sail out under the Golden Bay Bridge the ocean is full of huge swells. This is where most got seasick. In the dining hall that first evening there were half filled trays everywhere because so many got sick while eating and ran to topside. The decks were slimy.

They fed us three meals a day. They rotated the compartments. Breakfast started at 4 a.m. and the line was continuous to about 8 P.M. The end of the breakfast line got lunch. The end of the lunch line got dinner, so most of the time, you only got two meals. I never got enough to eat so I volunteered for K.P. This gave me something to do and I had plenty to eat.

The showers had only salt water in them. The sinks had regular water. What you did was fill your helmet at the sink, step into the shower stall, pour the water over your head, soap up, rinse off with salt water, go back to the sinks for another helmet of good water (I won't call it "fresh"), back to the shower stall and rinse off as best as you could. I think some guys never took a shower! The overall smell was so bad you never noticed. In the toilet and shower rooms, there was always several inches of water on the floor sloshing to and fro with the roll of the ship. I got a toenail fungus there that I have fought my entire life.

There was no place to show a movie. They tried to show one topside at the end of a large flat hold cover. Not one movie was ever completed. The wind would flap the screen so badly they always shut down the projector in the middle of the movie.

What few pocket books available passed through so many hands they were soon in tatters. There were dice crap games in progress everywhere, 24 hours a day. I didn't participate in these. A few sharpies got rich on that trip.

All this went on for 28 miserable days. Then we docked in Okinawa. (Twenty years later, I would spend a 3-year tour here). They wouldn't let us off the ship. Another 5 miserable days on the ship and

SA SEBO Navy Base
Japan

we docked in Sasebo, Japan. Boy, was I glad to get off that ship!

We were trucked to a processing center and I was then trucked to Johnson Air Base. I was assigned to 1st radio squadron, Mobile, USAFSS.

Thus began an interesting and fascinating tour in Japan and Korea.

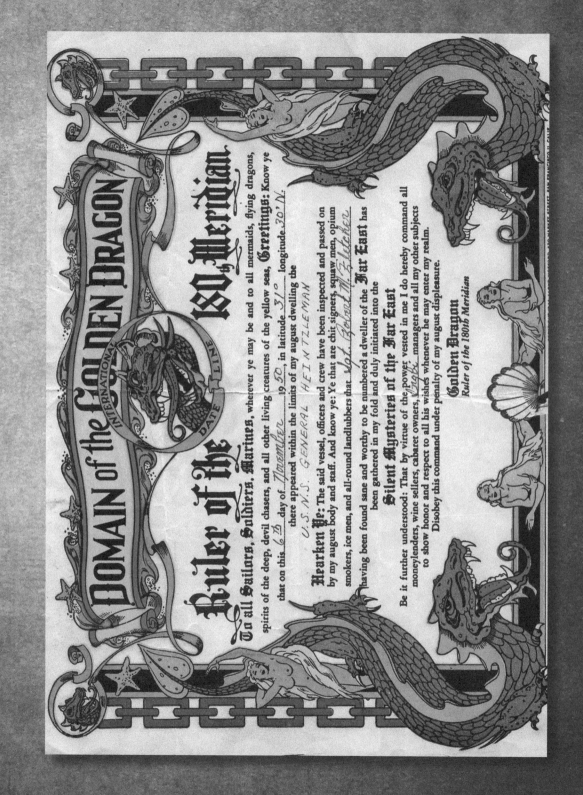

DOMAIN of the GOLDEN DRAGON

INTERNATIONAL DATE LINE

Ruler of the 180, Meridian

To all **Sailors, Soldiers, Marines,** wherever ye may be and to all mermaids, flying dragons, spirits of the deep, devil chasers, and all other living creatures of the yellow seas, **Greetings:** Know ye that on this 6th day of _November_ 19 50, in latitude 31° longitude 30' N. there appeared within the limits of my august dwelling the

U.S.N.S. GENERAL HEINTZLEMAN

Hearken Ye: The said vessel, officers and crew have been inspected and passed on by my august body and staff. And know ye: Ye that are chit signers, squaw men, opium smokers, ice men, and all-round landlubbers that _Sgt. Robert M. Fletcher_ having been found sane and worthy to be numbered a dweller of the **Far East** has been gathered in my fold and duly initiated into the

Silent Mysteries of the Far East

Be it further understood: That by virtue of the power vested in me I do hereby command all moneylenders, wine sellers, cabaret owners, _night_ managers and all my other subjects to show honor and respect to all his wishes whenever he may enter my realm. Disobey this command under penalty of my august displeasure.

Golden Dragon
Ruler of the 180th Meridian

OCTOBER, 1950 – FEBRUARY, 1952

▶ JOHNSON AIR BASE
JAPAN

WHERE I'VE BEEN IN JAPAN

JOHNSON AIR BASE

R&R FROM KOREA 5 DEC '51

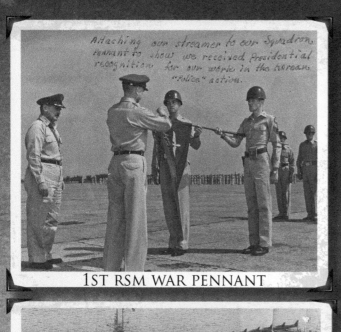

1ST RSM WAR PENNANT

AIR CRAFT CARRIER RETURNING TO U.S.

R&R FROM KOREA JAPAN 1951

Japan, Japan! A different world! Sight, smells, people… so interesting and fascinating! Really something for a country boy from South Georgia at the tender age of 20.

Johnson Air Base was a very large base. It had squadrons of our first jets, F-80's, F-84's, plus WWII B-25's and B-26's. All of Japan had a distinctive smell… charcoal, fish, rice patties, "night fertilizer", etc. All the sewer lines in small villages ran into a large, open-air tank. The farmers would dip this stuff out of the tank and put it on their crops. There were also "honey wagons" on the streets. They collected the "stuff" from individual homes. The air was so polluted from factories that a pall of smoke hung over the countryside.

My squadron was housed in dirty smoke-colored clapboard low buildings. The Japs had used them in WWII. The toilets and showers were in separate buildings from the sleeping areas. The buildings were joined by wooden walkways. We still had old WWII double decker cots. These shook often from minor earthquakes. The food in the mess hall was extremely good. All of the cooks were Japanese. Because of shift workers there was a 4th meal at midnight. Many guys were eating 4 meals a day.

As usual in those days, personnel procedures were screwed up. I was needed so badly that I was taken out of my medical career field. Yet, six of us showed up for the one opening.

I was assigned to the 1st Radio Squadron Mobile of the USAFSS (United States Air Force Security Service). This was part of a hush-hush secret organization. Everyone there had security clearances, top

JAPAN

NIKKO

secret or higher. It was an intelligence gathering organization and was linked to all the intelligence organizations in Washington, D.C. We had a large section that was behind a high security fence. It had a large group of guards. I was not allowed in there. It wasn't until I went to Korea that I learned what went on behind that fence.

Our squadron had about 400 personnel, so there was a lot of personnel work. Again, I was made the "morning report" clerk. The morning report was in a mess! The numbers of personnel in the report did not match the bodies present. It took me about a month of long hard hours to straighten it out. This paid off. I made staff sergeant early because of what I had accomplished.

While working in personnel I discovered how much work was involved when there was a fatality in the unit. We had two deaths. One guy was taking pictures while standing on top of one of the old buildings. The roof gave way and he fell all the way to the bottom floor and died immediately. Another died in bed, choked by his own vomit after excessive drinking. In Korea our guys were constantly doing dangerous things like fooling around with unexploded ordinance and hunting pheasants while walking through old mine fields. I warned them repeatedly because I knew how much paperwork I'd have to do if something happened to one of them.

Another job I had was processing marriage applications. This was very involved. The Security Service didn't take too kindly to its members fraternizing with the local girls. But it couldn't stop many of the stupid young airmen. Prostitutes were

65

plentiful. Guys were "shacking up" with these girls. In many cases it was the first time they had ever slept with a woman and they thought they were in love. They stupidly thought they wanted to get married. It was a lengthy process. They had sessions with chaplains and the commander. Their parents had to be notified and they had to have numerous interviews with me. I didn't pull any punches. I didn't mind calling their intended a "prostitute". Most changed their minds after all this counseling but some went through with it. There had to be a civil ceremony and be married by one of our chaplains. Once one was married, his clearance was revoked and he was transferred out of the security service.

I went through this again in a later time in Germany with stupid, young airmen marrying German girls.

MAUREEN

There was a fast train station right outside the gate. We would get into the heart of Tokyo in 30 minutes. They were packed! The platform men would shove people in tight. You couldn't move your feet. Everyone just swayed and swayed.

The Tokyo taxis were a riot! They were justifiably called "kamikazes". Each ride was an adventure. Some of the taxis ran by steam. There was actually a stove on the back bumper. The driver stopped every now and then and filled the stove with charcoal. Once, several of us took our dates home, and we didn't have enough yen among us to pay the bill. After much haggling between the girls and the driver, the driver accepted bags of charcoal from the girls as payment.

PERSONNEL OFFICE

VOLCANO ON MT. FUJI

FIRST BLUE
UNIFORM IN
JAPAN

Ah! Tokyo! No other place in the world like it! The main drag was called "Ginza Street". About 2 miles of it was used by U.S. military personnel. The largest BX in the world was there. We took over a department store building of several stories.

The Ginza was laced with bars, night clubs and shops for G.I.'s. Girls! Girls! Girls! Everywhere!!! And some were cute too. They would come up and grab your hand and try to get you into a bar or restaurant. Yes, I dated a few but none off the street. The ones I dated I met through my buddies' girlfriends.

The Tokyo NCO Club was a palace. It would rival the casinos in Las Vegas. It had slot machines, cheap food and booze (I didn't

STAFF AT A LUXURY HOTEL

MAUREEN AND FRIENDS

JOHNSON AB

drink other than a beer or two). There were great shows and dances. The military before and since never had a club like that one!

General Macarthur had his headquarters downtown. A large crowd would gather every morning as he got out of his limousine. The crowd would cheer and he would wave to them. I saw him twice. That limousine is in his museum in Norfolk, Virginia. I saw it there again.

I had a buddy that was billeted in a luxury hotel in downtown Tokyo… Wow! Unbelievable! There is nothing like duty in an army of occupation.

LUXURY HOTELS

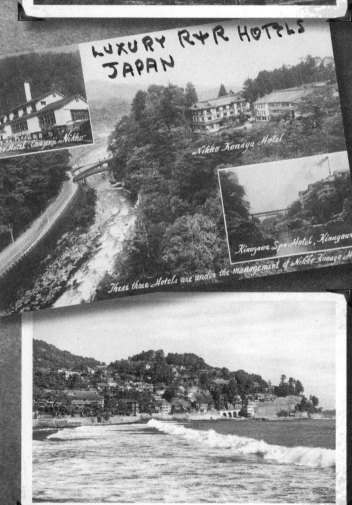

LUXURY R&R HOTELS JAPAN

Kanko Hotel, Chuzenji Nikko

Nikko Kanaya Hotel

Kinugawa Spa Hotel, Kinugawa

These three Hotels are under the management of Nikko Kanaya Hotel

We had taken over all the luxury resorts in the mountains and on the seashores. There were palaces too. I went to several of these. What a life! 50 cents a day! Scrumptious meals 24 hours a day, cheap drinks, bands every night, spas in the basements, girls giving massages in your room, etc.

There were in the basements two large pools of water. One was practically boiling and the other was ice water. What you did was lie in the hot water till you couldn't stand it any more and then you

LUXURY HOTELS
R+R JAPAN

MAUREEN

BUDDY–RAY EAST

CANADIAN GIRLFRIEND - JAPAN

← MAUREEN

MAUREEN

MT. FUJI—HIKED QUITE A WAYS UP IT

would run and jump into the ice water. Wow! It felt like you were hit by a million needles all at once!

I really enjoyed the baths and massages. The girls would actually bathe you. Then you would lie on a table and they would give you a great massage. Then you would lie on your stomach and the girl would stand on your back. These girls were really small. They would step all over you and massage you with their toes. Now, that was an experience!

It was en route to one of these that I met Maureen. She was Canadian and worked at the Canadian Embassy in Tokyo. I went to church with her and to embassy parties and picnics. We all played softball on Sunday afternoon in one of the beautiful Tokyo parks. We went together to several of those resorts. Separate rooms always! Dancing, sightseeing trips, sailing, and all kinds of wonderful activities. She was very smart. She wanted no serious relationship.

She was older (26), Catholic, and she knew I would rotate back to the U.S. We were just great friends having a lot of fun. Later, when my brother, Monte, who was in the Navy and visited Japan, looked her up. He said she kept calling him Bob. We never wrote and I lost track of her completely.

Rumor came out that the G.I. Bill would only be given to those who spent time in Korea. I really wanted the G.I. Bill. We had a small detachment in Korea, so I volunteered to go there. There was a regulation that stated that if a family member had been KIA (killed in action), no other member had to serve in a war zone. One of my brothers was KIA in France in WWII. So, I had to sign a waiver in order to serve in Korea.

So, off to a new assignment, a new experience, and what an experience!! Korea!

KOREA
JANUARY 1951 - JANUARY 1952

MY HOME
KOREA

SEOUL
KOREA

Seoul June 1951

I was at Johnson AB, Japan, happy in my work, good, easy duties, and run of the countryside and Tokyo. But it was rumored that a new G.I. Bill was in the works and only those who served in Korea would get it. So I volunteered to go to Korea. It turned out to be an interesting and exciting experience.

The Chinese had entered the war and pushed the U.N. Forces (mostly American) into the southeast portion of the Korean Peninsula. There was a big port on the southeast coast called Pusan. So, we finally quit retreating and formed a front line about what was called "The Pusan Perimeter".

I flew in on an old WWII C-47 into K2 Airfield in Taegu. A mountainous ridgeline in sight of K2 was the front line. I watched from K2 as our B-26's bombed the ridgeline. For some reason I wasn't scared or worried about "buggin' out".

I joined our Detachment 13 in a very large compound in the heart of Taegu. About 20 guys in the detachment had been near the Yalu River when the Chinese crossed the river and changed the course of the war. "Mobile" was part of our name and you had to be ready to move at a moment's notice. These guys had lots of stories about their "bugout" and retreat. I was glad I wasn't with them during that time.

Taegu was a sprawling, dirty city. It was packed with our troops, U.N. Troops and a couple of million refugees, plus thousands of South Korean troops.

What was really sad was thousands of orphan kids. In rags they gathered around campfires at night. During the day they would be begging for food. Each carried a small pail.

North Korean   Seoul   Korea   Jun 51

RADAR HILL KIMPO AIR BASE KOREA

HEADQUARTERS
1ST RADIO SQUADRON, MOBILE
APO 994

10 September 1951

SUBJECT: Meritorious Unit Commendation

TO   : All Personnel, 1st Radio Squadron, Mobile, APO 994
          Commanding Officer, Detachment 11, 1st Radio Sq, (M), APO 919
          Commanding Officer, Detachment 12, 1st Radio Sq, (M), APO 919
          Commanding Officer, Detachment 13, 1st Radio Sq, (M), APO 970
          Officer in Charge, Team "1", APO 970

    1. On Saturday 8 September 1951 this squadron was awarded the
Meritorious Unit Commendation. The ceremony consisted of a formal review
with fourteen squadrons of the base participating and was climaxed by
Brigadier General Charles I. Banfill afixing the appropriate streamer
to the Squadron Guidon.

    2. This award, which ranks high among those given to non-combatant
units, has been received by only two other units in the Far East Air
Forces since the outbreak of hostilities in Korea. It is, therefore, a
direct indication of the outstanding manner in which every member of the
squadron has performed his assigned duty. It is my desire that the
contents of this letter and the inclosed citation be brought to the attention of all officers and airmen of the 1st Radio Squadron, Mobile.

                                    CHARLES W. SHEPAR
                                    Lt Colonel, USAF
                                    Commanding

1 Incl:
  Citation

1ST RADIO SQDN MOBILE
DETACHMENT 13
MOTOR POOL

BRITISH OR S.AFRICAN AF

KIMPO RUINS

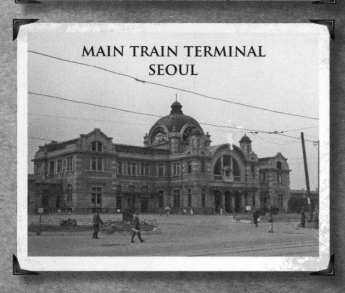
MAIN TRAIN TERMINAL SEOUL

In Korea if you helped an accident victim you were responsible for him. A child was killed by a truck and lay for days in the middle of the street covered by a straw mat.

The money exchange rate was 1,000 Won to a dollar. We would get a stack of Won notes and go down to where the kids were. We would hand out 100 Won notes to them. You had to insure you had an avenue of escape for they would soon mob you, and you had to "bug out".

We used military script for our money. Greenbacks were illegal. It was strange having paper 5c, 10c, 25c, 50c and $1 in paper money.

There was quite a black market in script and greenbacks. For a greenback dollar you could get $5 in legal script. Every month or so the script would be changed for a new version since so much of it was on the economy. The exchange was supposed to be top secret. One day everyone would be notified that the old version was null and void and what you had had to be turned in for the new version. Somehow, the civilians found out about the exchange early. They would be packed six-deep along our security fence holding up stacks and wads of the old script. They would be screaming. They wanted to give you script for anything of value. They'd pay ten times the worth for cigarettes, cameras, radios, watches, etc.

The black market was quite an operation. I once visited an area that covered a square mile. Everything was for sale, most of it stolen military hardware and goods. We had a small motor pool. For cases of beer our guys could get all the parts necessary to keep all our vehicles running.

Detachment 13 consisted of a captain (who was the commander and a big goof-off), another captain, a 1st LT (a brilliant guy who spoke several languages including Chinese) 4 men in the motor pool, two T/SGT intelligence analyst, about 10 world known code breakers.

We had the most advanced radio receivers in the world. The enemy, North Koreans, Chinese and Russians still transmitted by Morse code all their communications. But they had their own codes. Our radio operators would copy the intercepted transmissions and give this to the code breakers. They broke all the codes and wrote the results in English as best they could. My buddy and I would straighten out their English as best we could and type our results. The information would be studied by Lt. Gilbert, revised as needed, and then we would deliver the finished product to headquarters 5th Air Force and 8th Army. The intelligence we got was amazing! Lt. Gilbert had a huge chart on the wall with a setup of the complete enemy organizations and even the names of all their commanders. Later, during peace talks, the unit would intercept messages that the enemy negotiators sent back to their people each evening. Thus, our people were armed the next day with what the enemy negotiators were thinking about us and their own plans.

Another good example of our intelligence work! The Chinese and Russians kept all their planes in Manchuria north of the Yalu River. The North Koreans actually had an air force of about 14 planes. They kept them hidden. One day they decided to move all of them. We learned of this and gave the information to the 5th Air Force. We were waiting for them and shot down every one of them. We got

HIGH SCHOOL BUDDY

RADIO ROOM

DIGGING A LATRINE

LOADING C-119 TAEGU TO SEOUL

HEADQUARTERS
1ST RADIO SQUADRON, MOBILE
APO 994

27 August 1951

SUBJECT: Letter of Commendation

TO : Officers and Airmen
Detachment 13
1st Radio Squadron, Mobile
APO 970

1. I would like to take this opportunity to express my personal satisfaction and appreciation of the splended work which your Detachment has accomplished in support of air operations of the Fifth Air Force. Your outstanding efforts and superior results obtained truly represent a job well done.

2. This headquarters has taken action through Far East Air Forces to obtain recognition by an appropriate military award based upon the above mentioned activities of your unit.

3. It is my desire that the contents of this letter be brought to the attention of all personnel presently associated with your unit, those who were previously assigned and others whosesppport made these successes possible.

CHARLES W. SHEPARD
Lt Colonel, USAF
Commanding

**CAPT. HARRIGAN
LT. GILBERT**

HEADQUARTERS
FAR EAST AIR FORCES
APO 925

29 August 1951

GENERAL ORDERS
NUMBER   411)

MERITORIOUS UNIT COMMENDATION

As authorized by Executive Order 9396, 22 November 1943 (Sec I, WD Bul
22, 1943) superseding Executive Order 9075, 26 February 1942 (Sec III, WD Bul.
11, 1942 and pursuant to authority contained in General Orders Number 3, Department of the Air Force, 23 January 1951, the following unit is cited under
the provisions of Air Force Regulation 35-75, 7 August 1950, in the name of the
President of the United States as public evidence of deserved honor and distinction. The citation reads as follows:

The 1st Radio Squadron, Mobile distinguished itself by exceptionally
meritorious conduct in performance of outstanding service from 26 November 1950
to 13 July 1951. Throughout this period, the 1st Radio Squadron was of material
assistance to the tactical and strategic mission of all services of United Nations forces engaged in the Korean conflict. The unremitting and tireless efforts of this unit provided continuous support of such nature and extent that in
large measure it contributed to the success of the United Nations mission. The
outstanding efforts of this organization were of incalculable value to the Unit
Nations and to the security of the United States. The meritorious conduct and
devotion to duty displayed by the personnel of the 1st Radio Squadron, Mobile,
sustained the highest traditions of the military service and reflected great
credit upon the Squadron, the Far East Air Forces, and the United States Air
Force.

BY COMMAND OF LIEUTENANT GENERAL WEYLAND:

                                          L. C. CRAIGIE
                                          Major General, USAF
OFFICIAL: Vice Commander

s/E. E. Toro
t/E. E. TORO   A TRUE COPY:
Colonel, USAF
Adjutant General   Jim B. Hammons
                                          JIM B. HAMMONS
                                          2d Lt, USAF

HOUSE BOY LEE

KORIAN AIR FORCE FRIENDS

PART OF EWHA COLLEGE

KOREA
C-119

a direct wire from President Truman congratulating us. He also gave us the presidential unit citation. This meant we could wear a gold edged purple ribbon on our right chest.

Another example of our intelligence work: Our radios intercepted Chinese broadcasts. Each evening at the same time the Chinese would put on a program with our prisoners of war. Our guys would identify themselves and read a propaganda statement. The statements were so ridiculous it was obvious they were forced. Such as, "Mom and

CAPTAIN CHO.
WORLD REKNOWN CODE BREAKER

Dad, write your congressman. Stop this illegal war against the peace loving peoples of China and North Korea." You get the picture. It was obvious to us that the poor guy just wanted his folks to know he was alive. We would turn over these statements to the proper intelligence authorities.

We also intercepted the transmitted weather observations sent out by the North Koreans and the Russian and Chinese Air Forces. These were quickly given to the USAF weather personnel at Headquarters 5th AF. This was valuable information for our fighters and bombers.

Also we kept up with the latest American Hit Parade which came over the air from Radio Australia.

I arrived in Korea in January, 1951. It was cold! There was a lot of snow. We had great cold weather gear. We had a heavy, thick coat (parka), a fur-lined cap with fold-down earflaps, fur-lined gloves as well as boots!

Everything in our military was in a compound. Each one was surrounded by a high hurricane fence topped with barbed wire. There was one gate and you had to sign in and out. In my home compound we had about 50 12-man tents. The mess hall was in a huge wooden building. The latrine was in one tent, showers in another.

It was cold in that tent. We had wooden plank floors and a small pot-bellied stove dripped oil all the time. We slept on canvass cots and had no sheets or pillows. We had one huge comforter and a couple of G.I. blankets. We had a "tent boy" who kept the tent clean and guarded our belongings. He soon learned good English.

86

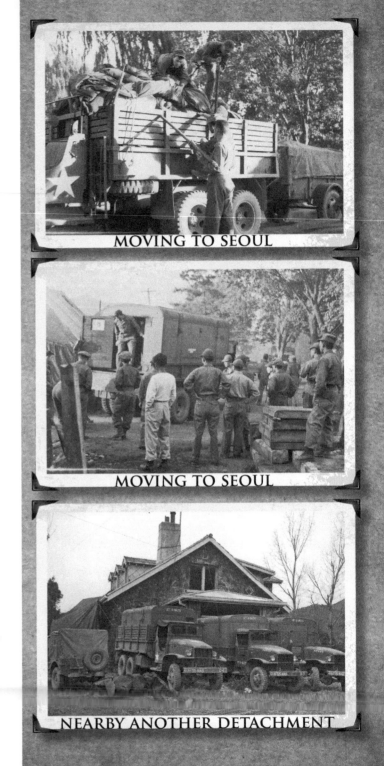

MOVING TO SEOUL

MOVING TO SEOUL

NEARBY ANOTHER DETACHMENT

Our latrine was a tent with open flap sides, with no heat. The toilets were long wooden benches with holes cut in them. Below were just trenches the Koreans with their "honey wagons", kept cleaned out. It was not a pleasant place and was freezing.

Our drinking water was in a tank on a trailer outside. We filled our canteens there. The water always tasted of iodine.

The shower tent was something! The sinks were holes in long wooden benches. Your steel helmet fit into the hole. It was used as a wash-pan. For hot water there was a gas heater on the roof. Several Koreans hauled buckets of water up ladders and dumped them into a huge tank. It wasn't unusual to get all soaped up in the shower, and the water would quit coming.

My office was in a building somewhere in Taegu. The radios were in tents near our sleeping tents. Someone would take the papers to the office. Then we would deliver the finished product to HQs 5th Air Force and 8th Army. We worked until 2 or 3am seven days a week. We wore a .45 on our hip and a 30-caliber carbine over our shoulder at all times.

Our Army finally broke out of The Pusan Perimeter, pushed rapidly north and recaptured Seoul, the capitol. Detachment 13 packed up and we moved to Seoul. It was sad leaving our tent boy. We gave him enough money to live on for several months. A lot of our equipment went by truck, but several of us plus equipment went by air in a C-119 "boxcar" transport plane. These were small, big body, twin booms with two propeller engines. Noisy and lumbering. We sat on canvas benches along the sides. We had a scary moment on takeoff. When the nose came up the load shifted toward the rear door. I thought we were about to be squashed, but it went straight back and stopped before hitting the rear door.

We landed at Kimpo Air Base (K-16) just outside of Seoul. We and the equipment were trucked to our destination. We set up operating in a huge stone building that had been a part of a girls' college. It was called EWHA College and covered several acres. All had been shot up pretty badly. There had been a major battle here. Old shell casings and spent ammo was everywhere. When rain washed out the gullies there were skeletons of North Korean and Chinese soldiers in them. There was unused ammo and land mines everywhere. The guys started using skulls for ash trays. Ghoulish!

Several of us put our cots in a very large room on the ground floor. The radios were also on the ground floor. The code breakers worked on the second floor. The Asians attached to us lived on the third floor. They were always cooking something that smelled up the entire building.

We ate in a small Army mess in the woods up from my billet on the side of a hill. We had to use our metal mess kits. These were used in WWII. The kit consisted of two small pans about 4"x6" with a small divider in the center, knife, fork, spoon and a cup for drink or coffee. All these snapped together and can hang from your belt. After eating you hooked them all together and dunked them several times in a G.I. garbage can full of boiling water. Very efficient really.

When we dumped leftovers in a garbage can, little kids would run out of the woods and get the garbage out of the cans. We soon learned to leave more food

S.KOREAN ARMY TROOPS

KOREA OUR LATRINE

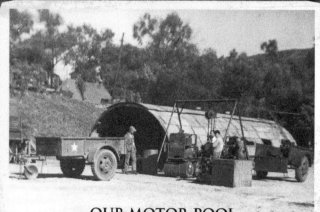

OUR MOTOR POOL

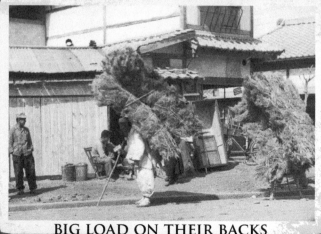

BIG LOAD ON THEIR BACKS

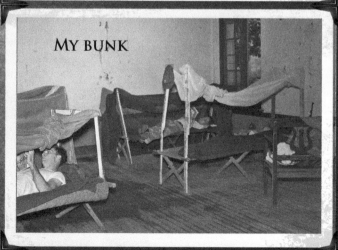

MY BUNK

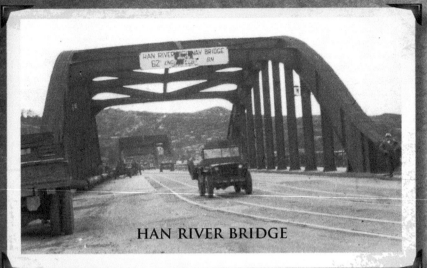

HAN RIVER BRIDGE

FAMOUS HAN RIVER BRIDGE

CAPITOL

BLACK MARKET

BX GIRLS

TAEGU P.X.

SCENE OUT FRONT OF OUR GATE

FRONT FULL OF BULLET HOLES

EWHA

EWHA

EWHA

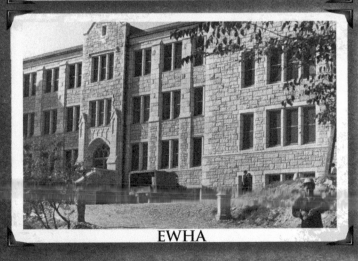

EWHA

OUT FRONT GATE

in our kit and try to lay it in the can instead of just dumping it.

One evening, I was running late for chow. I parked my jeep, ran inside, grabbed my mess kit and ran up the hill. While I was eating I suddenly thought, "Oh, No! I left a brief case full of top secret material under the driver's seat!" I ran back downhill to the jeep, looked under the seat – and the briefcase was gone!

Panic can't describe what I felt! I went inside and one of our officers was standing at the top of the stairs with the brief case. "You know what I could do to you, don't you?" "Yes, Sir!" Losing top secret material would compromise our entire mission. It could mean prison, loss of rank, courts martial, etc. I was scared! "Sgt. Fletcher, I think you and I are the only ones who know about this. I need you too much to lose you. I'll keep this quiet but I'll keep my eye on you!" "Yes, Sir, yes Sir. I will be more careful, Sir!" Wow! What a traumatic experience!

There was no running water in the building. A water trailer was parked outside for drinking and brushing your teeth. It tasted like chlorine and iodine. To drink it you had to drop a pill in your canteen.

For a toilet we had a 3-holer that was built overhanging a cliff. The refuse went way down there somewhere. It was scary to go to the toilet! We finally built a latrine like the one we had in Taegu.

We had no showers. Every few days we would load up a 6x6 truck and go out to a quarry a few miles away. But bodies of dead Korean soldiers started popping up and floating around. That was the end of that bathing spot. So we built a shower house like the one in Taegu and had Koreans and their buckets climbing up the ladders.

The motor pool guys had a separate building. The commander was constantly throwing women out of their quarters.

We had a small Korean military police unit in one of the buildings. One day I heard yelling and went to see what was going on. They were beating a guy up badly. I asked one what was going on. "He stole some gas." A few days later they were beating up another guy. The prior one they had beaten was all bandaged up and beating on the new guy! Crazy Koreans!

I had to take the work of our code breakers to my office downtown to work on it. It was quite a trip. I wore my steel helmet, a 45 pistol on my hip and a 30-caliber carbine on my shoulder or on the seat next to me. When I left the college gate I had to drive through several rundown areas on very narrow roads. The famous Han River Bridge was planks and one-way. Then through bombed and shelled-out city buildings and by the burned out shell of the main train terminal. There were burned out tanks and trucks everywhere. Sometimes the road was just two tracks through a lot of debris. Then down a wide boulevard with what at one time was a great view of the capitol building at the end of it. Now the capitol building was just a burned out shell. So sad. I turned right at the building and then a mile or two to where I worked.

Fifth Air Force headquarters was in what used to be the main city hospital. It was a huge complex.

FRONT LINES KOREA

BATTLE TAKING PLACE KOREA

CHINESE TROOPS 2   MOUNTAINS 3.

OUR TANKS 1   VALLEY

The main building my office was in was about 8 stories high and had many wings. The buildings had escaped heavy fighting and shelling and were in good shape. All the hospital equipment had been thrown outside in huge piles.

Across the street was the headquarters of the 8th Army. I think it had been a huge university. General MacArthur was a constant visitor. I took a lot of trips over there delivering top secret materials to their intelligence offices.

We had several high ranking air force security officers visit us. They wanted to visit the front lines. I volunteered to drive one of the jeeps. This was my first visit to an actual front line in a real war zone.

It was about a 60-mile drive to the front where we went. Hills and torn up roads. Land mines on the road were always on my mind. We went to an area near Charwon, North Korea, which was north of the 38th Parallel. We were on a high ridgeline overlooking a broad valley. The Chinese and North Koreans were on a ridgeline on the other side of the valley. We could see their soldiers moving about over there. Our tanks were down in the valley firing shells at them. Our artillery shells were whistling over our heads and exploding over there. It was like watching a war movie. Our soldiers lived in caves. It was a little scary and I was sure relieved to get safely back to Seoul.

At night there was an ancient biplane flying around over Seoul. It was North Korean. He would fire his pistol out his window as he circled around our hilltop radar sites. He would drop hand grenades out his window all over Seoul. There would be numerous searchlights on him as he circled about

95

and our antiaircraft shells would be bursting all about him. But we never could shoot him down! We called him "Bed-check Charlie". Everyone was cheering for him. It was very entertaining and was like the 4th of July.

In some of the makeshift billets around Seoul, spies would sneak up and toss hand grenades in the windows. One night I was sound asleep when "Crash! Boom! Bang!" I was covered in plaster. I thought a hand grenade had gone off. What happened was the entire ceiling plaster had come loose and fell on me.

Korea was a United Nations' effort although we bore the brunt of it. I really enjoyed meeting and drinking beer with soldiers and airmen from South Africa, Australia and England. I couldn't comprehend why the British liked warm beer. We had no refrigerators so we put our beer in laundry bags and lowered them into an old well which kept it pretty cool.

There were wild pheasants everywhere. Our guys would kill and cook them. They were good. I was in charge of personnel and administration. I warned them repeatedly about land mines. I was also worried about how much paperwork would be involved if something happened to one of them.

We had a new jeep stolen after being unloaded at Pusan. Months later the Korean Air Force guys attached to us were issued a used jeep by their air force. Our guys checked the serial numbers and discovered it was our jeep that had been stolen in Pusan!

CAPITOL

KOREA

5th AF HQRTS

Cold!!

OFF TO R&R IN JAPAN!

KOREA

South Korean Troops Parade for Rhee

ROK troops parade before the reviewing stand of South Korean President Syngman Rhee during ceremonies after his second inauguration. Fearing an assassination attempt, police kept the crowds away from the stand.
—United Press Photo

BATHING
KOREA

One day I was notified by 5th Air Force that the new jeep we requisitioned had arrived. I told the commander that I hadn't requisitioned a jeep. "Go get it anyway", he told me. "Give it to our motor pool guys and tell them to strip it". The jeep was brand new. The top was new, the tires, the seats, everything. Our guys replaced the windshield with our cracked one, changed the tires, the top, etc. The next day I received a call. "There has been a mistake. Bring that jeep back immediately". It would barely run and looked terrible. When I took it back the sergeant looked it over and shook his head. "Are you sure this is the jeep you picked up yesterday?" "Sho is", I told him. Look at the serial number". We got away clean to my surprise.

We had several real good USO shows. The one I remember most featured Danny Kaye. He was a big movie star at the time and with him was Monica Lewis. She was one of the original Hollywood "sweater girls".

We also had in a small theater a presentation by Raymond Burr. He was a big star in the TV series "Ironsides". He was a lawyer and was always in a wheelchair. He had the most intriguing voice I have ever heard before or since. We were spellbound on the edge of our seats!

In a war zone there is no such thing as a "day off". We worked 7 days a week and late into the night. About every six weeks we typed up a legal looking set of illegal orders and sent our guys TDY (temporary duty) back to 1st Radio Squadron, Mobile, our parent organization in Japan. This was really for "time off" purposes. It was called "R&R"

CAPT. CHO LATER BECAME A
MAJOR GENERAL AND HEAD
OF ENTIRE S.KOREAN AIR FORCE.

(rest and recuperation). Some guys called it "I&I" (intoxication and intercourse).

On my R&R trips I had to hitchhike on a lot of airplanes hopping to different bases in Korea and Japan, slept on the floors in a lot of planes and terminals. In most of the planes the parachutes were piled up in the rear. I made sure I was always close to them.

We maintained lockers at 1st Radio Squadron where we kept our uniforms and civilian clothes. We wore only fatigues and boots in Korea. I would go to Tokyo or one of the luxury hotels we had. After I met Maureen, I would see her often at one of the hotels or in Tokyo.

We bought cases of whiskey in Japan for $24. In Korea it brought $40 for each fifth.

We accumulated "rotation points" for every month in Korea. I was there 12 months and had enough to rotate back to the States. I returned to Johnson Air Base in January 1952.

At Johnson I had a lot of free time while awaiting a ship to the States. I decided to get a "circumcision". Don't laugh! I don't know why I never had one. In 1930 no babies were given circumcisions automatically. It was an experience! The guys on the ward were always depositing sexy pictures on my bed. The hospital was full of Army men recovering from battle wounds suffered in Korea. Some had actually been in hand to hand combat. One soldier said he was in hand to hand combat with some Chinese. He said he went crazy and was smashing heads with his trench shovel. Another said he was lying on a ledge with his finger on the trigger of his rifle in front of him. Suddenly the head of a Chinese soldier popped up in front of him right at the end of his rifle. He just pulled the trigger and blew his head off. I'm glad I never had to fire a shot in anger.

In Korea we lost around 50,000 killed in action and 200,000 wounded. Such a waste.

Finally I was sent to a "repo depot" to wait for a ship to the States. Strangely, about 200 of us were taken to Sasebo Naval Base and put on a small aircraft carrier. It was luxury compared to that tub "Heinzleman" I came over on.

It was a thrill to pass under the Golden Gate again. We landed at Yerba Buena Island in the middle of the bridge. We were given 3-day passes to San Francisco. Some guys weren't so lucky. We had a couple of dozen that were kept in isolation on the ship. They were kept under guard and immediately bussed to Fitzsimmons Army Hospital. They had V.D (Venereal Diseases). It was rampant in Japan and Korea. Some of these guys had types of V.D. never seen before. We had lots of lectures and training in Japan on how to avoid and prevent V.D. This group ignored the warnings.

I have always loved San Francisco. Strange that I would return 20 years later on my way to Vietnam and another war.

When we disembarked at Yerba Buna in San Francisco Bay, as soon as we could, we rushed to the Navy Exchange for milk, milkshakes, and real

MERRY XMAS

CHRISTMAS
1950

1ST RADIO SQDN MOBILE

Menu
Thanksgiving Day
Nov. 22 '51
Seoul, Korea

Maj. Gen. F.F. Everest, Com. General
Brig. Gen. J. Ferguson, Vice Com.
Col. W.R. Williams, Asst. Vice Com.
Col. J.J. O'Shea, Group Commander
Maj. C.V. Hull, Group Executive Off.
Capt. B.A. Segraves, Food Svce Off.
Capt. E.E. Morley, Mess Off.
1/Lt. L.P. Miller, Food Svce Adj.

—o—

American hamburgers. In Japan and Korea we only got some type of reconstituted milk - a whole year with no real milk! We couldn't get enough of real milk and real American hamburgers. Also, real vegetables! In Japan and Korea all the vegetables served in the military were grown on "hydroponic farms". They were grown totally in liquid! We couldn't eat anything grown locally because of the use of "night fertilizer" by the Japanese and Koreans.

I caught a Greyhound bus for a 4-day bus ride to home, family, and Mary Jo.

Thus ended my first of several trips overseas. I know I was changed forever by what I saw and experienced. I had experienced two new cultures. I had seen what conditions very poor people have to live in. I had experienced a real war. I had crossed the Pacific Ocean twice. Quite a lot for a 20-21 year old.

Civilian life is so boring!

So, on to new adventures!

HOME FROM KOREA

▶ En Route to Germany

BROOKLYN
TRAIN CAMP KILMER TO NAVY YARD

GOING OUT TO GERMAN

14 JUN 52

NEW JERSEY EER
ENROUTE TO EER

I returned from Korea aboard an aircraft carrier; I went through processing at Yerba Buena Island in San Francisco Bay; caught a Greyhound bus for a 4-day ride to home, family, and Mary Jo.

Mary Jo and I had a great time on my ten-day leave. We thought we were in love and even talked of marriage someday.

My brother, J.E., in Jacksonville, Florida, helped me buy a brand new '52 Ford Victoria. It was top of the line and cost $1800. I paid cash for it with the money I had saved in Korea.

After leave I had to report to Brooks Air Force Base, San Antonio, Texas. I drove my new Ford. There were no interstates in 1952. It was US-90 all the way and it was a very scenic route.

Brooks was a beautiful little base. San Antonio had grown up around it. No aircraft were active there. In WWII it had been a B-25 base. Every building on the base was wooden, old WWII. The USAF Security Service headquarters was at nearby Kelly AFB. Lackland AFB was just a few miles down the road to the south. I found out that Brooks was used by the USAFSS as a "repo depot". Several hundred of us there awaiting assignments all over the world.

I remember listening on my car radio to an instrumental "Blue Tango" by Leroy Anderson all the way from Georgia. It was playing when I entered Brooks. It was a lonely Sunday afternoon when I was assigned to a partly filled, old WWII wooden barracks. I'll never forget that day. Nothing is more lonely than a strange barracks on a strange base, knowing no one, on a Sunday afternoon. I have a copy of "Blue Tango". When I play it I am back on that lonely Sunday afternoon.

There was a large wooden mess hall. The offices were in wooden buildings. Hundreds of airmen were milling about waiting for assignments.

I have been back to Brooks. The base was given to the city. The city has done nothing there. All the buildings I knew are gone. The base is abandoned and neglected. So sad. I never want to visit there again.

I was there about ten days waiting for an assignment with nothing to do. An announcement was made that volunteers to Germany were needed. I wanted to do anything to get out of there. Why not?

I had orders for Germany. I was afraid to tell Mary Jo. I arrived in Fitzgerald and surprised her. I was the one surprised! "What are you doing back here so quickly", she wanted to know? "I'm going overseas again, to Germany". "Well, I'm not waiting for you anymore!" I really couldn't blame her for feeling that way. We dated a few times, but it was never the same.

Now I was going north up US-1 in my '52 Ford Victoria. I reported to the repo depot at Camp Kilmer, New Brunswick, New Jersey. New Brunswick is the home of Rutgers University, an old and famous school.

Camp Kilmer was a strange, small Army base. It was built in WWI. It was named for Joyce Kilmer, the poet best known for "Trees". (I think that I shall never see a poem as lovely as a tree, etc. etc.) He was killed in WWI in France.

I was very used to repo depots by this time. Again I had to wait a couple of weeks while they filled a ship. I was a Staff Sergeant now and didn't have to pull "crappy" details. I still had my Ford and explored the New Brunswick area. At the USO downtown, I met a local girl. Can't remember her name. Nothing serious. Pizza with friends, riding around, USO dances, etc., I met her family. I really enjoyed going to the beach at Perth Amboy with her and her friends. We both knew I was on borrowed time.

I had to take my Ford to the Brooklyn Navy Yard in New York City for it to be shipped to Germany, and I didn't like that city. Nothing but "Yankees"! I had to ride the subway and train back to Camp Kilmer. I had a hard time. I'd ask for help in getting on and off those darn subway cars, and people would ignore me or couldn't speak English.

At Camp Kilmer, they had dances at the Service Club. They would bring several bus-loads of girls from New York City. I danced with several. These weren't like any girls I had known! Most were dark Italians and really "Yankee". It was obvious they were looking for husbands and an escape from New York City.

The popular song at the time was "I'm Yours", by Vaughn Monroe and Eddy Fisher. I have these on CD's. When I hear them I am on US-1 or at Camp Kilmer. Strange how so many of my memories are tied to music and songs.

Finally, we were put on a train to some place in New York and put on a large ship to Bremerhaven, Germany. This was a 7-day trip. This was a lot nicer ship than those I had to Japan and return.

I was an enlisted Staff Sergeant, but I was still put "below decks". My only duty was night "C.Q" (Charge of Quarters). I just sat at a desk and took care of minor problems with the enlisted men. The officers and civilians were in staterooms topside. They had dances and parties every night and they ate in dining rooms. We would sit around on the deck, listen to the music, and watch them dancing. For the first time I thought about becoming an officer.

Finally we arrived in Bremerhaven, Germany. Thus begins a very unusual, interesting and exciting tour.

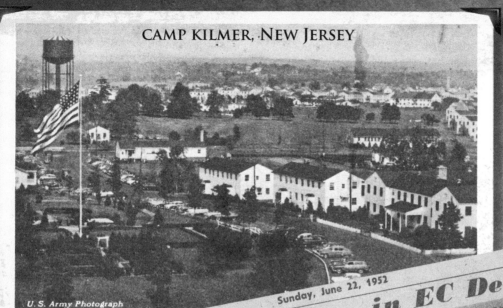

CAMP KILMER, NEW JERSEY

U. S. Army Photograph

LEFT N.Y., N.Y.: 14 JUNE 1952   ARRIVED BREMERHAVEN GERMANY: 22 JUNE 1952

Sunday, June 22, 1952

MSTS Ship Due in EC Debut

USNS BARRETT

New Barrett to Ply N.Y.-BPE Route

BREMERHAVEN, June 21 (Special)—The USNS Barrett, the latest addition to the Atlantic fleet of the Military Sea Transportation Service, is due to put in at Bremerhaven on her maiden voyage the latter part of this month, according to Commander Dillon R. McMullen, commanding officer of the MSTS port office. This will mark the beginning of her regular run, carrying troops and dependents, between BPE and the New York port.

Originally built for the American President Lines round-the-world service, the Barrett has never been sailed commercially. Her conver-

sion to a military transport was recommended by the Joint Chiefs of Staff following the outbreak of hostilities in Korea.

The 17,000-ton ship won the speed laurel of the MSTS fleet last April by attaining a speed of 21 1/2 knots on her trial runs. She has an overall length of 533 feet and 9 inches and a beam of 73 feet. She is completely air-conditioned and can accommodate more than 1,500 troops and almost 400 cabin-type passengers.

The conversion from commercial to transport status entailed lengthening and making additions to her superstructure as well as extensive changes inside the hull to convert her cargo holds into dormitories, galleys and recreation space for troops. Her facilities also

Service Scheduled For Troops, Kin

include a hospital, motion picture services, writing room, library and cafeteria.

Streamlined and modern in appearance, the Barrett is without conditional funnels, smoke and other exhaust gases being emitted through two kingpost-shaped stacks. The funnels and blue smokestacks of the MSTS are painted on the bridge house which has the appearance of a large funnel.

The ship was named in honor of Maj Gen Charles Dodson Barrett, U.S. Marine Corps, who died in 1943 while commanding the 3d Marine Div in the South Pacific.

WELCOME!

UNITED STATES AIR FORCE

HEADQUARTERS
12th AIR FORCE
(ADVON)

LANDSBERG AIR BASE

7030th HEADQUARTERS SUPPORT GROUP APO 61, PM. NY., NY.

LANDSBERG/LECH

BAVARIA, GERMANY

GERMANY 1952-1953

S/SG ROBERT FLETCHER.
AF 14264605
BUILDING # 4
EARNST LUDWIG KAZERNE
DARMSTADT GERMANY
DUITSLAND.

LANDSBERG AIR BASE

LANDSBERG AIR BASE

ENROUTE TO HOLLAND

Seven days on the troopship USS Barrett from New York to Bremerhaven, Germany. It was exciting to see the White Cliffs of Dover and the coast of France where "D-Day" took place.

We lined up early in the morning to disembark. The civilians got off, the Army and Navy got off, the ship's crew got off and the Air Force was left where we had lined up. We were totally forgotten! Someone in the Air Force had screwed up! Lunchtime came and we were still there. Some of the guys broke into the kitchen areas and hauled out food for everyone.

Finally that afternoon, trucks arrived and we loaded up and were taken to a train freight yard somewhere. It turned dark. We were loaded into old boxcars. They were made of boards and the sides had open slots. We sat on wooden benches. I'm thinking, "These must have been used by the Nazis to haul Jews in". It was a cold overnight trip to Wiesbaden. There we were put on trucks again and taken to a repo depot. It was an awful place! I got sick there, went on sick call, and was bussed to the Army 97th General Hospital in Frankfurt. That was a huge hospital. I was given some medicine and bussed back to the repo depot. A few more days and we were bussed to a kaserne in Darmstadt. Finally a permanent assignment. We were part of the 6910th Security Group. The headquarters was in Wiesbaden but personnel and security operations were in Darmstadt about 40 miles away.

Wiesbaden was a beautiful city. The Air Force had deliberately not bombed it because it planned on the city being used as Air Force Headquarters after the war. From the Bahnhof and down a beautiful tree lined boulevard, there was nothing but Air Force. There must have been 20,000 airmen on that

MARKEN ISLAND HOLLAND

ENROUTE TO HOLLAND

WINDMILL

ENROUTE TO HOLLAND

MY '52 FORD

avenue. Billets, clubs, mess halls, offices, etc. My Security Service Headquarters was one block off the main avenue. It was in a very large, old mansion. It had the most beautiful wooden stairs I have ever seen.

Heidleberg was spared from bombing too. It, too, was a beautiful place. It was saved for U.S. Army Headquarters.

Frankfurt wasn't so lucky. It was about 70% destroyed. Ruins everywhere. All the surviving buildings were used by our military. Many offices were in beautiful, old mansions.

Darmstadt had been a beautiful city before the war but now most of it was in ruins. It had been "fire bombed". There was a huge fountain in the city's square. During one bombing hundreds suffocated here trying to get into the fountain.

Nearby Darmstadt there was a hilltop castle known as "Frakenstein Castle". It is believed that this castle may have been the inspiration for Mary Shelley to write in 1818 the Gothic novel "Frankenstein". I toured it. It was a scary place.

The kaserne was a square of several huge stone barracks. The German army had used them. I was impressed. They were the nicest barracks I had ever been in. We had large two-man rooms. I shared mine with another Staff Sergeant. The personnel office was on the ground floor. I had only walk downstairs to go to work.

The officer in charge of personnel also did the hiring of civilians. Most of these were women. He would interview them with their backs to us. We would all give him thumbs up or down on the women. We had the best looking group of women workers

anywhere! In no time at all they would have G.I. boyfriends.

Work and life at the kaserne went smoothly. I was the morning report clerk again. No one else ever wanted this job but I liked it. I did it well and I liked the prestige that went with it.

I was also in charge of marriages again. It was very difficult for our guys to marry a German girl because of the nature of our security work. The typical case was a 19-year old airman and a beautiful German girl of 28 with two or three kids. And most of these kids had been fathered by previous G.I. boyfriends. It was so obvious that these girls wanted to get to the U.S.A.!

Our NCO (Non-commissioned Officers) Club was nearby. There was a pretty German girl working there who passed by our office on the way to work at the club. I can't remember her name. We started waving to each other. She started sending me cakes, sandwiches, etc. We got together, hit it off and started dating. She took me to German night clubs. Most were in the basement of bombed out buildings. German beer, German bands, German people. I really enjoyed this. I often think it was because I'm half German. Forgotten was the fact they had killed my brother in WWII.

We were parked beside a road one night for some reason. It was snowing. The car slid down a slope about 40 feet. The incline wasn't steep and the car was not damaged. We sought help. We found an all night street car garage open full of German men. She told them what had happened. They were laughing loudly! They got ropes, pulleys, and a couple of trucks, and we all went to the stuck car. They were laughing and joking so much it was like a fun party! Soon they got us on the road again and we were on our way.

I was suspicious that she was just another girl looking for a ticket to the States. She took me to meet her family. They all lived in the basement of a burned-out building. Well… she had a two-year old daughter – probably by another G.I.! She later told me she had found an apartment and I would pay the rent. That was "Auf Weiderzein" to her! In other words, "Goodbye"!

One of my buddies was rotating home and taking his car to Bremerhaven. I went with him and picked up my '52 Ford Victoria. That was the best looking car in Europe! Everywhere I went the civilians thought I must be very rich.

Women! Women! My goodness what a great situation for a young single man! Germany had lost about 6 million men in the war. It was now a nation of women, about six women to every man. No wonder they wanted to meet American G.I.'s!

The women stood on every corner at traffic lights. Some were prostitutes, but many were just hitchhiking. I'm serious, you had to keep your car doors locked! When you stopped at a red light several would try to open the door and get in. On the entrance to the Autobahn, there would be several hitchhiking to the next city. It was understood by many that they would pay for the ride with sex! My buddies took advantage of this all the time. I can honestly say I did not! I actually felt sorry for them.

There was a nightclub in Frankfurt that was very unusual. It was a great semicircle with tiered levels

of tables. On every table there was a phone. The tables were numbered and you had a diagram showing where they were located. You'd see a girl, or girls, sitting somewhere, you looked up the table number, called it on the phone, identified yourself and waved to her. Once you looked each other over, if you were interested, you carried on a conversation and got invited over. The girls called the guys too. Most of the girls spoke some English. Wasn't this a great way to meet a girl or guy? I think this would go over in the U.S.A.!

My buddies and I did a lot of traveling all over Europe. Everyone was crazy about Amsterdam, Holland, as everyone spoke English and they loved Americans.

There was something different about Dutch food. The bread, butter, milk, jam, eggs, etc. were distinctive. They were the best I ever tasted anywhere even in the U.S.A.

Two buddies and I met 3 Dutch girls in Amsterdam. Two of them spoke English. Mine, a sister, did not. Her name was Cory Kruyk and she worked in a diamond exchange. We met their families and they loved us. They all thought I was rich because of my car. Cory's Dad was a small man and loved cigars. We would buy him the biggest cigars we could find, for it was so funny watching him puffing on a huge cigar.

One day I asked Cory's sister, who spoke perfect English, why her dad was always walking around my car. Her reply: "He has never ridden in an automobile in his life. He wants to ride in yours but is too shy to ask". "Well, you get in and we'll give

ISLE OF MARKEN

HOLLAND '52

Scheveningen - Gezicht op Kurhaus

DUTCH BEACH

Cory

BARBARA

ISLE OF MARKIN
HOLLAND

BARBARA KENWORTHY
U.S. ARMY LT NURSE

HOLLAND 1953

BARBARA AND I - SWITZERLAND
MY '52 FORD

him a ride." He wanted to ride 'round and 'round the neighborhood so all his friends could see him. He was puffing on that big cigar and waving to his friends. I'll never forget that scene.

We took the girls to a movie once. We had our own "box" to sit in. The movie was "Gaslight" and it had many sad scenes in it. I have never seen anyone cry like those three girls. The music soundtrack was very popular. I have it. Every time I play it I can see those three girls just bawling away.

One day I received a letter from my Mom. It read: " I don't know what you are doing in Holland, but I think you shouldn't go there anymore." Cory's family, actually her sister, had written to my parents. My buddies had given them my address. They wanted to know my education, kind of employment I'd have in civilian life, etc. The sister was trying to get me to marry Cory. I liked Cory but not enough to marry her! My buddies had proposed to Cory's sister and her friend and they were trying to make it a threesome. They actually married the girls later and took them to the States. I didn't go back to Amsterdam to see Cory anymore.

I did go to Amsterdam again but it was with other buddies, and I didn't see Cory or visit my old haunts. We took in night clubs and restaurants and took sightseeing boat trips up and down the numerous canals. At the time everyone had to see "Canal Street". This was about a mile long red-light district. There was a large canal with numerous bridges. Along each side was a tree-lined wide walkway. All of the buildings had small fronts with open glass windows. In each was a woman, or women, lounging around in various states of dress, reading, knitting, looking out, etc. If a guy was interested he would tap on the window. Through sign language and gestures, a price was agreed upon. There was always an entry locked door. I've never seen anything like this anywhere. Prostitution was also legal in Germany. In Frankfurt, it was confined to one large hotel like structure.

On this trip we went out to the "Isle of Marken" on a ferry. This was a huge tourist attraction. Everyone on the island dressed and live like the Dutch did hundreds of years ago. They even wore wooden shoes. It was a very interesting place.

On the return to Amsterdam on the ferry was a car load of U.S. Army nurses. Of course we talked to them. It was good to talk with female Americans. We separated hours later and were looking for a hotel. We found one, and the nurses had stopped at the same hotel.

One of the nurses and I took a shine to each other. She was I/LT (First Lieutenant) Barbara J. Kenworthy from Ohio. She was a few years older than I (I was 22). We spent most of the night sitting in a stairwell talking. I got her address and phone number. She was stationed in Stuttgart, Germany, about 200 miles south of Darmstadt. I got in touch with her later and went down to Stuttgart to see her.

Stuttgart is a beautiful city, in a broad valley surrounded by mountains. Barbara and the nurses were billeted in quarters way up the side of a mountain. It was a beautiful site. She had roommates and I slept on a couch. It was a very large, nice apartment.

Barbara was an Officer and I was an enlisted Staff Sergeant. We were not supposed to fraternize. But nurses didn't care that much about military protocol. She took me to her officers club one evening, and we got a lot of stares.

We went on several sight-seeing trips. I recall one trip to Lacerne, Switzerland. Such a beautiful city. Any place in Switzerland will steal your heart with its beauty, mountains, lakes, old buildings, etc.

To see Barbara was a four hour trip on the Autobahn. It was a beautiful drive. But I met someone else in Frankfurt and we drifted apart. We didn't correspond and just went out own separate ways. I can't help but wonder what became of her.

My Dad's brother, Ed, had two sons in the military; James (Air Force) and Tommy (Army). Both were outstanding individuals and reached top enlisted rank. James was a member of the crew of Air Force One, the Presidential plane. Tommy was a Battalion First Sergeant and stationed in Frankfurt. In the future Tommy was head of the Boy Scouts in Georgia.

I found out Tommy was stationed about 20 miles from me in Frankfurt. A visit to him changed my life. We really hit it off. He lived in a two-story apartment in a large Army housing area. He had a wife, Betty, and a young son.

I once went with Tommy out to his army unit. He was the First Sergeant in the old sense of the term. He had a tough side of him that

was impressive. The troops treated him with great respect.

Tommy's housing complex was huge. It had its own PX (Post Exchange), commissary, chapel and theater. It bordered a river. Along the river was a stone wall. From the stone wall to the river was several hundred yards of a type of flood plain. It was planted in apple trees. When they were in bloom it was a beautiful sight. I mention this because my new girlfriend and I spent a lot of beautiful hours walking under those trees.

Tommy was superintendent of the Sunday school in the chapel. We got up early every Sunday morning and attended Sunday school and church.

The girl who played the piano and organ was an Army Staff Sergeant WAC (Women's Army Corps). She was extremely talented. We became good friends and went to a lot of places together. We went to youth meetings and church services everywhere. We once visited an old German church that had an organ whose pipes covered the entire end of the church. She got permission to play that organ. It was beautiful. I had never heard such an instrument before or since. Our relationship was just platonic.

I noticed a young girl in the chapel who was one of the prettiest I had ever seen. Her name was Phyllis. Her dad was an Army Technical Sergeant (T/SGT). Her mom was a sweet southern gal. They lived about 2 blocks from Tommy. Their apartment was right next to the river wall and overlooked the apple trees.

Phyllis was five feet two, eyes of blue and long dark hair and very, very pretty. The more I saw of her the

MY HOTEL

Z 8922 Zürich. Quaibrücke, Utoquai, Glarneralpen

Wiesbaden Hbf

HOLLAND
53

ROME
53
ROME ITALY '53

SWITZERLAND
1953

SWITZERLAND
'53

BING CROSBY
FRANKFURT
GERMANY
1953

more I fell in love with her. Everyone was in love with her.

For some reason Phyllis was in the hospital for a few days. I told a few people, "After church, let's all go see Phyllis and take all these beautiful flowers to her". She was so pretty sitting there in the hospital bed. I was falling madly in love with her. That day she indicated that she liked me too.

Things like this happen. Young men fall in love with young girls. This situation was very much like what happened to Elvis and Priscilla a few years later.

We met in Sunday school and church every Sunday. Then I spent time at her house with her family. She had two younger sisters. I was accepted (such a good guy – ha!) by all of them. I knew the rules in such a relationship and I kept them. We weren't alone very much. I took her, her sisters, and her friends on many rides around Frankfurt and nearby mountains. We went alone together for many walks along the river and among the apple trees. It was sweet, it was pure, it was romantic, it was just beautiful. Just being with her was pure bliss. Every guy should experience this type of love at least once in his life. Was this what is called "puppy love"?

I am certain I was the first boy Phyllis ever kissed. We did a lot of kissing but nothing beyond that. I would not violate her, or her parent's trust. Just being with her was enough.

Eddie Fisher was at the top of the vocal charts at the time. He was drafted and went into the Air Force. He was assigned to "Special Services", and all he did was go all over the world and put on stage shows. He was a teenage heartthrob. Phyllis and all her friends were crazy about him. He gave a show in

Frankfurt, and I took Phyllis and some of her friends to his performance. I really liked him too.

Soon my unit moved to Landsburg, Germany, in Bavaria. Such a beautiful area and base. The Alps surrounded us. When the sun came up or set the snow covered mountains looked like ice cream cones.

Landsburg was where Hitler was imprisoned when he wrote his famous book, "Mein Kampf". It explained how he intended to take over the world. Unfortunately, no one paid much attention to it.

From Landsburg to Frankfurt was a good six hour drive. It was mostly Autobahn and beautiful. We had large snack bars and gas stations about every 50 miles on every Autobahn. Like I said before, "Nothing like an army of occupation".

I had to work every Saturday until noon. Then I would get in my Ford and drive to Frankfurt. Phyllis and I barely had time for a movie and dinner before she had to be home by 11 p.m. I stayed with Tommy. We got up early Sunday morning for Sunday school and church. I would meet Phyllis there and then spend the afternoon together. At around 6 p.m. I would head back to Landsburg. It took me till midnight to 3 a.m. to get to my barracks. I was so tired and sleepy I would occasionally run off the road. I was lucky I didn't have a wreck.

I didn't do much work on Monday. I would pile up what I could and do it on Tuesday. I'd hit the sack about 6 p.m. and sleep till 5 a.m. Tuesday morning.

Tommy, Betty, their son, Phyllis, her Mom and I took a trip to Italy in my Ford. I was driving along, everyone was talking, and I noticed this unusual building that seemed to be leaning. It quickly dawned on me,

ANCIENT ROME

PISA

ROME '52

LEANING TOWER OF PISA

"the Leaning Tower of Pisa"! We had an interesting visit there.

We stopped for the night in a beautiful old seaside city. That night Phyllis and I walked down to the city square. Then we had one of the most romantic events of my life. We rode in a horse-drawn carriage along the seashore. It was like a scene from a movie, a foreign romantic place with two people really in love. I'll never forget that night.

We went to Rome and saw and did what tourists there usually do. The trip back through the Alps in Austria and Bavaria was wonderful. We stopped by my air base and I showed them my barracks and where I worked.

All over Europe and even Italy, we had military bases everywhere. I kept a 5-gallon gas can in the trunk of my car. We bought books of gas coupons in the BX (Base Exchange). Gas was 13 cents a gallon. Yes, I said 13 cents! The Army had stockpiles of gas everywhere. There would be mountains of 5-gallon G.I. gas cans full of gas. You just drove up, some Army G.I. would fill your tank and you would give him coupons. I don't think I ever had to buy gas on the economy.

I want to mention the "black market". In Europe in 1952-53 the WWII black market system was still going strong. It dealt in weapons, trucks, cigarettes, gas, etc. We all participated in it to some degree. I was allowed one carton of cigarettes a month. It cost $1.00. I was allowed two pounds of coffee which cost about $2.00. You'd just walk down the street with these items in your jacket. Soon a German would walk beside you and inquire, "Cigarettes, coffee, chocolate"? "Yes, how much?" He'd give you German marks and slip you the money.

You'd get $20 in marks for a carton of cigarettes or two pounds of coffee. There was a demand for greenbacks everywhere. We were using military script. All over Europe you could stay in luxury hotels and eat in the finest restaurants very cheaply if you paid in U.S. dollars.

Phyllis and I had several wonderful months together. I was scheduled to rotate back to the States for my enlistment was up July 9, 1953. Phyllis' dad still had another year on his tour so we agreed that I'd rotate, reenlist, and we would get married after she returned to the U.S. Pipe dreams of young people!

The church gave me a big going away party. I got up and sang "Auf Weidersehen". There wasn't a dry eye in the place. So many wonderful friends, Tommy, Betty, Phyllis' family!

The area where the housing was located was called Hedernheim. I went back there in 1966. All the quarters were gone, replaced by upscale German houses. The stone wall and the apple trees were still there. And, oh the memories of walking with Phyllis under those trees! The only familiar building left was a German biergarten that was across the street from the chapel. I am a nostalgic person. I can stand in such a spot and the memories engulf me.

I have been back to Frankfurt three times. The Bahnhof (train station) is still the same. The building that housed our large PX across the street is still there but is no longer used by us. Of course, all the ruins have been rebuilt. The city no longer swarms with American G.I.'s.

I had taken my car to Bremerhaven and rode back with G.I.'s who had picked theirs up. I said goodbye to everyone and caught a train to Bremerhaven.

ZURICH

KING LUDWIG'S CASTLE

ROME

VATICAN

HOLLAND '53

In those days, the American military had its own private waiting room in every bahnhof. We had a private car on every train just for us. Ah, nothing like an army of occupation!

Again, I was in a repo depot in the "Bremerhaven Enclave" where troops waited to fill up a ship. The Enclave was very small. A mess hall, some barracks, a service club and that was it. It covered only a few acres.

I arrived late in the evening. When I reported in the next morning I was told I was a day late, that the ship was full, and I had to wait until the next one. This would mean several days in that small place.

I knew the military phone system, so I would call Phyllis at her home and we would talk for hours.

In a few days we were assembled to board another ship. My name wasn't called! I wasn't on the manifest! When we looked into the problem it was just because my records had been accidentally misplaced! There was no space left on the ship and I would have to wait till the next one! Hell, what a snafu (situation normal – all f— up)!

I was going stir-crazy in this small base! I had an old pass so I started riding military buses in and out of the Enclave and all over Bremerhaven. One day Army M.P.'s stopped the bus and checked passes. Of course, mine was no good. I knew it wasn't valid and they did too. They took me off the bus, put me in a jeep and took me back to the Enclave.

I had to report to the C.O. (Commanding Officer) the next morning. I explained to him what had happened. "We have been discussing how to punish you", he said. "We thought about making you miss another boat." I almost fainted right there! "But you have missed two already, and we have to

MY BARRACKS

124

GERMANY

TOMMY

BETTY

GERMANY '52

get you back before your discharge date." I knew a lot about military regulations and administrative matters, so I told him, "Sir, give me an Article 15 and I'll volunteer to clean these offices every morning till I leave. He agreed to this, so I went to their offices every morning and cleaned them. Really an easy job. And, I kept checking to insure I was on the next manifest.

Finally, I got out of the Enclave and on a ship. It was a nice troopship. Seven days to New York and a train to Camp Kilmer in New Jersey where I had been before.

Nothing significant about this trip, but I do remember all the people in the cabins topside were Germans. They were all rocket scientists!

I looked up the girl I had dated there before. When she came to the door she had a baby in her arms! That reunion and conversation didn't last long!

When I went to personnel to reenlist I couldn't. Regulations had changed. To reenlist I had to go to an air base, find a vacant position, and reenlist there.

They wanted to discharge me on July 8th, one day short of my six years. I went to the C.O. "Sir, I am a personnel specialist. If you discharge me one day early, my records will be screwed up forever!" They were too lazy to change anything so I was discharged on the 8th. For the rest of my career I had problems! Personnel kept giving me an even six years and my pay was always screwed up.

For all the veterans out there I want to tell you about one of your greatest career problems – The APR (Airman Proficiency Report). During my enlisted career, I never wrote or received an APR. Each airman had a white folder in his records called his "201 file". Everything about him was put in this file, including his proficiency rating. Upon each transfer the commander would just enter a checkmark and sign the section. The proficient section was simple and looked like this:

POOR_____BELOW AVERAGE___AVERAGE_____
ABOVE AVERAGE_____SUPERIOR_____

In later years would come the dreaded APR. It was a headache for the preparer and the airman. I know for I would write dozens of them when I became an officer. You had to inflate them or the airman would never get promoted.

So help me, I think the old system was just as good if not better. You could get promoted to a vacancy in your unit, and the commander had the authority to promote you. There were not "Promotion Boards" or Air Force wide quotas.

My '52 Ford was waiting for me at the Brooklyn Navy yard. I picked it up, happy to have it again. I took my discharge and headed home to Fitzgerald. Down U.S. 1 most of the way. That was a busy road in those days. It would be replaced by I-95 years later. I didn't have air conditioning in that Ford. That summer was so hot, I'd stop by the road, find some grass under a tree and lie there for a couple of hours. I had to run the heater in the car to keep the engine from overheating.

I went to Robins Air Force Base in Warner Robins, Georgia, to see about reenlisting. This was 1953. I had been stationed at Robins in 1949 and 1950. I found a vacancy for my career field, AFSC (Air Force Specialty Code) 73270, Personnel Supervisor. I did

Germany
'57

all the paperwork, had a physical and was supposed to be sworn in in a few days.

I visited Mary Jo a few times. We had some good times, but nothing serious. Now there was Phyllis…

Now something happened that redirected my life. Phyllis was too attractive. Guys got to her and she was dating. She didn't want to get married to me anymore and felt we would never see each other again. So I got my "Dear John" from her.

Well, hell! What now? I was only reenlisting so I could afford to get married. I don't know what made me decide to go to college, but that was what I did. This was another redirection of my life. It worked out for the better I have to believe.

So, I applied to the University of Georgia and was accepted.

It turned out this was not the final end with Phyllis. She comes into my life again in a year.

So, back again with Mary Jo! We dated and got pretty close again.

I should mention why I have no pictures of Mary Jo or Phyllis. My future wife, Pat, destroyed them all!

So, off to college! Another episode, another adventure! And, I am not through with the Air Force. AFROTC (Air Force Reserve Training Corps) plays an important part in my college life and future life.

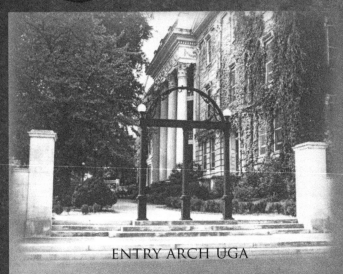

ENTRY ARCH UGA

UNIVERSITY OF GEORGIA

▶ AIR FORCE RESERVE OFFICERS
TRAINING CORPS (AFROTC)
SEPTEMBER 1953 – JULY 1956

ME

Arnold Air Society cadets look as Ralda Lefkoff and Clarice Coleman pass by.

ON THE WINTER DRILL WING STAFF were R. M. Fletcher (Commander), J. D. Higginbotham (Executive), and J. E. Harner (Operations Officer).

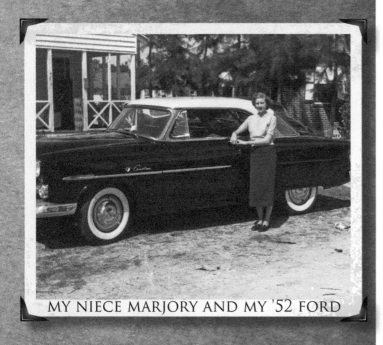

MY NIECE MARJORY AND MY '52 FORD

I had just returned from Germany. My girlfriend, Phyllis, in Germany, no longer wanted to get married. I changed my mind about reenlisting in the Air Force and decided to go to college. So, I applied and was accepted at the University of Georgia.

I was to receive the G.I. Bill to help me financially which was only $115 a month. My uncle, O.W. Fletcher, was very well off. He had only one son and he loved all my older brothers. In addition to large real estate holdings, he was a partner in a bank. He heard I was going to college. I don't know why he decided to help me financially. I think it was because he was proud that one Fletcher wanted to go to college. He gave me a stack of blank checks from his bank and told me to use them as needed. Of course, I was very prudent with the use of them. I used $15 a week to eat on. In registering for a new quarter, I'd use $100-$150. I worked every summer and that helped. When I finally was drawing money for being in the Air Force, I sent $25 a month to his bank until his death to repay him.

I wanted to major in optometry. One of the richest men in Fitzgerald was an optometrist. My dad always told me, "He buys a pair of glasses for $25 and sells them for $75. Great occupation!"

Optometry school was for six years. The nearest one was in Chattanooga, Tennessee. I found out you could go to a regular college for four years and then to the optometry school for two years. Of course, you had to major in science. So, I started taking classes that would lead to a degree in physics.

In the fall of 1953 a large new library opened at Georgia. Also, a huge complex for girls opened. It

131

248 Prince Avenue

599 Prince Avenue

530 S. Milledge Avenue

324 S. Milledge Avenue

654 S. Milledge Avenue

186 S. Milledge Avenue

FRATERNITY AND SORORITY HOUSES UGA

was known as South Myers and North Myers. There were large steps and landings at the entrances. All of us guys sat out there eyeing the freshman girls as they unloaded their cars. Of course we volunteered to help the good looking ones. I think we were called "bird dogs"!

Girls! Girls! Girls! I had never seen so many beautiful girls in one place at one time! To an ex-G.I., this was like dying and going to heaven! I made a mental note of a few. I got to know one in particular, a dark-haired beauty from South Georgia. Unfortunately she quit school after a few weeks and went home. This happened to quite a few students, male and female.

I was assigned a small room in Clark Howell Hall, a small dormitory just south of Myers Hall. The room was tiny. I had a roommate. We had double bunks, a small closet and a small table and chair for a study position. The toilets and showers were in a large room at the far end of the hall. The parking area for my car was just outside in back. I was but a short walk to the football stadium.

No one had air conditioning, but it wasn't too bad. I had a large window exposed to a wooded area, but the girls in Myers Hall were on an exposed, treeless hill and really suffered. All the classrooms had large, open windows.

The total student population was about 6,000. By today's standards that was rather small.

The college wasn't all that big but it was expanding. Georgia was one of the first land-grant colleges to open in the 1700's. The original square of the buildings was surrounded by Athens. Downtown was just across the street from the main entrance.

There are still trenches and earthen works that were built during the Civil War. The Yankees used the chapel as a horse stable. Sherman had moved just south of Athens on his march from Atlanta to Savannah, so most of the buildings on campus and the antebellum mansions in town escaped destruction. Many of these mansions housed fraternities and sororities. They were beautiful.

A main U.S. highway ran along-side the university. My dorm fronted this highway. The other side of the highway was not part of the school. It had several small eateries and restaurants along it. We called these "greasy spoons".

One of these greasy spoons was just in front of my dorm. This never changed in three years: for breakfast, I had a cup of coffee ($.10) and an egg sandwich ($.40). For lunch, I had a hot dog and a glass of milk ($.50). I didn't have a weight problem! For dinner many restaurants had what was called "plate dinners". They usually consisted of one meat, biscuit and two vegetables. Total cost: $.75 - $1.25.

A river ran along one edge of the campus. It had a lot of nice sandbars, shade and was cool. Couples would spread blankets on the sandbars and study, rest or "make out".

In those days, sex before marriage was taboo. Nice girls didn't "put out". There were only about six girls on campus who did "put out". Everyone knew who they were, and they didn't lack for dates. There was also one whorehouse in the shady part of town. The authorities let it function and didn't bother it.

The movie, "Mona Lisa Smiles", with Julia Roberts, took place in the early '50's. It was so much like the time I was at Georgia. As in the movie, most girls weren't interested in careers. They were there to find husbands.

I set out to meet as many girls as I could. I wasn't required to take P.E. (Physical Education). I discovered I could take ballroom dancing and that the girls outnumbered the guys 10 to 1. I liked those odds! I took the class and it was great! The girls did the cutting in. I met one cute blond that we danced well together and really hit it off. I thought this was the beginning of a great relationship. Pat (my future wife) was in this class. I hadn't known her before I met her here. She kept cutting in on me and my girlfriend. She said to my girlfriend, after we danced and my girlfriend cut back in on Pat and me, "You better enjoy him because I'll keep cutting in!" My girlfriend said, "Who in the world is she?" "I don't know her", I replied. Pat did cut in a lot. We danced well together. It was just friendly talk. She was a good looking gal too.

The girls' dining hall was just behind Myers Hall and not too far from my dorm. The freshman girls were required to purchase meal tickets at registration. The girls would line up at the door. I'd get in line and got to know a lot of them. I ate with the same group mostly. They would have a lot of unwanted food on their trays and they would give it to me. Great! I bought little in the serving line. After dinner I would take several for a ride in my car. It was girl heaven! I was 23 at the time. These girls were 16-19. They seemed to like an older guy, especially one who had a nice car and had seen so much of the world.

The girls would sit on benches in the last part of the line waiting for the dining hall door to open. I always chatted with the girls on either side of me.

One day I happened to be sitting next to my dancing partner, Pat. I had my legs crossed and I guess part of my leg was exposed. Suddenly, she reached over and pulled out some hair on my leg! "Wow", I am thinking, "This girl is really interested in me"!

So, instead of my usual carload of girls after dinner, I asked her if she wanted to go for a ride. She accepted. After riding around for a while, I decided to park and see if she would let me kiss her. I leaned over to kiss her. She threw her arms around me, squeezed me tight, and really laid one on! When I came up for air, I said the most stupid thing I have ever said: "I hardly know you!" That didn't slow her down and we had a great session right there! We spent a lot of time together after that. Great chemistry! But we weren't going steady... yet.

Pat was only 16! She was very mature both mentally and physically. She had skipped two years of school and still graduated #1 in her high school. She turned 17 October 9th. She could even play a piano well. She turned out to tbe the most intelligent female I have ever known.

Pat had two boyfriends back in Atlanta, her hometown. One would later come to Georgia. She would go to Atlanta on weekends, and I had plenty of dates at Georgia.

I had another way of meeting girls. The girls would stand in groups in front of Myers Hall and hitchhike to classes on the main campus about a half mile away. I would make several trips with car loads. I met several that way... Just couldn't get enough of all those girls!

The muffler on my Ford developed a large hole and made a terrible noise. The cheapest new muffler was a "gutted" model. It was loud and not too bad.

PAT

COOL ON THE RIVER

FUTURE TEACHERS OF AMERICA...

Education Convocation Sponsored by Group

FTA was established to afford an opportunity for education majors to share their ideas, problems and experiences in educational areas.

The organization sponsors the College of Education Convocation; and also it hopes to bring two honorary societies onto the campus—Kappa Phi Kappa for men and Kappa Delta Epsilon for women.

The officers were Pate Neese, President; Joy Putman, Evelyna Twitty, and Kathy Williams, Vice-presidents; Sally Van Buskirk, Secretary, and Gene Aiken, Treasurer.

Frank Miles, Betty Stubbs, Allen Brock, Jean Bridges, Bill Overton, Phyllis Duncan, Philip Posey, Barbara Stubbs, Edwin Rice, Elizabeth Logan, Phyllis Speir, Miss Ila Rooks, Marjorie Denning, Frances Harris, Rebecca Bee, Mary Ann One, Sally Van Buskirk, and Pat Logue practice class room technique.

I had picked up a load of girls in front of Myers Hall and was on the way to the main campus. A cop pulled me over. "What's the problem officer?" "You have a gutted muffler and it's against the law." "Sir, no one ever told me, and I didn't know it was illegal." Well, it is" he told me. And he gave me a ticket.

I really couldn't afford a fine. So I'm thinking: "I have never been in a court before. I think I'll see what it's like." So I went to court at the appointed time.

I sat with a large group of people. They were called one at a time upfront of the judge. Some very interesting minor things then, finally, my time. The cop who gave me the ticket told the judge about my muffler. Then it was my turn to state my case: "Judge, the officer makes it sound as though I am driving a pile of junk. I have a relatively new '52 Ford, and it is in great shape. I didn't know a gutted muffler was against the law. I only bought it because I couldn't afford anything else. Judge, I am a very poor college student. Can I take the fine and apply it to a new muffler?" Good idea," the Judge said. "No fine then. Buy a new muffler and turn in your receipt to the sheriff's office. Case dismissed." Whew! Saved myself some money! I found the experience in a court very interesting. It was my first and only time I was ever in front of a judge and in a court case.

Pat found out I was having a ball when she was in Atlanta, so she quit going. We started going steady. When a couple started going steady, the girl was said to be "pinned". Most guys belonged to fraternities and the girls, sororities, so they exchanged pins. Pat and I never joined these. They were really after her because of her grades, but she just wasn't interested in that kind of social life. I wasn't either. Pat and I lived in the dorms. When you joined those organizations you were expected to live at the "house".

The universities in those days were not as free and open as they are now. Sexual activity wasn't rampant. Freshman could not have cars. There were strict rules for freshman girls. The entrance to the girls' dorms had a large sitting area where dates would wait or they could sit and talk. There was an office and a very strict "house mother". Entry to the dorm rooms had a locked door. When you wanted a girl to come out you checked in at the office. They would call the girl and she came out of the locked door. If she left with you she had to sign out, time, destination, and expected time of return. Curfew was 9 p.m. weekdays and 11 p.m. Friday and Saturday nights.

In the waiting room was the first TV I had seen in my life. Black and white with rabbit ears. This was 1953.

The wearing of shorts on campus was prohibited by regular students. Next to the female dorms there was a large P.E. (Physical Exercise) field. It was gated and the fence was covered all around. The girls had to wear rain coats both to and from the P.E. field and dorms. No males were permitted inside the gate.

There was a parking area for cars next to the dorm. It was heavily patrolled by campus police. Two heads had to be showing at all times. Pat and I spent a lot of time there in my Ford. We would listen to the "Hit Parade" from W.C.K.Y, Cincinnati, Ohio. There was only A.M. radio and a lot of static.

I stayed busy. I had to study a lot. Pat didn't. I would study late in the evening after dropping her off at her dorm. I would spend most of Saturday studying in the library. She would join me to help me with my math.

Pat and I would graduate in 33 months. We took full summer quarter classes. It's difficult to graduate in four years these days.

My first summer, I took a full load at the Georgia Atlanta Division. It is now Georgia State. It was in an old parking garage in downtown Atlanta. We had to walk up the old curved driveways to change classes. All our classes were in the evening. I sold Fuller Brushes door-to-door all day in west Atlanta. I did pretty well at this and made about $100 a week. That was good money then. The Fuller Brush officers tried to get me to quit school and work there full-time. Pat worked as a secretary for headquarters at A&P Foods. They were so impressed with her, they tried to get her to stay. She was so efficient! She organized her full day position into a half day.

During my last year at Georgia we had a very famous freshman football player. His name was Fran Tarkenton. Pat knew him well. He went on to lead Georgia to the Southeastern Championship in 1959.

Fran was a small guy, but he had something special. When he retired from the NFL he possessed every major quarterback record there was at the time.

AFROTC

(Air Force Reserve Officer Training Corps)

I wasn't finished with the Air Force. I was drawing $115 a month from the G.I. bill. Uncle Lynn was giving me $15 a week to eat on. I

was always near broke and it was depressing. The AFROTC paid $30 a month. So, I decided to take AFROTC. This was to change my life forever! I had my uniforms already. I stood out wearing real ribbons on my uniform. I went from Airman Basic to Lieutenant Colonel (LT/COL) in a couple of months. My military experience was evident, was needed, and really paid off. We had a wing and two squadrons, about six hundred men (no women!) I was a Squadron Commander. The Wing Commander was a full Colonel, so I was the second ranking officer in the AFROTC.

I was really busy. I doubled up on my AFROTC classes, taking years one and two simultaneously and then, years three and four even more compressed. It was hard work... inspections, huge parades, marches in civilian events, etc. As Squadron Commander I had a lot of responsibility.

We had an honor's club called the "Arnold Air Society" (named after General "Hap" Arnold, famous WWII airman). I mention this because it had something to do with the first "filet mignon" I had ever seen or eaten in my life. We had a banquet one evening and filet mignon was served. I took one look at that tiny steak and blurted out, "What is this?" "That's a filet mignon, a steak." I learned something that night... filet mignons were too small and too expensive for me. Even today I still feel that way.

I loved ROTC. I saw that I would probably be designated as an AFROTC "distinguished graduate". This meant that if I were on active duty I could apply to be a "regular officer". In the military, at the time, you were either a regular officer or a reserve officer on active duty. There was a cloud hanging over the heads of all reserve officers on active duty. There

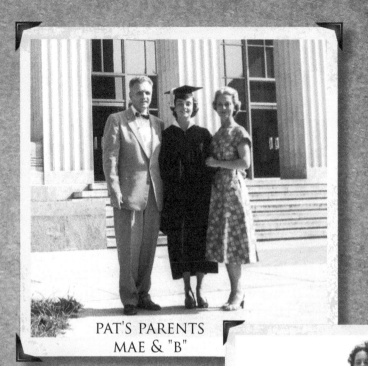

PAT'S PARENTS
MAE & "B"

DAYTONA BEACH, FL

was something called "R.I.F" (reduction in force). If there were a budget reduction some officers would be "rifed". So, if you wanted to make the Air Force your career, you should be a regular officer. When I was commissioned a 2D/LT it was for "active reserve". My serial number was AO 3070940 (AO means "Air Reserve Officer"). A couple of years later I applied for regular status and it was approved. My serial number was changed to 57874A. Promotion was also affected. All officers competed for promotions at the same time. All first promotions were "temporary". At certain time periods for regular officers, you received a "permanent promotion". I retired as a Major. If I had stayed in I would have automatically been promoted to a regular LT/COL in two years.

I got to thinking… "Why not go back into the Air Force? I already had six years active duty and I could retire in 14 years. Great deal!" However, at the time, the ranks were full. Some stupid rule came out that I could not get active duty because I was a veteran. This really upset me.

One day one of our "real" Air Force officers, who headed the AFROTC program, said to me, "There is a captain here from the USAF Air Weather Service. He is looking to sign up science majors for meteorology training. The Air Force has a serious shortage of weather officers right now. If you're qualified you might be able to get immediate active duty". I'm thinking, "What the heck is meteorology? But if it means active duty, I'll go for it".

I made an appointment with the captain. "Yes, we are in need of weather officers. If you are accepted you will be put on active duty immediately after you

are commissioned. You will also be sent to a civilian university for a year to major in meteorology." After looking over my school records, he told me I was highly qualified, so I applied and was accepted. After AFROTC summer camp, I was commissioned, put on active duty and sent to Oklahoma A&M for a year of meteorology.

BACK TO SCHOOL DAYS AT THE UNIVERSITY

Pat and I were really going steady now. All other girls were out of the picture. We were together every possible moment. I went to Atlanta with her and met her parents. Her mom was a pretty, gracious, southern lady. She was a school librarian. Her dad was an engineer with AT&T. She had a younger brother, Jimmy. Pat told me later that her mom had said, "Glad you are dating someone with some sense."

Well! Phyllis enters the picture again!!!

One day, I got a phone call from Phyllis. They had returned from Germany and her dad was stationed in Atlanta. She wanted to see me. Suddenly my world was turned upside down! I had loved her so much. I discovered that you can love different people in different ways. Pat and Phyllis were as different as night and day, yet I loved both deeply. Suddenly I was overwhelmed in emotional turmoil!

I should never have gone to Atlanta as it wasn't fair to Pat. But I couldn't resist the urge to see Phyllis again. Without a word to Pat, I rushed over to Atlanta. Phyllis was as cute and adorable as ever, and I felt I was still attracted to her.

141

During the next few weeks, I started disappearing a lot. Of course Pat was wondering what was going on. So I had to tell Pat all about Phyllis. She was extremely hurt, and I felt like a rat. We saw less of each other and broke up. She started dating other guys.

Phyllis' dad was reassigned to Fort Benning in Columbus, Georgia. Phyllis and her family moved to Columbus. Columbus was too far away for me to get there very often, so I saw less and less of Phyllis. Too, it turned out not to be the same as in Germany. I had changed. I realized how much I now cared for Pat. Being the wonderful person she was, and that she still loved me, she dated me off and on.

Pat and I decided to get married the last quarter of school before graduation. I couldn't get transferred this time! (Just kidding!)

During spring break we got married in Atlanta at the Decatur Methodist Church, March 13, 1956. I was 25 and Pat was 19. My mom, sister, Mattie Ola, and I spent the night before the wedding at the home of my cousin Tommy. He was the one I knew in Germany. Tommy lived in the south side of Atlanta, about 30 miles from the church. We had to cross Atlanta to get to the church. Traffic held us up and we were about 40 minutes late for the wedding. Everyone thought I was a "no show"! Pat's dad was pacing back and forth in front of the church. Pat said later that everyone was tired of hearing the same music over and over. Poor thing… she thought I had changed my mind.

We didn't have a honeymoon. We went immediately back to Athens after the wedding. We had rented an apartment in an old antebellum mansion.

142

THE JOINT PARADE held before the Ball.

Mr. and Mrs. James Bradford Neese
request the pleasure of your presence
at the marriage of their daughter
Patricia Louise
to
Mr. Robert Merrill Fletcher
Tuesday, the thirteenth of March
nineteen hundred and fifty-six
eight o'clock
East Lake Methodist Church
Atlanta, Georgia

and afterwards at the reception
Recreation Hall

Up until this time I had always slept in my underwear. I had never slept with another person. Now, I wore pajamas and had someone beside me. It took me a week to be able to get a good night's sleep. Also, I had never had access to a refrigerator. I started gaining weight. No more diet of egg sandwiches and hot dogs.

Pat and I both should have graduated with the class of 1957. But, since we went to school in summers and took extra classes, we were able to graduate in the class of 1956. Pat graduated on time in June. I was so proud of her. She was number one in the College of Education. I was one course short of graduation in June. I had to take one class and graduated in July. I had no graduation ceremony and my diploma was mailed to me. I didn't do too badly for a country boy with little academic background. I obtained a BS in physics and had a "B" average.

That one course changed my life. I didn't go to summer camp with my ROTC class. I went to the next one. This threw my commissioning in July into another promotion year. All my friends got promoted a year ahead of me and it seemed their quotas were always larger than in my promotion cycle.

Pat stayed in Atlanta with her parents while I went to AFROTC camp at Tyndall Air Force Base, Panama City, Florida. She came down when I finished camp. I had a commissioning ceremony and she pinned on my bars of Second Lieutenant. I was finally a USAF Officer. I was so proud.

So, off to a new life as a married USAF Officer…

POSTSCRIPT

Somehow, I wish I could capture in writing the essence, the way it was, the sweetness, the feeling of life in the 50's. Everyone had a good paying job. America was the number one manufacturing country in the world. Our dollar was supreme. No jobs were being shifted out of the country. The American dream was at its peak. Everyone could afford a nice car and a nice home. There was some poverty, yes, but the churches and communities handled it much better than the government.

There was the Korean War from 1950-1953. It was sort of isolated from American life. There was no mass communication. It was called a "police action", and it was away "over there" somewhere.

There were no drugs. There were little criminal activities. People rarely locked their house or car doors. In my hometown of 6,000 there were one to three policemen. Young girls still got pregnant out of wedlock but they disappeared and went to live with relatives out of town. They weren't allowed in school. A couple living together were "shacking up" and looked down upon. A child born out of wedlock was called a "bastard". Gays were definitely "in the closet" and were called "queers". So, all wasn't "sweet" but these things weren't exploited and thrown in the public's faces. Also, there were no "cuss" words or sex scenes in movies.

Families tended to stay in the same town. They gathered together every Sunday for dinner after church. The family members weren't scattered all over the world. All businesses closed on Sunday. The movies couldn't open until after churches were closed. People were more regionally concentrated. For example, southerners in the southeast tended to stay in the southeast. There were no great migrations from region to region. Persons from the northeast really stood out when they visited the south. They were branded "Yankees".

The southeast still had its "southern charm". Maybe this was idealistic and not true, but something was there. A lot of those scenes of early southern life as depicted in "Gone with the Wind" were still evident.

I sold Fuller brushes door-to-door in Atlanta during my summer college breaks. People were so friendly and kind. I would be offered a glass of water or tea or a cookie or snack. Some people wanted me to sit with them in a rocking chair on their front porches and tell them all about college in Athens. There were young people who looked forward to my coming each week. And, there were lonely, live alone women, who wanted to get too friendly. There is no such thing as a "door-to-door" salesman these days. He'd be shot or robbed in no time.

College in the 50's was a wonderful experience. Students were friendly and trustful. Sex wasn't rampant. Most girls were "good" girls and held the belief of "no sex before marriage". Most were there to find a husband.

I wish I could convey how beautiful and meaningful a college dance was. Every two or three months, a major performer and orchestra would come to the University and there would be a huge dance. Some included acts such as Charlie Spivak, The Dorsey Brothers, Ray Anthony and Sammy Kaye.

I distinctly remember Louis Armstrong "Satchemo" at one dance. He was great! That man could sweat and "slobber"! I don't know another word for his copious "spit" while blowing the horn. He used several large handkerchiefs to wipe the sweat off his face and the "___" off his lips.

The girls wore those large flared skirts held out by hoops. A large group dressed that way was so beautiful. Pat couldn't sit in the car with the hoop on. She carried the hoop separately and would have to go to the girls' dressing room to put the hoop on under the dress. They were all so beautiful. Where do you see such a sight anymore?

The Fox Theater in Atlanta was the most beautiful theater I have ever seen. The premier of "Gone with the Wind" was held there. The ceiling was a blue sky with clouds moving across it. There would be Sunday afternoon performances there. Before and after each performance, "Tara's Theme" from "Gone with the Wind", by Max Steiner, would be booming around the theater. It was so beautiful. I have a copy of that soundtrack and I can play it and I'm back in that beautiful theater with Pat.

In the late 50's society started to change, and I personally feel for the worse. You really can't blame Elvis, but I feel the deterioration started with him and rock and roll.

Across the hall from my dorm room, a buddy, Hugh Riley, had a large hand-made sign on his door which read "Elvis Fan Club Headquarters". Elvis had two big hits at the time, "Blue Suede Shoes" and "Heart Break Hotel". I told Hugh, "Are you crazy? That guy will never make it!" Boy, was I wrong! Up until this time, popular music was sweet, love song ballads. Slow romantic dancing was the norm. There was some swing and "jitterbugging". Now music started to be loud and wild and the dancing too. This seemed to lead into the rebellious 60's and the 50's way of life was gone forever.

There was one ray of light in the early '60's. This was a period in college life called the "Hootenanny". This was a type of musical variety show, originating from a different college campus each week, featuring various pop-folk groups of the period. The songs were folk, sweet and innocent, and the entire audience would sing along. This was a wonderful period in college life.

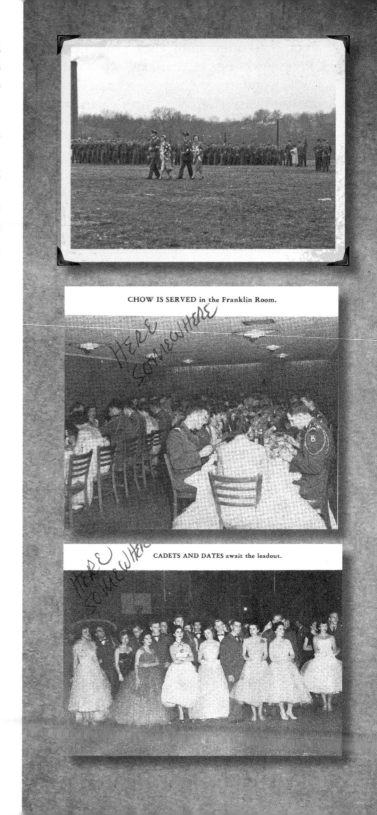

CHOW IS SERVED in the Franklin Room.

CADETS AND DATES await the leadout.

R. M. Fletcher, 104; H. M. Crane, 102; J. L. Fleming, 103; and M. L. Adler, 101 were the Fall Squadron Commanders.

MEMBERS OF ARNOLD AIR SOCIETY are *(first row)* M. Kersey, R. Fletcher, J. Fischer, H. Kimball, G. Fortson, J. Worley, E. Davis, C. Snyder, M. Cohen, D. Bishop *(second row)* W. Morris, M. Ross, Roberson, C. Cook, L. Cohen, J. Higginbotham, J. Harrold, G. Beall, D. Cummins, J. Mercer, J. Harper, and B. Crane.

SUMMER OF 1956

▶ Tyndall AFB,
    Panama City, Florida
▶ Tinker AFB,
    Oklahoma City, Oklahoma

T-33 FLIGHT TYNDALL

MY WEATHER CLASS OKLAHOMA STATE
1956 - 1957

METEOROLOGY CLASS OKLAHOMA A&M

SUMMER CAMP TYNDALL

I had to go one summer session at the University of Georgia in order to graduate. I wasn't able to go to AFROTC camp with my fellow cadets. All the cadets at the next camp were mostly from northern schools.

Pat stayed with her family in Atlanta and I drove down to Tyndall AFB, Panama City, Florida.

It was July and August. The buildings were not WWII types, but they were not air conditioned. I have never been so miserably hot in my life. The humidity was over 90% and it was hot. Our uniforms stayed soaking wet all day and it was difficult to sleep at night.

Summer camp was a joke. Nothing like I went through in basic training in 1947. We did some marching and mostly attended classes about the USAF and how officers were expected to perform as officers.

The barracks were now called "dorms" and the latrines "bath rooms".

Our dorm was inspected every day and we failed inspection every time. Finally I told the acting commander, "Let me take over getting the dorm and bathrooms ready for inspection." I had plenty of experience in cleaning barracks and latrines! We soon passed every day with flying colors.

We were given rides in T-33 jets. The pilot handed you a bag and said, "Use this if you get sick. If you mess up my airplane, you will clean it up!" I didn't get sick. I was shocked at the amount of sharks in the water. The water was full of people out to the first sandbar. Beyond that were hundreds of

149

sharks! I learned a lesson, "never go beyond the first sandbar!" I actually flew the plane in and out of clouds. I understood the physics of flight and it was actually easy to fly, just controls and throttle.

We were bussed over to Eglin AFB and toured the climatic hanger. Very impressive what they do there.

At the time inside the hanger was a MIG-15, a Russian jet used against us in the Korean War. They were testing how it held up in extreme weather conditions.

In Korea we had offered a $100,000 bonus to any Chinese, Russian, or North Korean pilot who would defect to South Korea with his jet. One actually took the bait. He said at the time he didn't know about the bonus but just didn't agree with his country on the war. He was brought to the USA and given the $100,000. He was made a US citizen and graduated from engineering at the University of Delaware.

At one of the bases we toured we experienced a pressure chamber. This is something you never forget. About 10 of us were put into the chamber, a large steel tubular affair. We were seated and given oxygen masks. There were two or three technicians who watched us carefully.

The air was sucked out of the chamber slowly to what it would be at 30,000 feet. At about 10,000 feet you feel dizzy and had to put on the oxygen mask and breathe oxygen. All gases leave your body. Then you get a bloated feeling. We were given a pad to write on. It became harder and harder to write or speak coherently.

150

NEW OFFICERS . . . Ten cadets in the ROTC encampment will climax their training today as they are presented with commissions in the USAF. The cadets are (left to right front row) Joseph M. Eller, Donald B. Goodrich, Andrew W. Hodge, Robert M. Fletcher, Robert R. Reeves, (back row) Norman H. Beachley, George A. Innis, George W. Linn, III., James T. Alvey and William H. Barnes.

Commissioned 2nd Lieutenants

Back row, left to right: Beachley, Innis, Linn, Alvey, Barnes. Front row, left to right: Eller, Goodrich, Hodge, Fletcher, Reeves.

MY NEW '56 FORD VICTORIA

Then they let the outside air in. There was an explosion and things started flying about. What an experience! I was to do this one more time in my career.

Pat came down from Atlanta for my graduation and commissioning. Once again I held up my hand and swore to protect the constitution and my country. It was one of the proudest moments of my life when Pat pinned on my shiny, new Second Lieutenant bars. I was now an officer in the United States Air Force!

I noticed a large group of NCO's hanging around during our commissioning ceremonies. It was a tradition that a new officer had to give one dollar to the first enlisted person to salute him. I knew about this and had my dollar ready. That was a proud moment too.

My first assignment was to Tinker AFB, Oklahoma City, Oklahoma. The personnel office there would maintain our records while we attended the meteorological classes at Oklahoma A&M (now Oklahoma State) in Stillwater, Oklahoma, about 50 miles north of the base.

Everything Pat and I owned fit into that '52 Ford Victoria. We spent the first night of our trip on Panama City Beach and the next night in Biloxi, Mississippi, on the beach. Then to New Orleans, the first time I had ever been there. Then, on to Oklahoma.

We stayed in the BOQ (Bachelor Officer Quarters) a few days while I was processed, I.D. for her, etc. There were 20 of us doing the same thing. They were from all over the U.S. and a wonderful group.

Several were married and had their wives with them.

Finally, we arrived in Stillwater. Several of us rented small apartments in an old house on south Main Street.

Stillwater was a wonderful Midwest small town. I fell in love with the place. The college was small too. I loved it too. Everything moved at a small, even pace.

USAF meteorology training was a new program. There were no military duties. We wore civilian clothes. Our checks came in the mail. We were like any other students. Occasionally we had a meeting with an officer from AFIT (Armed Forces Institute of Technology).

We took meteorology classes all day long. Our instructors were former USAF weather men. We learned weather codes, how to draw weather maps, atmospheric physics, all that kind of stuff.

At first we had several civilian students in the class. They soon realized that the people in this class were all college graduates, and that the standards were very high. Every one of them dropped out!

Pat found a teaching job in a high school in Cushing, Oklahoma, about 30 miles away. She taught math and English, had six periods a day with no planning periods, and over 200 students. She was busy! But she was up to it and loved it.

This was the fall of 1956. The university introduced the first computer classes ever. Some of my group took these classes. I didn't, and I have regretted it ever since.

OKLAHOMA A&M

The school did not offer a degree in meteorology at the time. But we did everything needed for such a degree.

I traded my beloved '52 Ford Victoria for a '56 Ford Victoria in Oklahoma City. It was a sad farewell for me. I loved that car… so many memories of Europe and the University of Georgia. I still think of that car and wish I still had it. But… that '56 was hot and I fell in love with it too!

There was plenty of weather in Stillwater. It was in "tornado alley"… tornadoes all over the area. Every house had a storm basement. Many times in the dead of the night, the alarms would go off and we had to go to the basement. We never did get a direct hit. First time I ever saw yellow and green skies.

At the end of the spring semester, my weather schooling was over. I asked for an assignment in the southeast. I got Pinecastle AFB, Pinecastle, Florida. Pinecastle was a small village to the east of Orlando. Orlando eventually grew around it.

I had really enjoyed Oklahoma. Pat had too. I kind of hated to leave but I was excited about being a weather officer at a real Air Force base.

So off to a new adventure!!!

12

ORLANDO, FLORIDA, 1957 – 1959

▶ PINECASTLE AIR FORCE BASE

▶ McCoy Air Force Base

I completed the meteorology course at Oklahoma A&M. I received an assignment to Pinecastle AFB, Pinecastle, Florida. Pinecastle was a small village just east of the small town, Orlando.

Pat had some time left in her teaching job in Cushing, Oklahoma. She would come to Florida later with the wife of one of the other weather officers who was from Ft. Lauderdale. So, I drove the '56 Ford to Orlando. Everything we owned fit into that car.

Orlando was a small town with a typical main street with shops such as Penny's, Sears, a movie theater, etc. Such a lovely place… fell in love with it immediately. The air base had been a B-25 base during WWII. There was also another base on the northern edge of town. The Navy had taken that one. Orlando grew up around both, and the Navy base ceased all flying operations. We went to the Navy base for medical needs.

When I first arrived on Pinecastle AFB, I thought it was one of the most beautiful areas I had ever seen. The base was huge, but there weren't many buildings. There was so much land the buildings were scattered around. The Officers Club was in a picturesque setting. There were pine and palm trees and many open green grassy areas with streams. The golf course was part of the base. All the SAC hangers were along the runways. The weather station was very isolated at the edge of aircraft parking aprons. It was a small brick building with large windows.

After Colonel McCoy was killed in an aircraft accident, the base was renamed McCoy AFB.

When the Cold War cooled down, SAC and the fighter squadrons pulled out. The base was given to the Navy. The Navy couldn't afford to keep the base maintained. Eventually the base was turned over to the City of Orlando. The base was renamed to "Orlando International Airport". The city renamed a large avenue McCoy. That is the only thing left to honor Colonel McCoy.

I visted the base several times over the years. The civilian airlines took over large areas. The beautiful grassy knolls became warehouses and parking lots. So sad. The weather station was there for a while, boarded up and deteriorating. The ditch that we used for forecasting fog was still there. But now all that is gone. The entire former base is now warehouses and parking lots. So sad.

Pinecastle AFB was in the process of expanding. The Cold War was heating up and the base became a SAC (Strategic Air Command) base. The base had a wing of B-47 bombers. They carried nuclear bombs. There was also a FIS (Fighter Interceptor Squadron). The FIS patrolled all the ocean areas around Florida and as close to Cuba as we could go. The B-47's deployed all over the world. Unfortunately, it was not a safe airplane. The long narrow fuselage was prone to breaking apart. We had a lot of accidents.

I think I'll tell now how the base changed its name to McCoy AFB. One year, Pinecastle AFB was host to a worldwide bombing competition. We had a lot of British Air Force bombers there. The SAC commander was Colonel McCoy, a great guy. I gave him weather briefings often. He was well known. IN WWII, he had bailed out of a plane over western Canada. His chute didn't open but he hit such a large snowdrift, he survived.

Colonel McCoy took up the British commander for a ride in a brand new B-47, I briefed him for the flight. A few hours later, the B-47 came apart over Orlando and all the parts fell onto the Orlando race track. All aboard were killed. It was thought that he was showing off and tried to roll the plane. So the base was renamed in his honor and became McCoy AFB.

I stayed in the BOQ till Pat arrived. She had applied for a teaching position in Orlando and all the nearby counties. She was offered a job in the Kissimmee high school. So we found a small apartment in a duplex in Kissimmee.

I loved Kissimmee. It was a small village on a huge lake, Tohopekaliga. The fishing was great! I spent every spare moment fishing. The largest crappie I have ever seen. Black bass were everywhere. I felt the place was undiscovered and that I would like to retire there someday.

Pat loved her job. The people and students were wonderful. I participated in a lot of school activities. This is where I first felt that I wanted to be a teacher someday. Pat and I became active in the First Baptist Church. There we met many town leaders and members of the oldest families. We joined a bridge club, made up of these individuals, and we really felt like a part of the community.

On Sunday afternoons we would ride around the areas bordering Kissimmee. The countryside was beautiful… rivers, lakes, citrus groves, etc. We particularly liked the area where Disney World is now… citrus groves and lakes. Lakefront lots were $3,000 to $4,000. We seriously thought of buying one for a retirement home one day. If only we had! But I got transferred rather early, so we didn't buy the lot.

158

There was a back road from Kissimmee to the air base. I was only fifteen minutes from work.

This was my first weather forecaster assignment. I was on OJT (On Job Training) status for a year. Everyone couldn't be a forecaster. You had to be a real salesman. And you had to be able to stand in front of an extremely intelligent group of people and give a good presentation. Forecasters had a comprehensive training program. You had to be certified by the detachment commander before you could pull duty alone. This applied to every local assignment. Every base had different types of weather and flying operations.

Being a USAF weather forcaster in the 50's, 60's, and 70's was not an easy job. So much depended on your forcasts. What you forecasted might affect the launch of hundreds of planes, or affect a large operation involving hundreds of planes and personnel. You were also responsible for the weather safety of base personnel and facilities. **You** were **personally** responsible.

If there was an incident because of a wrong forcast, and Accident Investigation Board would send a team to the weather station. It would examine all the weather information available that the forcaster had at the time, i.e., radar, observations, pilot reports, etc. If he had examined and considered everything available to him, and some unforseen act of adverse weather occured he was exonerated. If he had overlooked or neglected anything pertinent, he had to face an Air Weather Service investigation. This could result in his dismissal from forecasting duties and even from the USAF. **THIS WAS PRESSURE!**

I loved to brief fighter squadrons. They were young and so enthusiastic about flying. Wherever I was I was soon accepted as a member of their squadrons.

I was invited to their parties, participated in skits and all their activities.

We had an incident involving another trainee. It was obvious he was scared of briefing pilots. Whenever a group of pilots and crews came in the station for their briefing, he seemed to gravitate to another room. My commander told me to train him on how to brief the FIS. I drilled him over and over on how to do it. When he stood up in front of everyone, he started stammering. It was obvious he was nervous and scared. All of a sudden the FIS commander stood up and addressed him. "Son, we are all men here. You are expected to be a man too. Have a seat. Lt. Fletcher, give the briefing, please." The commander shouldn't have done that. The lieutenant was really shaken up. He had a degree in electrical engineering and had been through meteorological school. Yet, he couldn't talk to people. So he was not certified and he was transferred out of the Air Weather Service.

McCoy had a great golf course. It soon was obvious to me that to really progress as an officer you had to learn to play golf with the higher-ups. This was obvious during my entire military career. Pat bought me a set of McGregor golf clubs. I practiced and practiced. I could hit the ball okay, but I was terrible at putting. I just couldn't fall in love with the game. My first love was fishing. And this was my first love for many years to come. I never became a good golfer.

The weather station was a busy place. SAC and the FIS did a lot of flying. I also briefed the SAC wing and squadrons. I learned a lot about weather forecasting and how to stand up in briefings in front of flying personnel and high ranking officers.

I also learned tidbits of unorthodox methods of forecasting weather. Behind the weather station we kept a large metal plate in the grass. There was also a large deep drainage ditch nearby. These items were invaluable when heavy fog was a threat. We would go out several times each night and check the metal plate and ditch. If there was a heavy dew on the plate you didn't forcast fog. If the bottom of the ditch had fog, you checked it often. If the fog went over the lip of the ditch you forecasted fog for the entire base. This was and excellent forecasting tool. Also I could tell the speed of the wind outside just from the noise it made around the building.

Pat and I were very happy with the area, our friends, and our jobs... and then... WHAM! I received orders for transfer to NAHA Air Base, Okinawa, Japan! This was totally unexpected.

Pat had to finish her school year. Then she went to stay with her parents in Atlanta. I had to go to Okinawa, find a place for us to live, and then she could join me.

So, off to a new assignment and a new adventure!

(Note: All my pictures of McCoy AFB and Kissimmee were on slides. These were destroyed by hurricane Ivan, 2004, Navarre, Florida.)

13

1958-1961

▶ Naha Air Base
Okinawa, Japan

KYOTA, JAPAN

SHURI CASTLE, OKINAWA

NAHA

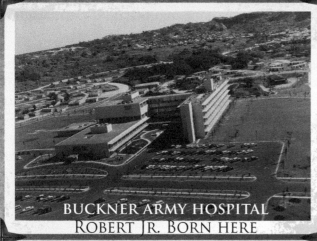

BUCKNER ARMY HOSPITAL
ROBERT JR. BORN HERE

Pat and I loved Kissimmee. I enjoyed my first assignment as a weather forecaster at McCoy AFB. We were thinking of buying a waterfront lot in the area that is now Disney World. We loved the quiet little village of Kissimmee and thought we might retire there someday. But, out of the blue came orders for Okinawa. Pat finished the school year and went to stay with her parents in Atlanta. She couldn't accompany me. There was some sort of rule that I had to find quarters for her on the economy before she could come.

I drove the '56 Ford to San Francisco. There were no interstates. I drove U.S. 80 to west of Dallas. Then, U.S. highways to Clovis, New Mexico, then NW to U.S. 66 in Albuquerque. Then in NW Arizona you turned NW to Hoover Dam and Las Vegas.

I stopped in Las Vegas to visit my brother Monte and his wife, Dorothy. There are lots of memories of my being stationed here in 1949. Vegas had grown. The base was now called Nellis AFB.

Monte and I went to a show on the strip. While waiting to get in we received a notice on the loudspeakers to call home. We called Dorothy and found out our Dad had just died back in Fitzgerald, Georgia.

Monte and I decided we could make the funeral if we left immediately and drove straight through. We immediately jumped in the Ford and headed to Georgia. We drove straight without stopping. We each drove 4 hours on, 4 hours off. It took us about 48 hours. Immediately after the funeral we headed back. There was not time for Pat to come down from Atlanta. I had to get an extension on my flight date out of Travis AFB. Again, we drove straight through to Las Vegas.

I was glad to turn that car into the port in San Francisco. I had driven 10,000 miles in less than 10 days.

I reported to Travis AFB for my flight to Okinawa. While there, I met a nurse I had known at Goodfellow AFB, Texas, in 1948. She was surprised to see I was now an officer.

When we flew out over the Golden Gate Bridge I thought of the time I had sailed under it in 1950 in that awful troop ship. Times had changed the way the military traveled overseas. I was a 20 year old sergeant then. Now I was a 28 year old 1st Lieutenant.

The plane landed at Tachikawa Air Base, Japan, just outside Tokyo. I was bused to our headquarters at another base for processing and orientation. Then, another flight to Kadena Air Base, Okinawa. In those days, Okinawa was still a WWII occupied island. We ran everything. Naha Air Base was just a few miles south of Kadena. Kadena was to enter my life again in 1972.

Okinawa was a strange and fascinating island. It was one of a string of islands that stretched from Japan to Formosa, now Taiwan. It was 3 to 5 miles wide and about 60 miles long. You could stand on any hill and see the ocean on both sides. It had a rocky, jagged shoreline. The only sandy beach was on the north end of the island. There was an officer recreation area with motel type quarters. It was a beautiful spot. It had an excellent harbor on both sides. The one most used was right next to Naha Air Base. The island was totally military. The civilians resided in Naha City and many small villages scattered around. Other than a few stores and bars, the natives worked for us. I might add, the

bars had hundreds of prostitutes. There was a huge marine base on the north end of the island. Kadena was a huge air base in the center of the island. The Army had bases everywhere. Naha Air Base was on the south end of the island right on the ocean. No matter where you were you had a view of the ocean.

Okinawa had quite a WWII history. We lost about 30,000 men while taking the island from the Japanese. Its occupation meant we had air bases within range of all of Japan. That's' why they fought so hard to retain it. This battle shaped future military planning for the Japan home islands. If they fought for Japan like they fought for Okinawa, we were in for a long, bloody campaign. Of course, the atomic bomb changed all that.

I read all I could find about the battle for the island. Then I visited all the battle sites like "Shuri-Line". There were still caves full of the remains of Japanese soldiers. "Hacksaw Ridge" was part of this line. There was an infamous cliff where hundreds of soldiers and civilians committed suicide rather than be taken by the Americans.

On the highest hill, maybe 3,000 feet high, was the remains of an ancient feudal castle. You could see the entire island from there.

The Okinawans buried their dead in huge tombs that are supposed to resemble a womb. Each family had one where all the family's dead were placed. After a period of time the women went into the tomb, cleaned and washed the bones and placed them in a basket. These tombs are quite large and dot all the hillsides.

Naha Air Base was right on the ocean. The runways were near a rocky coast. The base buildings were up the side of a hill. It was a beautiful setting. Everyone had an ocean view. In the weather station we could hear the waves crashing on the shore.

I was billeted in an old WWII Quonset hut. It was actually quite comfortable.

In 1960 through 1963 the Air Force tried out a radical new uniform for summer wear. We actually wore shorts! The uniform consisted of khaki shorts about two inches above the knee, calf length stocking, and a pith helmet. The pith helmet didn't last long. It was difficult to store and awkward to wear. The shorts lasted about two years. I loved the outfit, and for my size it looked great on me so I thought. However it looked terrible on tall guys and overweight guys. Also, older men wouldn't wear it. So the uniform was soon abandoned.

We had a brand new officer's club. It had a gorgeous view. Mixed drinks were $.25, beer was $.10. A big lunch was $.75 and a large steak dinner was $1.50. Haircuts were $.25. Wow! That was living! I never saw the likes of that again!

Duty in the weather station was easy. On base we had two fighter squadrons. The aircraft were sweptback winged F-102's. I loved presenting weather briefings to the pilots. I was soon a member of their squadrons. They had a lot of parties.

Naha Air Base was allowed to be used by civilian air lines. My weather detachment was tasked to provide weather support for them. And they flew all over the Pacific. Our runway was right on the shoreline. From the weather station you could hear and see the surf.

I was the forecaster on duty the day a potentially serious weather incident occurred. A strong squall

TRIP TO NIKO, JAPAN

日光觀光記念 於 陽明門 35.9.19

OUR ON-BASE QUARTERS NAHA AB

line was approaching the base. The runway was oriented north-south. Ahead of the squall line we had a southweast surface wind about 40 mph. Behind the squall line the wind was about 60 mph from the northeast. This represents a serious wind "shear" situation. Planes land "into" the wind. So a Japan Air Lines (JAL) airliner was approaching the runway from the north. The pilot was intending to land from the north into the southwest wind. He and the control tower personnel were not aware of the timing of the squall line passage. If he landed with a 60 mph tail crosswind he could possibly be blown into the sea!

I assessed the situation and notified the control tower controller. I advised the plane not to land and "go 'round". He agreed. We have a few 3-way conversations among me, the tower controller, and the pilot. The pilot agreed and changed his approach path. I heard him zoom right over us! That's how close he was! He gained altitude and later landed from the south into a strong northeast wind. Whew! It all ended well! A possible disaster was averted. The weather forecaster in the USAF can be under a great deal of pressure at times.

I sometimes pulled duty in the "block house". Naha was an air defense station. Radars from Japan to Taiwan tracked all aircraft within 1,000 miles of the island including civilian airlines. The F-102's would go up and investigate any aircraft that didn't report properly. In the block house was a huge, clear fiberglass board. Two airmen were behind it. They put on the board, writing backwards, the positions of all aircraft in the defense zone. Across the room was a 3-tiered row of positions where the controllers sat. I had a position on this, ready to answer any weather questions.

In the block house I became friends with Major Louis Vegias. Pat and I became close friends to him, his wife, Carolyn, and their two kids. They were the reason in the future that caused me to retire in Fort Walton Beach, Florida.

I had a lot of free time in the block house. I took correspondence courses. I completed the military courses of "Squadron Officers School" and "Command and Staff". I also took Calculus 1 and 2 again from Penn State. I didn't improve my scores from the University of Georgia, however. I made C's again. I also took a battery of tests to become a "regular" officer. I passed and was accepted. My career was now safe from a RIF (reduction in force). My serial number changed from "AO 3070940" to "57874A". This was my fourth serial number in the military. I was to have one more before retirement. In the future, everyone's social security number would serve as his serial number.

My '56 Ford arrived on a ship. I took it to a civilian garage, owned by Americans, and had it "salt air proofed". I went to check on it one day and almost had a heart attack! My beautiful car was in a thousand pieces! They coated every piece. I was assured it would be put back together. It was, and it was the quietest running car I ever owned.

The speed limit on the entire island was 25-35 mph. They let us use an old abandoned air strip to race up and down to blow out the engine now and then.

I found a small cement block house on the economy to rent. There were hundreds of very rich American businessmen on the island, and they seemed to own everything. One owned this house. It was in the midst of several American civilian and military families.

MY TRIP TO HONG KONG

HONG KONG

HONG KONG

HONG KONG

HOUSE ON THE ECONOMY

OUR OFF-BASE HOUSE — NAHA

OUR LIVE-IN MAID

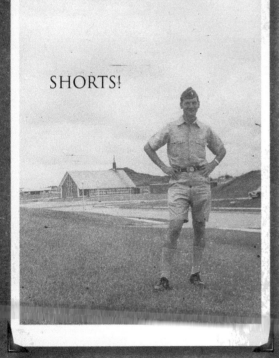

SHORTS!

DAMAGE AFTER TYPHOON

Pat soon joined me. She had flown from Atlanta to San Francisco, then from Travis AFB to Kadena AFB. We got settled into our small house. The house had a small fenced-in lawn and a garage. A "yard boy" came once a week. He cut the grass with handheld shears and worked all day for $1.00! Pat would cut out a picture of a dress from a catalog. A "sew girl" would come in and duplicate the dress exactly. She would work all day for $1.00! We had gorgeous raw silk drapes that were bought and made dirt cheap. We used them for years.

Pat soon got a job teaching in the American high school "Kawasaki". She loved it. Discipline in the American schools was no problem. If a kid caused trouble he and the entire family of dependents would be shipped back to the States.

We had a bad typhoon (hurricane) hit the island. I put the car in a warehouse at the port. The eye came right over the island. The wind was about 100 mph and the roar was deafening! All of a sudden it quit as the eye came over. I went outside. In a few hours you could hear the roar of the opposite side of the eye coming down the road.

First the picket fence blew away. Then the garage collapsed (thankfully, my car wasn't in it). Then the wooden shutters began to tear off and blow away one by one. The heavy wooden doors were bending in at the corners top and bottom. I nailed them to their frames. The windows were bulging inward. I was propping mops, brooms and chairs up against them. Water was everywhere on the floors. It was running down the stairs from upstairs. We were mopping and using towels as fast as we could. It did little good. Transformers were exploding all over the neighborhood. It sounded like we were being bombed. This went on all night. Came dawn the storm eased up. We were exhausted. Pat said, "I'm taking a bath." She turned on the faucets and black, oily, muddy water came out. That did it! She sat down on the floor and had a good cry.

Pat and I had been married four years. We decided it was time to start a family. We timed it so that the baby would be over a year old when we rotated back to the States. It was right on target.

I was watching "Rawhide" late one evening. There was a terrific thunderstorm outside. Pat announced, "I think we had better go to the hospital!" "O.K.", I answered, "Just as soon as 'Rawhide' is over." "No! Right now!" So off we rushed to Buckner Army Hospital just a mile or two away. It was March 25, 1960. Robert JR. was born that night. We had hoped for a boy. He had a head of dark hair and was a perfect beautiful baby boy.

We soon got base housing on Naha Air Base. It was a nice duplex, built "typhoon proof" with a gorgeous view of the ocean. The Vagias' were next door. We became great friends. We would babysit their two children and they would "Robbie". Carolyn was born and raised in Destin, Florida. Her family was one of the original Destin families. They owned several acres on Destin harbor next to the pass. Carolyn would become a multi-millionaire in the future. She was the most gracious southern lady I ever knew. Lou was a handsome dark-haired Yankee from Pennsylvania. He had a great personality and dressed to kill in his civilian clothes. All the ladies liked him. I could tell Pat did too.

The quarters were built with a maid's living area. The government set a maid's salary at $18.00 a month. We hired a full-time live-in nanny, cook, and

OKINAWA

OKINAWA

housekeeper. Her name was Kiko. She was about 20 and single. We learned to care for her dearly. She and Robbie loved each other. When we went out for the evening she would prepare rice dishes for herself and Robbie. Robbie was crazy about rice. Since we were only allowed to pay her $18 a month, we gave her lots of gifts. Dollars were used by everyone on the island.

I was able to take some great trips around Asia. I went to Hong Kong on a Navy PBY. It was a small plane and 14 of us were crammed into it. The approach to the Hong Kong airport was strange, and scary! You flew down long corridors between tall apartment buildings. You could look out the windows and see Chinese on their balconies. They were so close you could have talked to them.

Hong Kong! No other place in the world like it! Everyone loved that city. It was on a series of islands with boats and ferries everywhere. Large slum areas packed with Chinese. But large areas of mansions and modern businesses, apartment stores, restaurants and night clubs.

While in Hong Kong I was walking down a side street when I noticed this old Chinese man was sitting on the sidewalk and working with pieces of ivory. I stopped to watch him. What he was doing was unbelievable to me. With some simple tools he had a large ball of ivory about the size of a baseball. He was making rotating balls inside of rotating balls inside that large piece! Through tiny holes he was making another ball inside. Then inside that ball through tiny holes he'd make another rotating ball. There would be 3 or 4 rotating balls inside one another. It must have taken him weeks to complete one set of balls.

He was outside an ivory store. I went inside. The ivory products were astonishing! I bought two sets of ivory chess sets for $40 each. The king and queen were about 6-8 inches high. All the pieces were hand carved solid pieces of ivory. On the bottom of each where you placed your hand to move them was a ball of rotating balls inside. They were beautiful! And they were placed in a velvet lining inside a beautiful wooden box. My father-in-law loved to play chess. I bought one for him and one for my family. I also bought several pieces of jade jewelry. It was very cheap.

After a while in Okinawa I learned that what I did was illegal. You could not buy or possess any ivory or jade without a "Certificate of Origin". This proved the ivory or jade was legally obtained and independent of Communist China.

I was told by friends that I could not take the chess sets and jade home, and that household goods were inspected for such contraband. What to do? I decided to put the ivory sets and jade inside my household goods and take the chance that they wouldn't be confiscated. They actually made it home ok. My family now enjoys these beautiful ivory chess sets and jade jewelry.

In Hong Kong we befriended two English fighter pilots we met somewhere. They took us out to their airbase. It was one of the most beautiful small airbases I have ever seen. The Officers Club was like something out of a WWI movie. The British had ruled Hong Kong for hundreds of years. The military and government buildings were works of art. I cant help but wonder what happened to it all after the British turned Hong Kong over to the Chinese in 1999.

I had a suit tailored for me for $27. Every store you went into gave you free beer or cocktails. I was measured for the suit one morning, went back that evening for the final fitting and picked up the finished suit the next morning.

Because several of us used the same tailor business they gave us a free car and chauffeur for the day. He took us up to the border of communist China and we would peer over the fence at it.

We took the famous track rail to the highest peak. The view was breathtaking! You could see all of Hong Kong, the surrounding islands, and into Red China.

Because several of us stayed at the same hotel we were given a free banquet one evening. We sat on the floor in a semicircle and the food was brought to us. I didn't know it was a ten-course dinner! Each serving was so delicious, and I didn't know it would be followed by another. I ate too much! At the end of the meal they brought in a group of girls and anyone wanting one could have their pick. I did not!!

We went out to the famous floating restaurant. It was on a beautiful barge big enough to be called a ship. There were cocktail lounges topside. They had water pens filled with live seafood of every kind imaginable: eels, snakes, all kinds of weird creatures. You picked out what you wanted and later it was prepared and brought to your table. I chose a normal looking fish that looked like a sea bass.

The night clubs were fabulous…cheap drinks, good entertainment, and beautiful hostesses asking you to dance. Wow!!

I had another trip to Hong Kong. We gave the pilots of Japan Air Lines free weather briefings and charts. In appreciation they gave us 4 days in Hong Kong. Everything was first class and free. We flew first class on their planes. It was a fabulous 4 days! Hong Kong is still great. Wow!

I got a chance to take a hop in a C-130 to Duang International Airport, Bankok, Thailand, for 3 days. Duang was the airport for the city. It had been a British air base before and after WWII. The Japanese used it as a military air base during the war when they occupied Thailand.

As we were landing and the wheels touched the runway there was a loud explosion and the C-130 filled with smoke! The aircraft swerved a few times and came to a stop. The rear door slammed down and over the intercom came the order "Abandon aircraft"! What had happened was a wheel axle broke and the wheel lodged against the wheel-well. Good thing it didn't happen on take-off! Thankfully there was no fire.

We stopped in front of the terminal. Several officials came out and started screaming at the crew, "Move that aircraft! No military planes are allowed here!" It took a while to get it towed to another part of the airport.

It was put on an old WWII unused runway overgrown with jungle. We walked back to the terminal. Alongside the runway were a lot of wrecked old British and Japanese WWII aircraft. I wanted to see them up close, but there were signs everywhere, "Danger – cobras and snakes! Do not get off the tarmac (pavement)!"

ROBBIE

KIKO, OUR LIVE-IN MAID

In Bangkok a strange incident happened. There was an Air Force doctor in the group. He talked me into helping him do something. I thought it crazy and dangerous, but in the interest of medical science I decided to go along with it.

He wanted to study the effects of smoking opium. He was going to smoke it, and I was to observe how he acted and his responses to it and write it down for him. Crazy!!

So he rented a room in a sleazy hotel. After he found a supplier and a business partner we went to the room. One of them stayed in a taxi in the parking lot. So he lay on the floor and the guy mixed up the opium. Suddenly there was screaming from the parking lot. The guy with us starting screaming out the window to the guy in the taxi and they were screaming back and forth. It calmed down so the guy in the room got back to the opium. He couldn't get it to burn properly and there was the doctor lying on the floor. Suddenly the screaming from below started again! The taxi driver wanted some money and a lot of it. The guy with us gathered up his opium and paraphernalia and said, "I have to go! The police will come and arrest us all!" So off he went. The doctor was very disappointed and I was glad it was over!

One other event of interest happened (to me anyway). There are a lot of movies filmed in Thailand. They usually show nightclub scenes with many young women who are dance hosts and prostitutes. Many of these girls are sold by their families into this type of life. This was true.

We went to a couple of nightclubs. There was a large group of young women in each. They came to your table and asked you to dance. You had to pay them for each dance. While dancing they tried to get you to take them to their rooms. We didn't go for that! I danced with several because I would get them to tell me their life stories. These stories were unbelievable! They might have made some of it up for sympathy but I felt a lot of it was true. So, so sad!

Bangkok was a fascinating city with lots of water and canals. Motorcycles and modified vehicles of every type choked the roads. Pedi-cab (man-peddled bicycle taxis) were everywhere. We got a fairly good hotel to stay in. For our meals we went to a very upscale western-style hotel. It might have been the Bangkok Hilton.

Star sapphires are mined in Thailand. One in 1/2 inch diameter only cost $10. I bought Pat several. They are beautiful.

I thought I would see lots of "Siamese Cats" running about. I was disappointed. The cats looked like plain old alley cats in the USA.

Parts for the plane had to be flown in from Okinawa, so we got an extra two days in the country. It was quite a trip and experience, and I'll never forget it.

Another fascinating trip I had was to Taiwan. I was sent there for ten days TDY (temporary duty) to support a squadron of F-100's that were there on an exercise with the Taiwanese Air Force. It all took place on a Taiwanese air base named Chaiyi. It had been a huge Japanese air base during WWII. The ruins of the hangars and buildings were still visible, overgrown with jungle.

The island is tropical in nature with some pretty high mountains too. We had loads of bananas and pineapples in the mess hall. The best I have ever tasted.

The Chinese that ran the island and the Air Force had escaped the communist takeover of China. The government and all important functions were headed by the Chinese from the mainland. Taiwan had native peoples like our American Indians. They were Asian but different.

The Chinese Air Force weather station was very similar to ours. The Chinese weather forecasters spoke very good English. I would go to the station early each morning and discuss the day's forecast with them. Their weather maps were great works of art. I would prepare my briefing and go to the operations room of the F-100 squadron. Those Chinese forecasters were good. After all, they had been on the same base for 10 years. I used their forecasts and I never had a problem. The USAF forecaster that relieved me made up his own one day and 3 of the F-100's got into trouble. He changed the time of breakup of a heavy fog. Two went elsewhere and one had the pilot bail out and the F-100 was lost. There was a court of inquiry and he was found negligent. His forecaster status was cancelled. He was reassigned out of the Air Weather Service and that was the end of his Air Force career.

I became good friends with a Chinese forecaster. The group of people I was working with were tall people. They came from an area of China where the people were large. My friend's wife was a very tall woman.

I was invited by my friend to a local festival. The villagers collected on a huge rock and earthen dam on a full moon night, sang songs, ate a fruit that was a cross between an orange and grapefruit, and set off fireworks. Each family took its own fireworks. I told my friend I would pay for the fireworks. I gave him the equivalent of about $5.00. He had a strange look on his face, but I insisted he take my money. He came back with a huge basket, 3 feet across and 3 feet deep filled with fireworks! I hadn't realized they were so cheap! So we carried as many as we could to the dam. It was a fascinating spectacle - a different world - and I'll never forget it.

General Eisenhower came to Okinawa while I was there. He had just visited Korea and was visiting all the major US military installations in the Far East. This was in June, 1960. There was a huge parade for him through the streets of Naha. We were in the crowd and watched him pass by about 20 feet away. In my military career he and Kennedy were the only presidents I ever saw.

There was a famous restaurant on Okinawa called the "Teahouse of the August Moon". Marlon Brando made a movie there called by the same name. He played an Okinawa native who was always making fools of the US military officers. The movie made this restaurant very famous. It was a great place to eat and have parties, and we ate there often. The favorite dish was a huge sea bass cooked whole and served whole on a large platter. It was like "sweet and sour". It would be cut up and served at the table. Loved it!

There were several war movies made on Okinawa while I was there. I watched some of these being filmed.

Dolphin slaughter: When you "ride around" you have only the coastal highway to do it on. The road is narrow, twisting and, for the most part, congested with Okinawans and their goods. However, parts of it in the north half of the island are cliffs and the scenery is breathtaking.

On one of our trips, as we descended into a small bay area, we saw a large crowd gathered in the inlet and on a small beach. There was a net stretched across the inlet, and the water was full of people. The water looked like blood! There were dolphins leaping and thrasing about! The people were clubbing the dolphins to death! It was a sickening sight, and we didn't linger. We found out later this is an annual event. To them it seemed a fun holiday. There has been an international outcry from animal rights protectionists to put an end to the event.

Mongoose-snake fights: On Okinawa there is a very poisonous green snake called a "Habu". A Mongoose is a small furry animal about two feet high that looks like a prairie dog. For some reason this little animal likes to kill snakes.

The Okinawans love, and have often, Habu-Mongoose fights. They are a draw, sort of like cock fights in other parts of the world. I decided to attend one of these.

You sit in a tiered seat bleacher around a small circular arena. In the center is a large platform upon which sat a large wire box-like pen. A large 4 foot Habu was in the pen. they opened the door and let a Mongoose in. The snake coiled in the center, head six inches high, hissing, and long tongue darting in and out. It kept its eye on the Mongoose. He seemed to sense this would be a life and death struggle.

The Mongoose walked 'round and 'round the pen eyeing the Habu. The snake followed the Mongoose with its eyes. Then, like lightning, the Habu struck out at the Mongoose! The Mongoose was unbelievably quick at darting away from the snake. I have never seen any creature move as fast! This went on for several minutes-striking-darting! The Habu finally

tired first. Then the Mongoose grabbed the Habu by its head! Assisted by its paws and using its teeth, tore out the fangs of the Habu! At this point the attendants separated the two. It was a fascinating spectacle.

Dog-Lion fights: This was another strange attraction to Okinawans. I decided to see what it was all about.

There was a large circular tiered seat arena about 30 feet in diameter. First they let in a lion. After a while they let in a pack of dogs. The objective was, of course, for the dogs to attack and kill the lion. This lion was old and feeble. It could be no match for the dogs. I suddenly realized, "What am I doing here? This is obscene and inhumane!". So I hurriedly got out of there!

Pat and I had a great experience in Japan. People needed to get off that tiny island for a change, and the Air Force was very good about flying you anywhere. We wanted to tour Japan. We flew to Ashiya Air Base in southern Japan and took a train to a large ship port on the inland sea. We were taking a large ship all the way up the Japanese inland waterway.

Friends had told us to get a 2nd class ticket and that the boat always put Americans in 1st class. Well, we bought 2nd class tickets and that's where they put us!

We were assigned to a huge room that had tiered bunks on each side. It was full of Japanese. You had to put your luggage on your bunk. You pulled a curtain across the opening for a little privacy. We slept in our clothes. During the night I would peek out and there was a Japanese gentleman sitting on the bottom bunk across from us. I would swear he sat there all night staring at us!

The toilets were nearby in another room. In the room was a large concrete tank about 6'x6' and 4' deep full of hot water. "Well", I thought, "This must be one of those community baths. I'll just come in here early in the morning and get my bath before anyone else". So I'm in the tub washing myself. Japanese men would come into the room, take one look at me, and go back out. Something wrong here! I found out that this was not a bath tub! What you were supposed to do was get a small metal pan, dip the water out of the tub, and wash your hands and face. Boy, was I embarrassed! I felt like an "ugly American"!

We landed the next day and took a train to Tokyo. While waiting for the train I had to go to the bathroom. I saw a sign that said "lavatory", so I went in. It was a trough with a lot of small pipes spurting water into it. So, I was taking a pee in the trough. Japanese kept coming in, staring at me, and departing! Oh! Oh! Something wrong here! I found out you were only supposed to wash your hands in that trough! So much to learn about other customs.

We had a great trip to Japan. On Okinawa we went to the military resort center on the north end of the island. Beautiful beach and area. We really enjoyed it there.

Our tour came to an end in 1961. At this time the airlines were converting to jets. Some people lucked up and got a jet home. Unfortunately we got a 4-engine propeller plane, a DC-6. We flew to Tokyo and then to Travis AFB, California. It was a long trip.

Oh, I almost forgot… I worked hard at trying to catch fish on the coast. I had never done any salt-water fishing, and I didn't know how to do it. The Okinawans used only nets. The only success I ever had was next to a huge sewer pipe that emptied into the ocean. I caught some weird perch-like fish there. I threw them all back because they were feeding off the sewer stuff.

Mae and "B" met us at Travis AFB. "B" had picked up my '56 Ford at the port. They really were excited about seeing Robbi for the first time. We drove to Yosemite National Park and spent the night there in a tent. We almost froze to death! Then we went to Las Vegas to see Monte and Dorothy. We went to a show and saw Connie Francis. It was great!

No interstate in those days. We went to Flagstaff and the Grand Canyon. Then down to the petrified forest, the Meteorite Crater, Silver City, New Mexico, El Paso, San Antonio, and into New Orleans. We went on a night club tour and saw some of the old fashioned "stripper" first class shows. Then… on to Atlanta.

I had asked for an assignment in the southeast but had received one to Grand Forks AFB, North Dakota.

Another unusual adventure!

14

1961-1964

▶ **GRAND FORKS AIR FORCE BASE**
GRAND FORKS, NORTH DAKOTA

P at, Robbie, and I returned to Atlanta from Okinawa. While in Atlanta I did something I have always regretted. I traded in my '56 Ford Victoria for a Ford Comet station wagon. The Victoria with no center door post turned out to be an all-time classic. Only 6,000 of them were made. They are worth a fortune now. The Comet, though, was cute and ideal for the three of us.

Pat stayed in Atlanta with her folks and I drove to Grand Forks AFB. No interstates in those days. The route was Atlanta, Chattanooga – Nashville (U.S. 41), Evansville, Indiana – Chicago, Illinois – Madison, Wisconsin – Minneapolis, Minnesota – Fargo, N. Dakota – Grand Forks. I had to spend 2 nights on the road. It was a wonderful trip and it was my first time through this area of the U.S. We were to make this trip several times in the next 3 years.

Grand Forks was a small town of about 10,000 people. It was on the Red River of the North which was prone to flooding. Many years later the town was wiped out by a disastrous flood. The Red River flows north. One of only two that do this. The other is the St. Marys in Jacksonville, Florida.

The air base was about 8 miles west of Grand Forks on U.S. #2. The Red River valley is as flat as a pancake. It was an ancient sea bed. It was very good farming country for wheat, Irish potatoes and sugar beets. They said the top soil was several hundred feet deep.

The Cold War was at its peak in the early 60's. The U.S. built SAC (Strategic Air Command) bases all across the northern U.S., Great Falls, Montana, Eilson AFB, Alaska, Glasgow, Montana, Minot, North Dakota, Grand Forks, North Dakota, Selfridge, Michigan,

Plattsburg, New York, Loring, Maine, and a couple of others in Maine. These were B-52 bomber bases. On each base there were also fighter-interceptor squadrons. There was also a string of radar stations across Alaska, Newfoundland and Greenland and even in the ocean off the U.S. coast. My weather station supported a SAC bomb wing of 3 bomber squadrons, and two FIS (Fighter Interceptor Squadrons) of F-104's and F-106's. So you can see we had a lot of work to do.

The Air Force at the time had a constant stream of B-52's flying along the Russian coast on the North Pole, from Greenland to Alaska. Our B-52's took part in this. They had 22-hour flights… Grandforks to air refueling off New York City – to air refueling off northern Greenland – to air refueling over Alaska – to air refueling over Seattle, to home. We had a lot of weather work connected with this.

Working with the B-52's was hard, detailed work. I mentioned the 22 hour trips along the Russian Arctic frontier.

If we attacked Russia the B-52's would have to go in as close as possible to the surface and to try and avoid Russan radars. Low level radar has "ground clutter" reflections from hills and mountains. The B-52's would attempt to "hide" in these.

There were many movies at the time concerning the "Cold War" with Russia. Some featured low level bombing attacks on Russia. One of the best was "Doctor Strangelove" or "How I Quit Worrying and Learned to Love the Bomb". It had Peter Sellers, George C. Scott, and Slim Pickens in it. It was about a B-52 raid on Russia. It was serious but awfully funny. It put SAC in a bad light and was banned on all USAF bases.

Our B-52's did a lot of low level training flights all over Colorado, Wyoming, Montana, and the Great Lakes areas. We had to forcast something called the "D-Factor". It dealt with variations in air pressure near the surface. They would fly as low as 500 feet above the surface. In one instance turbulance ripped part of the tail off a B-52. The accident investigation board said the problem "was not forecastable".

I'm glad most crews had a good sense of humor. A navigator said to me one morning, "That D-Factor you gave me over Lake Michigan was way off! We were supposed to be at 500 feet above the surface of the water. Waves were hitting the bottom of the aircraft!" I am sure he was stretching his complaint a bit, but he was letting me know he had a problem with the D-Factor I gave him.

In another instance a crew member came in to the weather station with a big ball of ice he could hardly carry. He slammed it down on the counter, "Fletcher, here's a piece of your 'light' rime icing!" This type of ice can be very dangerous to the control surfaces of an aircraft.

I stayed in the BOQ (Bachelor Officers' Quarters) while the base was finishing an area of dependent housing. Meanwhile, I rented a duplex in town. Pat and Robbie flew into Fargo. I picked them up there and we moved into the rental unit.

Eventually the base dependent housing was finished and we moved into a brand new 3-bedroom unit of a 4-plex. It had a full size basement designed to be used during winter. It came in handy for kids because they couldn't play outside in sub-zero temperatures. All utilities in North Dakota had to be put 10-12 feet below the ground's surface. It could, and did, freeze the ground 9 feet down.

I had an enclosed garage on the end of the building. In the winter, I kept a 100-watt bulb under the battery. The wind was always strong. The garage entry doors would have 3-6 feet of drifts up against them in the morning. I would just take my snow shovel and throw the snow up into the air, and it would blow away.

This would be a good place to discuss the weather in North Dakota. It had profound effects on me and my family.

Weather in North Dakota

Forecasting the weather was easier than at Eglin AFB or McCoy AFB, Florida. Here, a cold front was a cold front! Rarely was it stationary. Rarely was there tropical air to complicate the issue. The cold fronts moved steadily across Canada and through North Dakota to mid-Minnesota. It stretched north to Winnepeg and Goosebay, Canada. Cold air flows like syrup because it is very dense. And when it's really cold it is even denser. So it would pour down the valley like syrup.

The general west side of the valley had a small town named "Devil's Lake". The general east side of the valley was "Bimiji" (of Paul Bunyan fame), Minnesota. This area, on the average, has the coldest weather in the United States. August is the only month that North Dakota has never had snow. The wind was very strong most of the time. Speaking of wind… when a base is built, the runways should point in the direction of the prevailing wind direction. Somebody screwed up here! The direction of the prevailing wind was about 30 degrees off from the main runway. The B-52 had wheels that could change direction. It was a sight to see a B-52 land with the wheels aligned down the runway and the place cocked at 30° to the runway! It took some excellent piloting to take off and land under those conditions.

In the winter zero degrees actually feels warm! It routinely got to -20°F to -40°F. Some unusual things happen at these temperatures.

After it turned really cold (below 20 degrees Farrenheit) you could not leave the base without a "winter survival kit". You had to keep this in your vehicle. The AP's (Air Police) would inspect this when you passed out the gate. You had to have: (1) a shovel, (2) blankets, (3) some type of high energy food such as candy bars, (4) flares, (5) several candles (you can keep from freezing in a vehicle by burning one candle).

The local farmers would have rows of posts in the ground to all the locations around the farm yard. These would be connected by ropes. This kept them from getting lost in a blizzard or whiteout conditions. In spite of this, every winter some would get lost in their own farmyard and freeze to death.

To my knowledge, this was the only SAC base that had permission for the B-52's to be late taking off during an alert. The instruments had trouble coming on, the tires were flat, and hydraulic leaks would pop up everywhere. At -40°F exposed flesh would freeze in less than a minute, so guards and flight-line personnel had to be kept in warm vehicles. Frostbite was common. In fact, Robbie got frostbite on his cheeks one day. They turned white. But we got him in on time and he was O.K.

Hoar Frost - This accumulated on everything outside. Everything would have a ¼ to ½ of frost on it. The wire fences were quite beautiful.

Ice Needles - All moisture was ice. On some days the air would be full of glistening lengths of ice from 1mm to 1cm long. It even formed rainbows (ice-bows?) You could feel them when they entered your nose. Our coats (parkas) were designed to zip so that you had a 6-inch tunnel of air in front of your face. Your lungs would freeze if you breathed the air directly. The gloves had a patch of fur on the top to wipe the ice off your nose. The ice needles were actually very beautiful.

Sun Dogs - I had read about these in Indian history where they were worshipped by the Indians, but I really didn't know what they were until I saw them. When the sun was setting there would be a "row" of suns on the horizon. They are very unusual but very beautiful.

Northern Lights - When I was "bacheloring" I went to a movie in town and it was dark while I was returning to base. All at once the sky turned green! What's happening! I pulled over and I couldn't believe it! Suddenly it came to me – the "northern lights" or "Aurora Borealis"! I had never seen anything like it! The entire northern sky was aglow. It was like huge green fountains or curtains rippling across the sky. On base people would sit outside for hours watching this phenomenon. This is a lifetime experience. I wish everyone could experience this! I saw them again later when I was stationed in Alaska.

Ice Fog – Super cooled air is strange. It could be clear and any air disturbance would create an ice fog. Nothing could fly as the plane taking off would create a wall of ice fog. The SAC commander had to go somewhere one day and we warned him. As the plane went down the runway the fog he created covered the runway. He had an emergency and had to go to Minot AFB because we were fogged in because of him.

We didn't get piles of beautiful soft snow. Because of the wind we had drifts. Our quarters were two-story. The snow would pile up to the roof line and we had to dig through a large drift to get out the front door. The poor airmen had to put their cars in a large open parking lot. Sometimes the entire parking lot was covered by 6-10 feet of snow. It would take days for some of the airmen to get their cars uncovered. The entire engine compartment under the hood would be caked with snow. Some days nothing could move. I would be picked up by a tracked vehicle and taken to work.

You had to have a special anti-freeze. You had to use 10-weight oil. You put a piece of cardboard in front of your radiator. You drove off very slowly because you had a flat side on your tires. Also, the transmission fluid was "mush". I kept a 100W bulb under my battery at night to keep it from freezing. When I worked night shifts I would go out and run my engine every 2 hours. Then I would throw a G.I. blanket over the engine. Your windshield defogger wouldn't work. You had to scrape frost off the windshield in front of the steering wheel to see out. Robbie and Brad had a good time in the rear of the station wagon scraping pictures in the frost on the inside!

You approached your car with arm extended with your key pointed at the car (you never locked your car for the lock mechanism would freeze). As you

182

approached you got a 10-20 inch static electric charge between the key and the car. Sometimes just walking by a car you got zapped on the leg. You couldn't get too close to another person without fear of getting zapped. Once I turned to speak to Pat and we got zapped nose to nose.

We made sleigh runs and ice skating rinks for the kids. All you had to do was pile up the snow and spray water on it.

There was a funny, popular saying… "Never eat yellow snow".

Our Quarters: We were in the center of a 4-plex. There was an upstairs and a full basement. The furnace was in the basement. In such cold temperatures the air has near zero moisture or humidity. It is actually hard to breathe. The furnace had running water in it and there were baffles hanging in the water. The air blew over the baffles and picked up some moisture to distribute into the house but it was never enough. We put a pan of water over every vent with a small towel hanging over the side. It was amazing how quickly the pan would empty of water. We boiled water all day long on the stove. This was quite a change in the everyday living that most people are used to.

The Birth of Bradford Alan Fletcher: Pat and I decided, since we were so confined anyway because of the cold, it would be a good time to have another child. This time it would be a girl, Kimberly Clark, and our family would be complete. We planned on having it in the fall so that it would be older in the spring. This worked perfectly! It was born October 3rd but we didn't get a girl! It

was a boy! So we named him Bradford, after his granddad "B". The "Alan" wasn't based on anything. It just seemed to sound good.

The base was so new that the hospital wasn't set up for delivering babies. The Catholic Hospital Downtown Grand Forks was used. I couldn't get leave or days off at the time Pat went to the Catholic Hospital. So I had to put Robbie with a neighbor each morning while I had to work. So "Brad" was born in the Catholic Hospital on October 3rd, 1962.

Seeing Brad for the first time was a real shock! His face was covered in purple (whatever they used to clear mouth and lungs). Evidently the forceps they used had mashed his face and the back of his in flat! I was really worried! When Pat wanted to get him from the nursery, and they asked his sex and name, she jokingly told them, "Just bring me the ugliest one in there". It didn't take long for his head to adjust and he became a handsome young boy.

Sometimes we would dress Robbie and Brad in boots, hats, scarves, padded snow suits, and try to walk around the block. It was so cold and the wind so bitter many times we couldn't make it around the block. The large basement came in handy. The kids did their playing down there.

The University of North Dakota

Again, the cold was so confining. I decided to work on a degree in education. I thought I might want to teach after retirement. So I volunteered for a lot of night shifts at the weather station. I drove to the University of North Dakota which was located in downtown Grand Forks.

It was a small school, maybe 4,000 students. I really loved it there. The head of the College of Education had lost a son killed somewhere in the Air Force. We became good friends. I was 32 at this time. Of course, I was 10-14 years older than the other students. The instructors all treated me as one of them.

The college atmosphere was different from University of Georgia and Oklahoma A&M. North Dakota was considered at the time to be isolated from the rest of the U.S. No one ever thought about North Dakota. It was a forgotten icebox somewhere up north. It was agricultural. There were no large cities. Some kids spoke only German when they started school. Large areas of the state were Indian reservations. They didn't see many outsiders.

The new air bases in Minot and Grand Forks brought in many "outsiders" for the first time and changed the culture of the state forever. In time, missile silos would be built everywhere and oil would be discovered.

I was sort of a curiosity in my classes. The students were from isolated farms and ranches and they weren't used to a college atmosphere. They seemed so insecure about everything. Here I was with two degrees already, mature (by their standards), an Air Force Officer with a career already. They actually wanted to "hang out" with me and seek my advice on life and career problems.

On my first day of basic education class, about 2/3 of the class were girls. When class was over a group of girls surrounded me in the hall. "What's going on?" I couldn't believe how they acted… "We just love the way you talk." Evidently I was the first southerner they had ever encountered. Of course,

after this revelation, I really laid the southern accent on in all my classes!

The girls would actually vie to sit next to me in classes! Wow! Male vanity! Miss North Dakota was in one of my classes. She was gorgeous! She sought me out and wanted me to drive her downtown after classes. When she talked to you she got right up in your face. I had to fight the urge to grab her and kiss her! I never did!! I asked her, "You are just getting over a romance, aren't you?" "Yes, how did you know?" Well, I quit taking her to town and actually avoided her. I was a happily married man, deeply in love with my wife and two sons. I didn't want anything to change that. President Kennedy visited the air base and there was a parade. She was in the car with the President. I was in the stands. She saw me and waved to me. I have to say, knowing her was a unique experience.

The civil rights activists were really getting active in the early 60's. There would be protest groups at the University. I got in trouble a few times because I would address some of these gatherings. "Look you people. You don't have the slightest idea about what's going on down South with the black people. I see how you treat the Indians here in North Dakota. They live in mud huts. You talk bad about them. You treat them worse than any black people are treated in the South!" That's the way I felt about it. I had seen the same treatment of the Mexicans by the white Texans.

I completed all the courses required for a degree in education. I only needed to practice-teach in a school to get a degree. This was not possible. However in a few years I did practice-teach in Germany when I got a Master's Degree in Education.

When Pat was pregnant with Brad, Mae and "B" came up and we took a long road trip. It was just a day trip to Winnepeg, Canada, and we did that. We made a bed in the back of the station wagon for Pat. No interstates in those days. We drove into Montana and visited the site of Custer's Last Stand. That was an interesting experience. I would recommend it highly for anyone. Then we drove to Yellowstone National Park and stayed in the famous Old Grand Hotel. It is still being used. We saw "Old Faithful", etc. Then… on to the Grand Teton National Park and Jackson Hole. Truly a gorgeous area. Then… on to the Black Hills of South Dakota, Deadwood, Mount Rushmore, etc., and then, back to North Dakota through Bismark. Quite a trip!

Another trip was to Bimiji, Minnesota which is where there is a giant statue to Paul Bunyan and his ox, Babe. Nearby is a small lake that is said to be the headwater of the Mississippi. There is a small stream that you can jump over so that you can say you jumped over the Mississippi River.

The fishing in Minnesota was great. The lakes froze over in the winter. I had to try ice fishing so I went with a civilian friend. He had a small wooden hut out on a frozen lake. He used a special drill that drilled through the ice to the water. The ice was about 2 feet thick. He cut a hole about 2 feet in diameter. You lowered a hand line into the hole. We caught several fish. He tossed them outside where they immediately froze. I did not care for this type of fishing and didn't ice fish again.

When the ice melted the fish would go crazy! They would bite anything. The northern pike was a great sport fish. It was really fun catching them. Brad and Robert enjoyed catching blue gills and catfish.

We gave a large southern type fish-fry often. Some of our Yankee friends had never experienced such a meal. I still have a couple of reels we used back then – that was 50 years ago!

I took up coin collecting. It was something to do when so confined inside due to the cold. I was mainly interested in pennies. I had 10-20 rolls of pennies in bank bags. I would put my name, address, etc. on the rolls. Then I would travel to small banks in the rural areas and swap out the bags. I wore my uniform. With that and my southern accent, people trusted me. Brad and Robbie and I would sort through those pennies and keep anything older than 1950. They filled little coin books for all the years. It was fun and entertaining..

I applied for "Squadron Officer's School" (SOS). I had already done it by correspondence on Okinawa. But it meant 3 months TDY (Temporary Duty) at Maxwell AFB, Alabama. Anything to escape the cold.

Pat and the boys went with me. Brad was just a baby, about 5 months old. We rented an apartment with several other SOS students.

The school was tough! Competition, competition, competition in everything! We had lecturers from every branch of military and government. After lectures we divided into groups of 12 and went over the subject matter in the lectures. All the groups were in competition with each other. We even met on weekends to study.

There was an aggressive physical exercise program. We played soccer, my first time ever. I wasn't very good at it. I could run fast but I could never hit the ball with my head or chest. We also practiced running. Before graduation we had to run one mile in 7 minutes. I actually was able to do this by the end of the course.

I was having problems with the Comet station wagon so I traded it in on a 1964 Ford station wagon. It turned out to be a good vehicle. We later traveled all over Europe in it.

I was driving to class at the University of N. Dakota on a snowy stormy day. The road was covered in ice. The ditches were wide and shallow so that the wind would just keep snow moving and not pile up in drifts. I was going slowly with caution and people were going around me. Suddenly I hit a patch of ice and slid off the right shoulder of the road. The vehicle hit on the right front fender, then went end over end. I had no seat belt but my heavy parka kept me under the steering wheel. The vehicle came to a stop on all 4 wheels. I remember thinking as I was turning over in the air, "This is just like the movies". I got out to check the Ford over. The right front fender was bent and the luggage rack on top was flattened. That was the only damage. I was unhurt. I drove the Ford to classes. When I took it to the garage for repair the mechanic said he had to report the accident to the police. A policeman came, wrote up a report, and really got on to me for leaving the scene of the accident.

Back to SOS (Squadron Officer School)… Brad got sick with pneumonia and had to go to the hospital. His condition was serious and he was in an oxygen tent. We were really worried but he pulled through O.K.

We had several visits to Atlanta and Mae and "B" came down a couple of times.

SOS was a great experience. Then… back to the cold country of North Dakota.

I had had enough of cold. My family too. So, I volunteered for "remote" duty just to get out of there. My commander told me, "There could be worse places". I replied, "I know that, but I will just take my chances". I came to work one day and he was waving a piece of paper and grinning ear to ear. "I told you there were worse places!" I was being assigned to Shemya Air Force Station, Shemya, Alaska. I knew where Shemya was. On our large weather maps of the North American continent that we used in our SAC briefings, Shemya was a tiny island right on the left edge of the map. It was 2,000 miles west of Anchorage and at the western end of the Aleutian Islands. It wasn't far from the Russian Peninsular of Kamchatka.

Just before I took Pat and the boys to Atlanta my mother died in Fitzgerald, my hometown. We were all able to go to the funeral.

A new assignment, so be it. I found an apartment for Pat and the boys near her parents in Atlanta.

This assignment turned out to be an amazing adventure every weather man should spend some time in and experience the "Aleutian low".

15

1964-1965

▶ Shemya Air Force Station
Alaska

EARTHQUAKE DAMAGE

I had volunteered for remote duty to get out of frigid North Dakota, and this was my assignment.

Pat took me to the Atlanta airport. I asked for military standby, and I was put in first class to Chicago and Seattle. I was feeling no pain when I arrived in Seattle for I drank champagne all the way.

I had a couple of days before I had to report to McChord Air Force Base for my flight to Alaska. I visited downtown and went up the Space Needle. I rented a car and drove completely around Mount Ranier. Beautiful trip. Flew Alaskan Airlines to Elmendorf AFB, Anchorage, Alaska.

The bad earthquake of spring, 1964, had just occurred. Many buildings on the base were damaged. In Anchorage, the first row of mansions, on the bluffs of Cook's Inlet, were 200 feet below the cliffs in the mud. There were several circular holes around town in which several homes had tumbled. One side of the main street in Anchorage had sunk until only the roof tops of the stores were visible. Strange… you could drive down the street – one side was normal – the other just rooftops. South of Anchorage were square miles of farms under water. Half of the telephone poles stood out of the water.

A river ran right through town. People were snagging 10-pound salmon right out of the river. The air was crisp and cool. I had never seen such clear air. You could see clearly snow covered mountain tops miles away.

I was at Elmendorf Air Force Base for about two weeks of orientation. There was an intensive course on cold weather survival. The base was beautiful. Darkness only lasted for three hours. You learned

EARTHQUAKE DAMAGE

TSUNAMI DAMAGE AFTER EARTHQUAKE

EARTHQUAKE DAMAGE

EARTHQUAKE DAMAGE

EARTHQUAKE DAMAGE

TSUNAMI DAMAGE AFTER EARTHQUAKE

BILLION DOLLAR JUNKYARD

to live by the clock. You had heavy curtains over your windows to keep out the sun at 3 a.m. The first morning I reported to work at the weather station, the sun woke me up. I thought my watch was wrong. The forecaster on duty wanted to know why I was coming to work three hours early.

I was scheduled to give a weather briefing to the small SAC unit on the base. At the end of my first briefing, the SAC commander blurted out, "Where did you come from? We have been trying to get a briefing like that for months!" His remark made me feel good.

I saw the "Sound of Music" for the first time in downtown Anchorage.

At last it was time to fly out to Shemya. It was a ten hour trip, over 2,000 miles, in an old lumbering C-124 cargo plane. You could see a lot of small smoking volcanos in the islands below. When I got off the plane the first thing I noticed was how white everyone was. No sun here.

The last U.S. island in the chain was Attu. Attu was about 10 miles by 30 miles big. It was the scene of heavy fighting with the Japanese in WWII. Shemya was about 40 miles east of Attu. It was only 3 miles by 5 miles big, which is really small.

The weather was so bad the air base on Attu couldn't be used. The field was small and surrounded by mountains. The highest point on Shemya was only 400 feet high. Our runway was built right on the beach. The planes would come in to land just a few feet above the water. There was a lot of wreckage at the end of the runway of planes that didn't make it.

Some nights, vehicles were lined along the runway with their lights on. It was frightening hearing the planes drone 'round and round' in the "soup" above.

Shemya was 2,000 miles from Elmendorf. Once the planes passed a point of no return they didn't have enough fuel to go anywhere else. The pilots would tell us, "Give us one weather report above minimums and no more. We will find a way to land."

The supply and mail planes came out twice a week. Some of these were commercial contract planes and had female flight attendants on them. There were no females on the island. A crowd of guys would gather to watch the girls get off the plane. The girls would be loaded in a van and taken to rooms where they could not leave and guards were posted around them.

Life on the tiny island was really confined. I lived in a huge hangar. The Navy had a huge hangar. There was one huge concrete block building that held all the other personnel. It held the B.X., dining hall, laundry, etc. You rarely saw the sun. The wind blew 40mph every day and would get to 80mph every third day. The temperature was 28 degrees all winter and never got above 38 degrees all summer. The "Aleutian Low" is a permanent low pressure area that covers all of the northern Pacific in the Gulf of Alaska. It was "bad weather" year round.

In WWII, if a German soldier "screwed up", he was sent to the Russian front. In the American Army he was sent to the Aleutian Islands. These were always considered the worst duty stations in the U.S. military.

There were remnants of the old wooden WWII barracks on the island. There was a part left of the old hospital. Beside the steps at an entryway was a fir tree about 5 feet tall. It had been planted during WWII. It was 20 years old and only grew 5 feet tall. There were no other trees on the island… just a type of sawgrass about 4 feet tall. Drinking water came from a small depression that caught rainwater. It had to be treated and filtered quite a bit.

There was a small cliff on a rocky shore where all the ammunition from WWII was dumped and set on fire. It was an interesting pile of debris.

There were mountains of 55-gallon drums. Hundreds of blue fox lived there. Nothing ever left the island. There was a junkyard called the "billion dollar junkyard". You could spend all day looking at the stuff dumped and stored there since WWII. That stuff would be worth a fortune in the States.

Everyone spent a lot of time scouring the beaches for large glass balls that were used by the Asians on their fishing nets. They were beautiful. I spent a lot of time fly-fishing for Dolly-Varden trout in a small lake. The fish were about 6 inches long and never grew any larger.

We had a lot of blue fox on the island. They lived in the huge stacks of 55-gallon gas drums. They had a blue tinge to their fur. They were a protected species because they had been hunted for their fur to near extinction. They were quite pet. In the weather station we fed them sardines and they hung around quite often.

SAC CREW WEATHER BRIEFING

Another pastime was digging for Aleut-Indian artifacts. These Indians had lived here for thousands of years. The Russians would capture them and make slaves of them. When we bought Alaska from the Russians all the Aleuts were taken off the islands and moved to mainland Alaska. Digging up their relics was illegal, and I never did it.

We held Sunday services in a small wooden chapel left from WWII. We had a small theater which showed the same movies over and over again. We had closed circuit TV but the programming was terrible.

The food was terrible. Vegetables, milk, etc. were flown in weekly. Once a year, a giant barge came in with food-stuffs. We ate well for a few months after it arrived. Then, it got terrible! There was a lot of green meat served. We had a great Sunday meal in the Officer's Club. We had a large beef round flown in weekly. It was good.

I had a partial plate in my mouth that wasn't working too well. I decided this was a good time to get the rest of my teeth pulled. We had a young lieutenant dentist fresh out of dental school. For some reason, he was scared to pull my teeth. An older, experienced dentist came out from Elmendorf to assist him. They took a couple of hours! The older dentist would pull one and tell the LT. all about the procedure. Then, the LT. would pull one while being supervised by the older. This was a horrible experience! But after healing for a long time and getting new dentures, everything worked out O.K.

The island shook all the time! We kept a large, flat pan of water in the weather station. It was interesting to watch the water shaking from the tremors. We had one really bad earthquake nearby. We were eating dinner. At first I thought the guy across from me was lifting the table with his knees. Then the coat hangers on a rack started banging. I had experienced this before in Japan. I stood up and yelled, "Earthquake! Everyone outside!" Once outside, we felt the ground upheaving about 3 feet. The large building we were just in was moving up and down. This was a weird feeling! You can't imagine what it's like if you have never experienced it.

We had a 30-foot tidal wave that night. It washed out most of the road around the island. The quake put a huge crack in the runway. A large crack ran right under the weather station.

A couple of amusing incidents happened during the quake. A van load of SAC guys were headed from the headquarters building to the hangar where we all lived. The van was swaying so badly, they asked the driver why he was driving so badly. "I don't know what's going on", he said. "I can't keep it on the road!" A warrant officer who worked with me was with the SAC commander, a colonel, in the day room upstairs in the hangar. The hangar started swaying. The colonel told my man, "Mr. Reber, you told me the wind wouldn't be this strong today." (Warrant officers were called "Mister".) Mr. Reber went over to the window and looked at the windsock we kept outside. It was motionless. Then he looked out into the hangar where we kept a huge iron ball suspended from the rafters. It was swaying in a large arc. He told the colonel, "Sir, that's no wind! It's an earthquake and we'd better get out of here!"

The hangar we lived in was huge. We kept the KC-135 inside and there was still plenty of room to house 40 men, a jogging track, a badminton court, basketball court, etc. I was the island badminton champ for several months. That can be a tough game. I was always quick and agile all my young life. I could drive that shuttlecock very hard and close to the net or just poop it barely over.

What was my mission there? It was very important and different. My sole job was to support that one aircraft. The weather station was manned by civilians. I had a sergeant and warrant officer under me. I was the commander of a detachment of three.

That aircraft was a modified KC-135. It had special windows for special cameras. It was loaded with electronic gear. It was handled by SAC (Strategic Air Command) and had a crew of fourteen. It costs a lot of money and was one of a kind. The weather out there was so terrible that we three were assigned to take care of that one plane.

The Cold War in 1965 was very real. We had just gotten over the Cuban Missile Crisis. The Russians had their main missile operations on Kamchatka. They fired them into the Pacific and they impacted at sea just north of Hawaii. They kept a fleet of ships in the impact area. Our electronic surveillance people on the island could tell when a missile was to be launched. Our plane would wait for the missile, follow it downrange and get all kinds of photographs and electronic information from it. The weather was so nasty at Shemya that sometimes we had to divert the aircraft to Eilson AFB, Fairbanks, Alaska. That was a huge SAC base. Eilson AFB was to affect my life in future years.

196

MY ROOM IN HANGAR

SAC WEATHER BRIEFING

MY ROOM IN HANGAR

MY ROOM IN HANGAR

OUR KC-135 SPECIAL OPS AIRCRAFT

I was on duty the day an Air Force SR-71 jet was attempting a "round the world" speed record. He was following the jet stream in the Northern Hemisphere. From the Tokyo area to the Anchorage area the jet stream is always very fast. I talked to the pilot for several minutes while he was near Shemya. I had been sent a lot of info about the flight, so I was ready to brief him. I gave him the jet's altitude and position and how to stay in it till he passed over the Gulf of Alaska. The aircraft set a new world record. I was very proud to be a part of this historic mission.

There was an amusing incident that happened. One day, a commercial aircraft going from San Francisco to Tokyo had to make an emergency landing on our airstrip. It had about 8 or 10 female stewardesses on it. We opened the mess hall, fed them, took them to the Officers' Club, and danced with them all night long! And I do mean ALL NIGHT! The poor girls were so exhausted the next day that I'm sure they had a hard time doing their jobs.

As my tour ended I put in for a "consecutive assignment" to Germany. This was a type of deal where you counted two tours as one. The main advantage was that you got a year on the base housing list. At the time, the Air Force was cutting back in Germany, so it was difficult to get an assignment there. I guess I was able to get it because a tour on Shemya was considered so bad. I received an assignment to Ramstein Air Base, Germany. I flew to Atlanta, had a great reunion with Pat and the boys, and we got ready to go to Europe.

As a meteorologist, I am glad I went to Shemya. It is considered the weather asshole of the world, but I learned a lot about weather forecasting there.

On to another great experience!

16

GERMANY
1965-1968

▶ RAMSTEIN AIR BASE

WEATHER STATION IN CAVE

SALZBURG SALT MINE

OUR BASE QUARTERS

From Shemya Air Base, Alaska, I got a concurrent assignment to Germany. Base housing was difficult to get. But, because I was "concurrent", I had a year on the housing list and we had an apartment waiting.

I picked up Pat and the boys in Atlanta and we drove to McGuire AFB, New Jersey. But, first we went to New York City. The World's Fair of 1965 was there at the time. We stayed in the Holiday Inn in New York and I was shocked at the price of a room- $70 a night. All over the U.S it was only $8-$12 at the time. I was also shocked at how much hotel security there was. We rode a special train out to the fair and spent the entire day there. They had a rest area for children and Robbie and Brad had naps in the afternoon. Brad was two and Robbie was five.

Back to McGuire AFB. I turned in our '64 Ford Fairlane station wagon somewhere for shipment and we spent two or three days in guest quarters waiting for our plane to Germany. Robbie and Brad had their own little bags of toys, snacks, etc. and they were really cute kids.

We were met by our sponsor, Captain Bill Muir. I was a Captain at the time. Bill now lives on the same Bay I do in Navarre, Florida and I see him now and then.

Bill took us to Ramstein AB, about 40 miles from where we landed in Frankfurt. It was afternoon. We had bad "Jet Lag" and slept all afternoon, all night and into the next day. Then, we moved into our quarters, which were partially furnished.

Our apartment (Quarters in the military) was on the 5th floor of a very large building. It was 5 storied. There were 3 or 4 stairwells with 8 apartments on one stairwell. We could see the small town of

Ramstein out our kitchen window. It had a small kitchen, a huge living room, a large master bedroom, another small bedroom and a large bath. It was really very comfortable. It was wired for 220 volts instead of 110 volts and we had to use electrical converters for our appliances. The bathtub was the largest I have ever seen.

The schools were great. Pat spent a lot of time educating the boys. Robbie could read well at 3 years of age. He was put in the second grade immediately. Skipped the first. His teacher was the wife of an officer I worked with.

The kids had a large play area behind the apartment building. It was here we discovered that Robbie could throw things very hard and very straight. The kids built forts out of snow and had lots of snowball fights. We finally had to stop Robbie from participating. His hard straight throws into kid's faces brought a lot of complaints from the kids' parents.

Robbie was ready for T-Ball. I coached his team. All teams were named after cartoon characters and our team was the "Menances". Robbie played the entire infield. We had a kid on first who could catch Robbie's fast throws. Robbie and another kid hit home runs at every bat. Our games were always around 4 p.m. I knew the kids were hungry, so I mixed gallons of milk with chocolate syrup, had lots of cookies, so my team was all fired up. We won the base championship that year (our last year in Germany).

MY JOB

I was assigned to a weather forecast and warning center. We made forecasts and weather advisories for every U.S. base in Europe. Overall, the weather in Europe was terrible. We also prepared top secret forecasts for all the Russian "cold war" bases in Europe behind the "Iron Curtain". It was exciting and important work. We worked in a cave network beneath a mountain in a small town called Kindsbach. The caves went on for miles under the mountain. They were made for and used by German forces in WWII. We were about 300 feet into the mountain. All the other tunnels were sealed off.

Satellite weather was in it's infancy at this time. We actually had to spend hours decoding reams of paper covered with codes in order to plot the actual path of the satellite. Then, we had to operate a radar that tracked the satellite as it went overhead. It was fascinating. Our first path was over Eastern Russia and the Bearing Sea. The next path was from the North Pole, over Central Russia, down to China. The next path was over Germany, Poland, down to Egypt. The next path was over England, Spain, down to North Africa. The next path was over Greenland, Iceland, Mid Atlantic. The last path was over Newfoundland and Atlantic. Each path was approximately 90 minutes. We printed the pictures of each path into Mosaics. By the end of the day, we had a large portion of the Northern Hemisphere. These were the first weather satellite pictures ever. What a boon to forecasting!

There was an International Air show held in Paris. The US had a large contingent of aircraft there. We were assigned the task of providing them with the weather information and severe weather forecasts. A very severe squall line was approaching the city. We issued a timely severe weather warning of thunderstorms and high winds to the US group there. They heeded the warnings, tied down their planes and took their precautions. Evidently the other countries didn't have weather warning capability or ignored French advisories. There was significant damage to the other aircraft at the show. Ours were the only ones that suffered no damage. We received high commendations from the US contingent authorities.

I bought a small green Fiat. The engine was tiny and sounded like a washing machine. But, it got me to Kindsbach and back home.

I went to the Air Force dump and found all kinds of lumber. I used it to build a tree house. Unfortunately, the trees were outside the nearby border fence and a German state forest of some type. There was an unauthorized gap in the fence. The German kids would slip up at night and tear our tree house down. It became a type of game. I must have rebuilt that treehouse at least six times!

We loved the local town's restaurants. We went to many. Everyone had it's own brewery. I loved their beer. The Germans make, to me, the best beer in the world.

I loved their weiner schnitzel. It was a fried breaded veal cutlet. And, their sauerkraut was great. You could get a first class meal for 6 Marks (about $1.50 then). I loved stopping in little sandwich shops and having a local beer with bratwurst and brotchen. This was a sausage served with a hard roll and German mustard. Nowhere in the world can you find sauerkraut and mustard like that found in Germany.

Johnny Mathis came to the NCO Club every year. I saw his show once. It was really good.

Pat was a den mother for a cub scout troop. Of course, I assisted. I remember the car races. Once a year, you had to carve out a small racing car from a block of balsa wood. We spent a lot of time on

that car, and I knew we would win. While I wasn't looking, Robbie let a boy put oil on the axles and wheels. Well, the oil actually slowed the car and we didn't win.

Pat was the president of the Officer's Wives Club. They put on a lot of bazaars and shows. She worked with a budget of over $200,000. Most of it was donated to scholarships. Sometimes, they would have over 100 European vendors. They all loved Pat. The Germans especially were quick to recognize ability and efficiency. Several told me that Pat was the best they ever worked with.

My squadron commander, a Colonel, had a crush on Pat. He and his wife got Pat to represent our squadron in the "Miss Ramstein AB Pageant". She was beautiful. Slim and long dark hair. She placed second I think. I was really proud of her.

Pat and I enrolled in the University of Southern California extension (USC) on Ramstein to get a Masters degree in education. We attended two evenings a week for 18 months.

The Air Force actually gave me 6 weeks TDY (temporary duty) to do my practice teaching at the junior high school on Ramstein Air Base. It was for physical science. My teacher supervisor spent 2 days with me and I saw him rarely after that. I took to the job naturally and really enjoyed it.

I can't remember Pat's thesis, but here is mine. I looked up a lot of foreign words, made up a lot and made a high school multiple choice test. There were no such words. I told the students I was trying to test their innate ability to recognize language. What I was really after is to see how they guessed A,B, C, D on a multiple choice test. It was interesting, my instructors liked it. Of course, I had to discuss possible outcomes, percentage errors, etc. etc.

Turned out "C" was the guess choice. (Somehow, I already knew that for myself)

At Ramstein I became eligible for promotion to Major. The board met. I was passed over! It was a shock! This couldn't be! My friends and commander were shocked! I got busy to find out why. I secured copies of all my officer efficiency reports (OER's). Found the problem!

When you work for someone and do a good job, you expect to be taken care of. Boy, was I naïve!

Overall, throughout the Air Force, OER's (Officer Efficiency Report) were inflated. Everyone was above average or superior. You had to have a great OER to be promoted.

On Okinawa, I did a great job with the two fighter squadrons I supported. They always asked me to give their briefings and to deploy with them. Same with the navy squadron we supported. My commander was a Lt. Colonel. He was real short and had the "Small Colonel Complex". This was a term used in the Air Force to describe a small Colonel who was obnoxious and always ordering his subordinates around. The only thing he had going for him was that he was a pilot in WWII and had shot down 5 Japanese planes. Other than that, he was obnoxious, boisterous, loud… you get the picture. He knew he could never make full Colonel and was a big goof off. He never did anything in the detachment. It was obvious that the OER's he submitted on me had been composed by our Airman First Class (AIC) Clerk. They were terrible! This hurt my chances of ever getting promoted. I was never shown my OER's. I challenged these OER's. I had affidavits and letters of recommendation from the fighter squadron commanders and the commander of the

air defense blockhouse. The Air Force turned down my request to throw out the OER's.

Now. Following Okinawa and at Grand Forks AFB North Dakota. Again, I supported 2 fighter squadrons and a large SAC (Strategic Air Command) wing of B-52's. I felt I did a great job.

Our Commander had just made Lt. Colonel. It just so happened that the Air Force promoted every eligible Major on that go 'round. He was promoted. He should have never been promoted. He was a bigger goof off than my commander on Okinawa. Again, it was evident that his OER's were written by our clerk. They were terrible. I was never shown these OER's.

Again, I obtained documents from the squadron and SAC commanders to help me get the OER's thrown out. Again, the Air Force refused to do so.

Somehow the news of my "passover" reached the commander of the USAF Air Weather Service, Major General Russell K. Pierce. He wrote an indorsement to my next OER which read:

*"I have been personally aware of Captain Fletcher's performance for several years now and am anxious to fully support this evaluation. He is not only an outstanding manager and technician, but a superior officer as well. It is indeed unfortunate that due to one or two misguided and unfair OERs in the past, he has not been selected for promotion by previously convened selection boards. He is of great value to the Air Force and it would be near tragic if we were to lose him because of continuing promotion passovers. In this regard, the continued disappointments he has endured have had **no** adverse effect on this attitude or performance."*

General Pierce and I, though a strange trail of events, actually knew each other.

During the first of several years of my weather assignments the Chief Meteorology Scientist at Air Weather Service at Scott AFB was a civilian named Robert Fletcher. He had a son, Robert Fletcher, Jr., who was an Air Force Officer and weather forecaster like me. I was often mistaken for this son.

General Pierce, then a Colonel, was the Commander of the 1st Weather Wing in Japan, my parent organization. He came to Okinawa often, and we always had a party or a large dinner for him. He sought me out and asked me if I was *the* son. Of course I was not. For some reason he liked me, and we had long conversations together.

After he became Commander of the Air Weather Service he loved to visit units "in the field". It seemed he visited every weather unit I was assigned to. We would have long friendly conversations. So we got to know each other quite well.

I was thrilled to see his indorsement on my OER, and I am sure this had a lot to do with my promotion to Major.

So, on the next go 'round I was promoted to Major!! God helps those who help themselves!

Because of all my extra hard work I was recommended for and received the Air Force Commendation Medal. I'm sure this helped my promotion to Major. I completed several studies of forecasting problems we had in Europe, and I revised many of our forecasting techniques to improve our forecasting procedures.

OUR TRIPS

One nice thing about being stationed in Germany was that you could easily visit most of Europe.

We had several luxury hotels (rest centers) in Germany. Bertchesgarten in Southern Germany was one gorgeous hotel and area. It was a famous ski resort in the winter. Another was Chiemsee. It was on a lake. A boat would take you out to an island where there was one of King Ludwig's famous castles. He was chastised and hated for spending so much money and resources on castles, but they paid for themselves many times over because they became huge famous tourist attractions. The most famous was Neuschwanstein. This one Disney copied for Disney World. It was absolutely beautiful. It sat on the top of a mountain. The valleys were full of lakes. It had a gorgeous view from every window.

Europe was a land of castles. We traveled up and down both sides of the Rhine and Mosel Rivers and visited every one of them.

When we traveled, we usually had to rent a room with only one bed. So, I put two canvass portable cots in a suitcase for the boys. This worked out well.

We went to Liechtenstein, one of the 5 "postage stamp" nations in Europe. They were called "postage stamp" nations because most of their money came from printing and selling myriads of elaborate and beautiful postage stamps. The other 4 are: 2. Luxembourg, 3. San Moreno - between France and Spain, 4. The Vatican, 5. Monaco.

I love such places as Liechtenstein. It looked as it did in the Middle Ages. I loved drinking beer in gasthouses (bars) that had been used for centuries.

In Overndolt bei Salzborg in Austria, we visted the small church where the Christmas Carol, "Silent Night", was written.

In Nurenberg, we stood in the bleachers of a large stadium where Hitler made most of his famous speeches.

We went to the most famous Christmas town in the whole world in, I think, Regensburg, and it was Christmas time. Acres and acres of shops and booths. A torchlight parade up and down a mountain near the city. What a wonderful experience.

At one of the German cities, we were introduced to a "Gluehwein" (sweet wine). The hot wine was poured over a column of sugar. It really warmed you up.

Heidelberg, the old University city, was a beautiful city. On a bluff, overlooking a river, and lots of castles. This was the headquarters of all our Army forces in Europe, so it was full of our military.

We went to Salzburg, Austria, and rode the slides down into the salt mines on a leather pad.

We went to the "Eagle's Nest" in Southern Germany where Hitler hung out. He had an elevator from the base of his mountain through solid rock to the top. It can't be used, so we rode a bus to the top. That was a harrowing experience!

In one of the rooms was a large marble fireplace on which American soldiers in WWII had chiseled their names. In the 82nd Airborne Division Museum at Ft. Bragg, N.C., there are a lot of items on display that came from the "Nest".

We went to Luxembourg. There we visited the American WWII cemetery. Patton's grave is there "at the head of the troops". Across the highway was

the German cemetery. Their crosses and plaques are different. So sad.

We visted both ends of the "Remagen Bridge" on either side of the Rhine River.

In WWII the first crossing of the Rhine by American Forces was made here. It is said this shortened the war by many weeks.

Fascinating history associated with the crossing. The war movie "The Bridge at Remagen" with George Segal does a great job of showing what happened.

A German engineer, a gallant German Army Major, was sent to the bridge to destroy it before the Americans could cross. Upon his arrival he found that all the explosives sent to do the job were agricultural and not Army. He had to use these. When they exploded the bridge was still intact. The Americans were able to get across.

Hitler personally ordered the immediate execution of the German Major. The execution was a touching scene in the movie. The Major was played by Robert Vaughn.

We explored the caves at either end. Much of the bridge was still there. I don't think the bridge was ever rebuilt. A great historical place.

We went to Amsterdam and to Brussels, Belgium. Just outside Brussels is the battlefield of Waterloo, where Napoleon was defeated by the British. For some reason this is not a tourist attraction. The Belgiums don't play it up. The only thing on the battlefield is a huge stone pyramid about 400 feet high with a huge bronze English lion on top. Downtown Brussels kept part of it's city from the Middle Ages. It is beautiful. We also visited the site of the 1958 World's Fair. The giant sphere is still there.

I think this is where the "pissing boy" statue is. It is a fountain on a corner. This is a worldwide tourist attraction.

Bastogne Belgium was the scene of one of the largest final battles of WWII. The Germans had our Airborne Divisions totally surrounded. When the German commander demanded our surrender General Anthony McAuliffe gave his famous answer, "Nuts!"

There is a very impressive huge monument in Bastogne to our forces. It has tall marble columns, maps etched in marble walls and the names of all the American units that fought there. There are four Sherman tanks guarding four corners of the monument.

My brother, Johnny, US Army Infantry, was in one of the units that broke through German encirclement and liberated our trapped troops.

This monument to the "Breakthrough" is a must visit for anyone going to that area.

Also in Holland is another famous tourist attraction. A miniature city called Medurodam. The buildings are 2-4 feet high. It covers acres. There are paths for walking. It is an entire city in miniature!

We went to Metz. I think part of the city is in Germany and partly in France. We visited the trenches and pill boxes of the "Maginout Line" of WWI. There is this famous (infamous) trench where shell explosions buried a whole line of French soldiers in formation. There is a row of rifle bayonets sticking out of the earth. They left them buried there. So sad.

There are monuments to battles and wars all over the roadsides and fields of Germany and France along the border. There is this huge church that is built upon a base of storage areas with windows all around. You can look through the windows and see bones. The farmers over the years have uncovered so many bones from so many battles that they bring them here and they just store them there as an monument and memorial to them all.

Pat and I went on a 3 day bus tour to Paris. Went up the Eiffel Tower. Went to the Lido de Parie Night Club. Dozens of nude artists on stage, but it was tastefully done. Went to the Louvre, the largest museum. Saw the Mona Lisa, the Winged Victory (no head) and numerous famous things. We had a nightclub tour and saw many amazing acts and shows.

A pilot friend of mine flew me down to Moron Air Base near Seville, Spain. Seville is a beautiful city. The Moors (Arabs from North Africa) occupied this city for a long time. All the buildings were trimmed in the most beautiful old painted tiles. There were numerous shops filled with silver. Every store and bar was closed from 1p.m. to 5 p.m. Then the city came alive for all night. I saw several shows where they do those "stomping dances" with cassonettes. They are something. These are the real thing. It doesn't seem possible that a human body can tap dance (stomp to me) like that. It was a sight to see and experience. I think the dances are called Flamenco. The streets are lined with silver shops. I have never seen so much silver in my life.

May and "B" came over and we went to France and Italy and we drove through Switzerland down through the Rhone Valley of France into Monaco (postage stamp country) to Nice, France, on the Riviera. Nice is a beautiful old city. The large boulevard along the water was lined with those old beautiful hotels you see in the movies. The beach was mostly pebbles. There were numerous topless ladies sunning themselves. Alas! Mae and Pat wouldn't let me and "B" linger there! Also, Robbie and Brad were with us.

We had a tourist book entitled "France on $5 a Day". It really came in handy. We had a hotel a block off the Riviera that was reasonable. It also told us where to find restaurants. It was interesting to see so many bottles of wine on all the tables.

Then, we went to Monaco. The entire country is just one big city, very beautiful. We went to the famous casino that was in a James Bond movie. They let us see the lobby, but we were not allowed inside.

Princess Grace was alive then. Her castle was open to tourists on certain days. Of course you were not allowed to see most of it. She would come out and greet tourists some days. She was out of town the day we visited the castle.

We then headed to Rome. There were no super highways in those days. The roads followed the coast. They were narrow and curvy and wound around mountains. It was a hard drive. There were many small towns on the coast and built up the sides of the mountains. We spent the night in one of these and fell in love with the place.

In one restaurant they tried to rip us off on the price of our dinner. "B" spoke some French. He was able to get our bill cut in half.

We were just toolin' along and suddenly saw an American soldier sitting on a bridge side. We stopped and talked to him. This was Leghorn, Italy. We found out there was an American Army Base there. We got directions and went to it. Went to the PX and gorged ourselves on American hamburgers and milkshakes! We were tired of French and Italian food.

We stopped at the Leaning Tower of Pisa. Old memories of being there 15 years before with Tommy and Phyllis really overwhelmed me. Rome and Venice did this to me too.

We arrived in Rome. Stayed at an old hotel where the bath rooms and tubs were of solid beautiful marble.

We stopped in one area where marble and alabaster were mined. They had stores full of the most beautiful marble and alabaster we had ever seen. We bought several pieces there.

Rome is fabulous! So much history. We visited the Colosseum. It was full of feral cats and we were covered with fleas! We got out of there in a hurry!

We went to a sound and light show in the ruins of the original old city. It made you feel like you were witnessing the triumphant return of a Roman Legion.

We went to The Vatican (another postage stamp country). St. Peters Cathedral was a sight to see. All the Popes were mummified and on display on a bottom floor. Each dressed in Ermin robes with jewels all over them. The Vatican museum covered acres, so we couldn't see all of it. So much gold and jewels! Priceless! We saw the balcony where the Pope stands and blesses the crowds below. He wasn't there that day. Witnessed the changing of the Swiss Guard.

Visited the catacombs. Gloomy and scary. Thousands of skeletons of people buried there for centuries.

Visited and walked down the "Apian Way", the road leading from Rome to the sea. It was rather narrow. It was lined with all kinds of statues and monuments. History, history.

One evening we decided to have a genuine Italian pizza. Couldn't find one! Finally, we were directed to an area of restaurants that catered to American tourists and found a pizza. Evidently this is an American dish.

Then on to Bologna. Museums, museums. The boys didn't want to visit any more museums.

Then on to Venice. The city lives up to all it's hype. It is something to see. Walk the bridges and along the canals. Took a tourist boat ride, but not a gondola. Beautiful old buildings and monuments. Lost Brad in St. Marks Square. We were afraid someone had abducted him. Finally found him. He had been chasing pigeons and left us.

Then up through the famous Brenner Pass to Austria and Germany. The Germans had heavily fortified this pass and many battles were fought there. It was one of the most beautiful scenic areas I have ever seen.

Went to Vienna, Austria. Beautiful fascinating city. I would love to go back.

BERLIN

I decided to see the Soviet sector of Berlin. Only military personnel could go. You had to be in uniform. You were instructed to show your military I.D. and nothing else. You were told to answer no questions and make no conversations with the Russians. You could not carry a camera.

The night before I went into East Berlin, I stayed at the Berlin Hilton. The U.S. military got a special rate. The "people watching" lobby was the best in the world. Diplomats, movie starts, rock bands, etc. All the world's noted persons stayed at the Berlin Hilton.

There was a bus load of us. We went through the famous "Check Point Charlie". The bus stopped on the U.S. side and an officer got on and briefed us on the do's and don'ts while in East Berlin. Then the bus stopped on the Russian side. A Russian army officer got on. He looked at our I.D. cards. He stared at each of us for a few moments. Meanwhile, another Russian soldier checked under the bus. It was quite exciting and a little scary.

Then the bus and a tour guide carried us around the city. The Russians had cleared a 100 foot lane of houses and everything. The outer wall (the "Berlin Wall") was stone topped by barbed wire with a guard house about every 100 feet. The inner wall was quite tall, of metal fencing, and topped with lots of barbed wire. The cleared lane was a mine field. It would be very difficult for anyone to breach that set up. The few people that did escape did so through tunnels.

Where Hitler's last days had been spent in his bunker was a cleared field with huge mounds of earth.

The Soviet Park with the huge monument to their soldiers was quite impressive.

We went through the Berlin's famous zoo.

Then, the museum. This is one of the largest in the world. At the time, it had the largest collection of Egyptian antiquities in the world. It was fascinating! Seems they have everything there but the pyramids! I don't see how they accumulated all that stuff.

We stopped at an East German bar. It was full of beautiful blue-eyed German girls. They pounced on us! I wanted to talk to one about her life in East Berlin. So, I told her "O.K., I'll pay the whiskey price for your glass of tea." We had an interesting conversation. They had a hard life under communist rule.

In East Berlin there were miles and miles of destruction from WWII. The area was dirty, gloomy and depressing. No wonder people risked their lives to escape to the West.

We saw several instances of Russian soldiers at their "changing of the guard." They put on quite a show of military precision.

OCTOBER FEST – MUNICH GERMANY

For some reason I had a few days TDY to a small Army base near Munich. It just so happened, the world famous "October Fest" was going on. It was nowhere as large as it is now. Now, millions of people from around the world attend it.

At the time, there were 3 huge tents, each holding about 6,000 people. There were 3 elevated band stands in each tent. The bands were called something like "Oompah" bands. They were dressed in the traditional dress of Bavaria. Green hats with a large feather, green suspenders, flowered, green leather pants (lederhosen) high top leather shoes and high white stockings. They played only horns of every type. The Germans have a lot of songs that are for beer drinking parties only. I love them! Maybe it's the German in me. I'm half German.

Beer and Bratwurst and Brotchen were the fare. The beer was dark, strong, and served only in 2 liter mugs.

It didn't take long till everyone was half drunk. Everyone was singing the songs and waving the mugs. We sat on long benches along huge tables. The servers passed among us keeping the mugs

CROWN PRINCE LUDWIG, LATER TO BECOME KING, MARRIED PRINCESS THERESA OF SAXONY ON 12 OCTOBER 1810. HE THREW A BIG PARTY IN THE FIELDS IN FRONT OF THE CITY GATES. HE ORDERED THE BEST BEER OF THE LAND TO BE SERVED.

Gruß vom Münchener Oktoberfest

THE PARTY WENT ON FOR 16 DAYS. THE CELEBRATION BECAME "OKTOBERFEST".

full and serving the Bratwurst and Brotchen. Soon everyone locked arms and swayed left and right. Then people started standing on the benches with locked arms, swaying to and fro, spilling beer everywhere and singing loudly. I didn't know that much German, but I mouthed the words and sang along too. I was careful not to drink too much and lose my senses.

This was the party of all parties! And it was great fun. I wonder what it is like now. It is a lifetime experience!

TRIP TO DENMARK,
NORWAY AND SWEDEN

There is so much to see in Europe.

We had our blue-green '64 Ford Fairlane station wagon. Lots of room in the back for the boys and a good luggage rack on the roof.

So, we were headed to Copenhagen, Denmark. Such a beautiful wonderful city. We went to the famous "Tivoli Gardens". Very large. Sort of like a Disney World.

We saw the famous "Little Gold Mermaid". She sits on a rock about 50 feet from the shore. She is about 2 feet high.

We saw the original statue of "The Thinker", by Rodin I think.

While traveling down a small hill, I noticed smoke billowing behind the vehicle. We pulled over and soon a man in a car stopped behind us. He spoke perfect English (most in Denmark do). He was one of the nicest men I have ever met. He called a tow truck and it took us to a huge Ford dealership and garage. It turned out we had a blown seal between the transmission and the engine. The transmission fluid flowed into the engine and thus the billowing smoke. A part had to be ordered so we had two nights to spend there. The gentlemen took us to a hotel. He came back later and took us to a restaurant. He checked up on us, and the Ford, the next day. What a guardian angel! We finally got the Ford repaired and said our goodbyes. I'll never forget the kindness of that man. Everyone in Denmark was wonderful to us.

We finally reached Skagen, a small seaport on the very North end of Denmark. There we boarded a ferry over to Kristiansand, Norway. It was about a 4 hours trip over open water. From Kristiansand, we drove all the way across Southern Norway to Stavenger, on the West Coast. There we boarded a ferry, which took us up the Sognefjord, one of the longest fjords in Norway. What a trip! Green mountains, waterfalls, small villages clinging to the mountainsides, a fairy land. This was an all day trip, and at the end you are almost halfway across Norway.

In an Oslo Norway museum is the famous boat, the "Kon-Tiki". The boat is made of reeds and balsawood. In August 1947 this boat made a famous voyage of 4,300 miles from Peru to near Tahiti. It was to show that South Americans could have colonized the Polynesian Islands by drifting across the Pacific Ocean.

There are also displays of all sorts of old Viking ships. Some were partially burned funeral ships.

We got off the ferry late afternoon and headed to Oslo. Again, such beautiful scenery. Especially interesting was the old Viking churches. It got dark on us and we were looking for a hotel. Couldn't find one. Stopped at a place that had lots of lights and several cars outside. I went in and there in a huge room was a real smorgasbord! The table was about 20 feet long and covered with cheeses and all types of meat, fruit, etc. It turned out to be a restaurant and a private party was going on. No rooms! We were invited to stay, but had to be on our own way. Found a little country inn. All room were taken. But, they had pity on us and gave us a tiny room in the attic. It looked unused and no heat, but they gave us lots of covers.

The next day, we arrived in Oslo. Such a beautiful city! It was on the ocean with a wide curved white sand beach that stretched for miles. Snow covered mountains ringed it to the West. So clean and beautiful. The people were friendly and helpful. We got a room at the University. The students were on holiday. Staying at a University in Europe is quite common. They just put you in a vacant dormitory room. But, these rooms are like small apartments.

We carried our own coffee pot. Each morning I would go to a nearby neighborhood bakery and buy rolls and milk. These were great.

After Oslo, we went into Sweden. Here I had to drive on the left side of the road. Boy! That took some getting used to! I finally got the hang of it before running into someone. I would have loved to go over to Finland, but we were running out of time.

We stayed in Gothenburg, Sweden, at a University dorm there. Toured the city. Another real old fascinating place.

Then back to Copenhagen. Had to ride a ferry from Sweden to Denmark. From Copenhagen home to Ramstein. What a glorious trip!

The European Alps Mountains are beautiful wherever you go or whatever the season. The cable cars are famous. In Switzerland, the cable car at Role Nase was (is?) the longest cable car ride in the world. It consists of two sections. The first ride goes to the top of a high mountain. Then you switch to another that goes to the top of even a higher peak. What a view! You feel like you are on top of the world. Snow covered peaks as far as you can see. There is a large building there containing a restaurant and toilets, and large walkways. The ride up and back is quite scary. You are thousands of feet high gliding through the sky. Makes you "pucker".

Another great cable car ride is up the Zugspitze, Germany's highest mountain. A cable car ride is a must for anyone visiting Europe.

I think I have covered our sightseeing and our trips in Europe. This helps to explain why everyone wanted to be stationed in Germany.

All good things must come to an end. Our 3 year tour was up. I took the Ford to Bremerhaven to be shipped to Charleston, South Carolina. (Lot of memories about Bremerhaven in 1952-1953)

I ordered a new '68 Pontiac Sedan to be waiting for us in New Jersey.

Again, I asked to be assigned to the Southeast. I received an assignment to Simmons Army Airfield, Ft. Bragg, North Carolina.

This turned out to be an unusual assignment!

Next – Ft. Bragg, North Carolina and another interesting and fascinating assignment.

WEATHER OFFICERS EFFICIENCY REPORTS AND AWARDS

THESE ARE INCLUDED TO DEPICT:

1. DUTIES OF A USAF WEATHER FORECASTER

2. THE MANY DIVERSE SITUATION AND OPERATIONS A USAF WEATHER FORECASTER HAS TO BE INVOLVED IN

3. THE PRESSURE A USAF WEATHER FORECASTER HAS TO ENDURE AND OVERCOME TO BE SUCCESSFUL

OER

THE AIRFORCE
COMMENDATION
MEDAL

RAMSTEIN
FORECAST
CENTER

RAMSTEIN AIR
BASE, GERMANY

OFFICER'S EFFICIENCY
REPORT

PAGE 1 OF 3

I. IDENTIFICATION DATA (Read AFM 36-14 carefully before filling out any item.)

1. LAST NAME—FIRST NAME—MIDDLE INITIAL	2. AFSN	3. ACTIVE DUTY GRADE	4. PERMANENT GRADE
FLETCHER, ROBERT M.	FR57874	Captain	Captain

5. ORGANIZATION, COMMAND AND LOCATION	6. AERO RATING	CODE	7. PERIOD OF REPORT
Det 21, 31 Wea Sq (MAC) Ramstein AB, Germany	Nonrated		FROM: 1 Feb 68 THRU: 7 Jun 68

8. PERIOD OF SUPERVISION	9. REASON FOR REPORT
128	CRO

II. DUTIES—PAFSC E2524 DAFSC E2524 PRESENT DUTY: DET FORECASTER TEAM CH. Supervises the performance of six forecasters and five observers. Responsible for forecasts issued in support of inter and intra-theater deployments, joint Army-Air Force maneuvers, 17th Air Force and 4th Allied Tactical Air Force air offense capability. Routinely makes professional analyses of synoptic weather charts, upper level constant pressure charts, nephanalyses and weather soundings. Frequently gives personal and telephonic briefings.

III. RATING FACTORS (Consider how this officer is performing on his job.)

1. KNOWLEDGE OF DUTIES
NOT OBSERVED | SERIOUS GAPS IN HIS KNOWLEDGE OF FUNDAMENTALS OF HIS JOB. | SATISFACTORY KNOWLEDGE OF ROUTINE PHASES OF HIS JOB. | WELL INFORMED ON MOST PHASES OF HIS JOB. | EXCELLENT KNOWLEDGE OF ALL PHASES OF HIS JOB. | EXCEPTIONAL UNDERSTANDING OF HIS JOB. EXTREMELY WELL INFORMED ON ALL PHASES. ☒

2. PERFORMANCE OF DUTIES
NOT OBSERVED | QUALITY OR QUANTITY OF WORK OFTEN FAILS TO MEET JOB REQUIREMENTS. | PERFORMANCE MEETS ONLY MINIMUM JOB REQUIREMENTS. | QUANTITY AND QUALITY OF WORK ARE VERY SATISFACTORY | PRODUCES VERY HIGH QUANTITY AND QUALITY OF WORK. MEETS ALL SUSPENSES. | QUALITY AND QUANTITY OF WORK ARE CLEARLY SUPERIOR AND TIMELY. ☒

3. EFFECTIVENESS IN WORKING WITH OTHERS
NOT OBSERVED | INEFFECTIVE IN WORKING WITH OTHERS. DOES NOT COOPERATE. | SOMETIMES HAS DIFFICULTY IN GETTING ALONG WITH OTHERS. | GETS ALONG WELL WITH PEOPLE UNDER NORMAL CIRCUMSTANCES. | WORKS IN HARMONY WITH OTHERS. A VERY GOOD TEAM WORKER. | EXTREMELY SUCCESSFUL IN WORKING WITH OTHERS. ACTIVELY PROMOTES HARMONY. ☒

4. LEADERSHIP CHARACTERISTICS
NOT OBSERVED | OFTEN WEAK. FAILS TO SHOW INITIATIVE AND ACCEPT RESPONSIBILITY. | INITIATIVE AND ACCEPTANCE OF RESPONSIBILITY ADEQUATE IN MOST SITUATIONS. | SATISFACTORILY DEMONSTRATES INITIATIVE AND ACCEPTS RESPONSIBILITY. | DEMONSTRATES A HIGH DEGREE OF INITIATIVE AND ACCEPTANCE OF RESPONSIBILITY. | ALWAYS DEMONSTRATES OUTSTANDING INITIATIVE AND ACCEPTANCE OF RESPONSIBILITY. ☒

5. JUDGEMENT
NOT OBSERVED | DECISIONS AND RECOMMENDATIONS OFTEN WRONG OR INEFFECTIVE. | JUDGEMENT IS USUALLY SOUND BUT MAKES OCCASIONAL ERRORS. | SHOWS GOOD JUDGEMENT RESULTING FROM SOUND EVALUATION OF FACTORS. | SOUND, LOGICAL THINKER CONSIDERS ALL FACTORS TO REACH ACCURATE DECISIONS. | CONSISTENTLY ARRIVES AT RIGHT DECISION EVEN ON HIGHLY COMPLEX MATTERS. ☒

6. ADAPTABILITY
NOT OBSERVED | UNABLE TO PERFORM ADEQUATELY IN OTHER THAN ROUTINE SITUATIONS. | PERFORMANCE DECLINES UNDER STRESS OR IN OTHER THAN ROUTINE SITUATIONS. | PERFORMS WELL UNDER STRESS OR IN UNUSUAL SITUATIONS. | PERFORMANCE EXCELLENT EVEN UNDER PRESSURE OR IN DIFFICULT SITUATIONS. | OUTSTANDING PERFORMANCE UNDER EXTREME STRESS. MEETS THE CHALLENGE OF DIFFICULT SITUATIONS. ☒

7. USE OF RESOURCES
NOT (M)(P) OBSERVED | INEFFECTIVE IN CONSERVATION OF RESOURCES. MATERIEL PERSONNEL | USES RESOURCES IN A BARELY SATISFACTORY MANNER. MATERIEL PERSONNEL | CONSERVES BY USING ROUTINE PROCEDURES. MATERIEL PERSONNEL | EFFECTIVELY ACCOMPLISHES SAVINGS BY DEVELOPING IMPROVED PROCEDURES. MATERIEL PERSONNEL | EXCEPTIONALLY EFFECTIVE IN USING RESOURCES. MATERIEL ☒ PERSONNEL ☒

8. WRITING ABILITY AND ORAL EXPRESSION
NOT (W)(S) OBSERVED | UNABLE TO EXPRESS THOUGHTS CLEARLY. LACKS ORGANIZATION. WRITE SPEAK | EXPRESSES THOUGHTS SATISFACTORILY ON ROUTINE MATTERS. WRITE SPEAK | USUALLY ORGANIZES AND EXPRESSES THOUGHTS CLEARLY AND CONCISELY. WRITE SPEAK | CONSISTENTLY ABLE TO EXPRESS IDEAS CLEARLY. WRITE SPEAK | OUTSTANDING ABILITY TO COMMUNICATE IDEAS TO OTHERS. WRITE ☒ SPEAK ☒

IV. MILITARY QUALITIES (Consider how this officer meets Air Force standards.)
NOT OBSERVED | BEARING OR BEHAVIOR INTERFERE SERIOUSLY WITH HIS EFFECTIVENESS. | CARELESS BEARING AND BEHAVIOR DETRACT FROM HIS EFFECTIVENESS. | BEARING AND BEHAVIOR CREATE A GOOD IMPRESSION. | ESPECIALLY GOOD BEHAVIOR AND BEARING. CREATES A VERY FAVORABLE IMPRESSION. | BEARING AND BEHAVIOR ARE OUTSTANDING. HE EXEMPLIFIES TOP MILITARY STANDARDS. ☒

AF FORM 77 JUL 62   PREVIOUS EDITIONS OF THIS FORM   12 JUL 1968   COMPANY GRADE OFFICER EFFECTIVENESS REPORT

V. OVER-ALL EVALUATION (Compare this officer ONLY with officers of the same grade.)

SPECIFIC JUSTIFICATION REQUIRED FOR THESE SECTIONS					SPECIFIC JUSTIFICATION REQUIRED FOR THESE SECTIONS	
UNSATIS-FACTORY	MARGINAL	BELOW AVERAGE	EFFECTIVE AND COMPETENT	VERY FINE	EXCEPTIONALLY FINE	OUTSTANDING ☒

VI. PROMOTION POTENTIAL

1. DOES NOT DEMONSTRATE A CAPABILITY FOR PROMOTION AT THIS TIME. ☐	2. PERFORMING WELL IN PRESENT GRADE. SHOULD BE CONSIDERED FOR PROMOTION ALONG WITH CONTEMPORARIES. ☐
3. DEMONSTRATES CAPABILITIES FOR INCREASED RESPONSIBILITY. CONSIDER FOR ADVANCEMENT AHEAD OF CONTEMPORARIES. ☐	4. OUTSTANDING GROWTH POTENTIAL BASED ON DEMONSTRATED PERFORMANCE. PROMOTE WELL AHEAD OF CONTEMPORARIES. ☒

VII. COMMENTS

FACTS AND SPECIFIC ACHIEVEMENTS: Capt Fletcher has performed in an "Outstanding" manner during the period of this report. As a Forecaster Team Chief he supervises six forecasters and five observers. The scope of his responsibility includes extensive and highly varied weather support to all USAFE, U.S. Army and NATO units in the European theater. Because of his outstanding professional skills and superior management techniques his team has been consistently the top performer in the USAFE Forecast Center in all of our products. He has provided many new and improved techniques and procedures for our forecasting section. Most recent and noteworthy is a study he initiated and developed for using ESSA VI weather satellite pictures in conjunction with surface and 850MB charts and the 850MB temperature fields to identify and track European air masses. His study is a major achievement and has aided immensely the analysis of sparse data areas. The results are being used in daily operations and have materially improved our forecast products. Capt Fletcher's outstanding ability to plan ahead and budget his time and that of his people, enables him and his team to produce with less manpower far more than our other teams. I have recently received several letters commending Capt Fletcher for outstanding support he has provided to field units. STRENGTHS: Capt Fletcher continually displays outstanding initiative, aggressiveness and technical competency in solving the most complex forecasting problems. As a leader he is unsurpassed. He is a creative thinker and is the most mission-oriented officer I have known. SUGGESTED ASSIGNMENTS: Capt Fletcher should be assigned as a detachment commander to expand his command experience and utilize his management skills. SELF-IMPROVEMENT EFFORTS: Capt Fletcher completed ECI Command and Staff College with very high grades. OTHER COMMENTS: Capt Fletcher is highly active in Cub Scouts and other youth activities. This officer has outstanding potential for the Air Force and should be given temporary promotion to major immediately. He has been consistently outperforming many majors I have known.

VIII. REPORTING OFFICIAL

Date of latest performance counseling _____

NAME, GRADE, AFSN, AND ORGANIZATION	DUTY TITLE	SIGNATURE
EUGENE B. LEWIS, FR26424 Lt Col, Det 21, 31 Wea Sq (MAC) Ramstein AB, Germany	DET COMDR	Eugene B Lewis
	AERO RATING Command Pilot	CODE 1	DATE 11 June 1968

IX. REVIEW BY INDORSING OFFICIAL

I agree. I am personally acquainted with Capt Fletcher's OUTSTANDING duty performance and personal conduct. He has been the driving force that stimulated and guided his team to clear superiority over all other teams in this large forecast center. He should be promoted to temporary Major immediately.

NAME, GRADE, AFSN, AND ORGANIZATION	DUTY TITLE	SIGNATURE
LLOYD C. HUGHES, Colonel FR15267, Hq 31 Wea Sq (MAC) Ramstein AB, Germany	SQ COMDR.	Lloyd C Hughes
	AERO RATING Command Pilot	CODE 3	DATE 12 Jun 1968

☆ U.S. GOVERNMENT PRINTING OFFICE : 1962 O—647040

LAST NAME-FIRST NAME-MIDDLE INITIAL	AFSN	ACTIVE DUTY GRADE
Fletcher, Robert M.	FR57874	Captain

(CHECK APPROPRIATE BLOCK AND COMPLETE AS APPLICABLE)

[X] SUPPLEMENTAL SHEET TO RATING FORM WHICH COVERS THE FOLLOWING PERIOD OF REPORT	[ ] LETTER OF EVALUATION COVERING THE FOLLOWING PERIOD OF OBSERVATION

FROM 1 Feb 68	THRU 7 Jun 68	FROM	THRU

Precede comments by appropriate data, i.e. section continuation, indorsement continuation, additional indorsement, etc. Follow comments by the authentication to include: name, grade, AFSN, organization, duty title, date and signature.

ADDITIONAL INDORSEMENT

I concur in the high rating of Captain Fletcher. His professional skills and talent for imparting instruction have contributed much to the professional growth of the young officers assigned to his team. Staff members of my headquarters have made specific comments on the effectiveness and enthusiasm of Captain Fletcher's team. I fail to understand why this officer has not been previously promoted to Major. He should be promoted now.

ROBERT R. OSBORN, Colonel, FR33334, 2 Wea Wg (MAC), Vice Commander, 28 Jun 68, Wiesbaden AB, Germany

ADDITIONAL INDORSEMENT

I am personally well aware of Captain Fletcher's performance and am anxious to lend my full support to this evaluation. He is an exceptionally capable, dedicated and mature officer who certainly should have been promoted before now. His record, when considered in light of today's inflated standards, definitely does not reflect his true performance or potential. I STRONGLY RECOMMEND HIS IMMEDIATE PROMOTION.

RUSSELL K. PIERCE, JR., Brigadier General, USAF, FR18118, Command Pilot-3, Commander, Air Weather Service (MAC), Scott AFB, Ill., 12 July 1968.

AF FORM 77a FEB 65   PREVIOUS EDITION OF THIS FORM WILL BE USED UNTIL STOCK IS EXHAUSTED   SUPPLEMENTAL SHEET TO AF FORMS 77, 707, 900, 910, 911 AND 475

CITATION TO ACCOMPANY THE AWARD OF

THE AIR FORCE COMMENDATION MEDAL

TO

ROBERT M. FLETCHER

Captain Robert M. Fletcher distinguished himself by meritorious service as a Forecaster Team Chief, Detachment 21, 31st Weather Squadron from 15 December 1966 to 8 July 1968. During this period Captain Fletcher provided new and revised concepts and procedures which stimulated the growth of professionalism and contributed materially to the outstanding mission accomplishment of the USAFE Forecast Center. The distinctive accomplishments of Captain Fletcher reflect credit upon himself and the United States Air Force.

THE AIRFORCE COMMENDATION MEDAL

RAMSTEIN FORECAST CENTER

RAMSTEIN AIR BASE, GERMANY

FORT BRAGG,
NORTH CAROLINA,
1968-1970

▶ SIMMONS ARMY AIR FIELD

I was surprised to find that the Army had no weather personnel. Air Force weather personnel were attached to the Army units. In the case of airborne, all weather guys had to be parachute jump qualified. At this time, to be in "jump status" meant extra pay. To get this pay, you had to jump at least once every 3 months.

Before I got this assignment, no one ever asked me if I wanted to jump! I would have said "no"! So here I am in a unit where everyone was jump qualified! And I am expected to go to jump school on Ft. Bragg and become jump qualified. More on this later.

I was the commander of the weather detachment. My first command. I loved the job, but it came with a lot of unusual responsibilities, like bailing one of your airmen out of jail downtown in the middle of the night or fending off creditors after your men, etc.

I was the staff weather officer to the 18th Airborne Corps (3 Star General) and the commander of the 82nd Airborne Division (2 Star General). I had to learn a lot of Army protocol.

The Generals' wives threw a lot of outdoor tea parties and social events. They thought I was their personal weatherman. I really sweated out a lot of forecasts for their outside activities! They would call me personally for their needs.

The Army Officers' Club was the largest I had ever seen, lot's of activities. The professional stripper, Gypsy Rosa Lee, gave a talk at the club once a year. She didn't put on strip shows anymore and was on a lecture circuit. The Army actually flew her to and from the base. The Airfield Lounge was next to my office. I talked to her twice. She was quite a woman and a real lady.

This was the period of the hippies and Vietnam War protests everywhere. The country was in turmoil. Also, there was something going on in the Congo in Africa at the time. The students were rioting and taking over the Universities. The airborne units were on constant alert. I was busy 7 days a week giving weather to them. They were ready to deploy to these universities at any time. Also, at one time, it looked as if the 82nd Airborne division would deploy to the Congo. I would go with them if they did.

This was the headquarters of the Green Berets. John Wayne filmed part of his movie "Green Berets" here. There were funerals and memorials going on 24 hours a day at every chapel on the base. So sad.

Doctor McDonald killed his family while I was here. He blamed their deaths on hippies. It was a famous case and went on for years. I think his quarters are still boarded up.

The airborne units were constantly going on maneuvers. All my guys (except me!) would jump with them and set up the weather facility. I would come later with the General. Most of the exercises took place in the jump zones and woods on Ft. Bragg. It was a huge base about 10 miles wide and 30 miles long.

The Generals went first class. They had their own compound with fences and guards around the perimeter. I had my own tent in the compound. I had a desk in the tent, which I used to make my forecasts and briefings. I stood in front of the General and his staff every morning and evening to present the weather for the exercise.

The General had his own mess tent. Only he and his staff ate there. I ate with them, for I was on his staff. We had silverware and china plates. Soldiers took our orders and brought the food. (I couldn't help but think of the contrasts with what I experienced in Korea).

We went on a 10 day deployment to Puerto Rico. Again, my guys jumped in and I came in the General's plane. This was a great trip. We were billeted in tents on the huge U.S. Navy base, Roosevelt Rhodes. There had been a lot of rain and we (weather unit) were ordered to get there as soon as possible. Well, the rain stopped and I had beautiful weather the entire week I was there. It was great! After the morning briefing, I went to the nearby officers club and beach. Both were beautiful. Had an evening briefing and then was free again. A vacation really.

All the Army staff members were jealous of my association with the Generals. They had a strict chain of command and could never approach a General directly. I could request and see him most anytime. After all, I was just attached (on loan so to speak) to the Army. I'll never forget one occurrence. We were camping out on an exercise in the woods of Ft. Bragg, and it poured rain for two days. The briefings were all about the rain and when it would stop. On the morning of the 3rd day, it was still coming down during the briefing. But, a good clean cold front was coming and I told the General it would stop by 2 P.M. I could sense the feeling of the staff members, "Ha ha, Fletcher's really gonna get it now! This stuff ain't stopping!" At 2 P.M., the rain stopped, the sun came out. I was walking across the compound. The General was on the other side. He yelled out loudly across the compound, "Great job, Captain Fletcher, great job!" I could sense the

disappointment of his staff members. I was a lucky forecaster!

We were in Army housing. A duplex and it wasn't too bad. Ft. Bragg is huge. Several P.X.'s and commissaries. And there was a Pope Air Force Base adjacent to Ft. Bragg,

The Army had a famous parachute team called the Golden Knights. They had always taken off from Simmons Air Field. I had to keep an eye on them. They knew I didn't jump and threatened to kidnap me and throw me out of a plane! They would have done it too.

The manner of doing things by the Army was quite different from Air Force procedures. My airmen were billeted in old WWII wooden barracks. Army sergeants were constantly inspecting our barracks by mistake. I have to say the airmen weren't as neat and proper as the Army soldiers. So, I was constantly having to explain to some Army officers why our barracks weren't up to Army standards. My airmen pulled shift work and some were always sleeping.

The Simmons Air Base was commanded by a Lt. Colonel. His office was a few doors down the hall from mine. He was constantly chewing out the Army pilots for buzzing locations, flying too low and landing in unauthorized locations. The pilots were pretty loose!

One day I told the airfield commander I had to go to Charleston, S. C. to pick up my '64 Fairlaine station wagon that had been shipped from Germany. He volunteered an Army plane and pilot to take me to Charleston Air Force base. It was a small plane and it was an exciting flight. From Charleston Air Force

Base, I caught a bus to the Navy yard and picked up my Ford. Again, the Army Air Force was pretty loose.

My weather observers called me one Sunday and told me a storm had damaged some Army planes. "Oh no, I thought. I am in deep trouble tomorrow!" Our weather observation post was in a tower. This tower had one solid wall. On a sleepy Sunday afternoon a thunderstorm formed in this direction. The weather observer was goofing off, not doing his duty, and didn't report the thunderstorm. The storm tore some small army planes from their tie downs and one was totaled.

I was ordered to report to the airfield commander. If this had been an Air Force Base, I would be in deep trouble. There would be an accident investigation board meeting and I could possible be canned and lose my job. I was shocked at what transpired!

The commander. "You know we lost a plane to a thunderstorm and we were not advised or warned." "Yes, sir." "Colonel _____ is quite put out with you about this. You better see him and apologize". Apologize!! Here I'm expecting my career to end and all I have to do is apologize!?! What a difference in Air Force and Army! "Yes sir. Right away, Sir!" So, I called the Colonel, explained about the visual problem, etc. He just said, "O.K, but don't let it happen again." Whew! What a relief!

My squadron headquarters was at Fort Monroe, Virginia. A beautiful, old place that has been active since the Civil War. This squadron handled all the Air Force weather people attached to the various army commands. The commander was an elderly full colonel.

My commander called me one day and told me there was a TDY (temporary duty) school class position open at the "Air-Ground Operations Center" at the Hurlburt AF Base in Ft. Walton Beach, Florida, and would I like to go?. A week in Florida in the middle of February! Yes!

This was to change mine and my family's lives forever!!

There was an Air Force shuttle plane that daily went around to several bases in the Southeast. I didn't think I needed an auto at the school, so I caught the shuttle at Pope AFB and flew to Hurlburt Air Base.

The school was very informative and interesting. Basically, it taught how the services cooperated with each other in battlefield situations.

Ft. Walton Beach, Florida

WOW!

My good friend from Okinawa, Louis Vegais, was stationed at Eglin AFB. He and his wife, Carolyn, lived in Piquito Bayou, Shalimar. He was now a Lt. Colonel. I visited them. He loaned me his motorcycle for transportation. He was part owner of a private plane and he flew me all over the area. He had flown me all around Okinawa when were were there. I was captivated at how beautiful the area was. He took me water skiing. I couldn't get over how clear the water was, and every time we got out of the boat, we stood on white sand. On all my previous water skiing over the past years, there was mud, mud, mud.

223

The city of Ft. Walton beach was dead on a Sunday afternoon. You wouldn't see 3 cars downtown. I'm thinking, "Wow! Just like Kissimmee was, this is an undiscovered paradise! I think I'll retire here someday."

Waterfront lots were $6,000 to $8,000. This was 1968. I thought that was too much. Those lots would be worth a half million later. I bought two lots behind Lou's house in Piquoto Bayou. They were each 100 x 200, almost an acre covered by huge pines.

Later we would build on those lots and make Ft. Walton Beach our permanent home.

As I said, at Ft. Bragg, I was in a jump position. The school was right there. Every time I got up enough courage to apply for the school, there would be a paratrooper killed, and I would chicken out. So, finally, I was told that since I wouldn't jump I would be transferred to Pope AFB and a jump qualified officer would take my place.

We lost our Army quarters and moved into a nice house in Cottonwood, a housing area of Fayetteville. It was a nice house and area.

We loved Ft. Bragg and we loved Pope AFB. The boys were involved in football and baseball. Pat taught at the Jr. High School on base. We were members of a bridge club group that consisted of some wonderful couples, both Army and Air Force.

We were involved in education. I participated in many school activities. I became the president of the PTA at Robbie's elementary school. The principal and I became good friends. I sold him our '64 Ford Fairlane station wagon. So many memories

associated with that vehicle. North Dakota and all over Europe.

I was notified that since I was not jump qualified, I would be replaced with someone who was. I was transferred over to Pope Air Force Base. Pope was adjacent to Fort Bragg. I really didn't mind getting away from the Army and getting back to the Air Force.

For some reason the Simmons Air Base Commander, The 82nd Airborne Division Commander, and the 18th Airborne Corps Commander liked me. I guess they were pleased with my support. They presented me with the Army Commendation Medal. This was an unusual thing to do for an Air Force officer. (Maybe their wives appreciated my help to them too!) Of course I was very proud to get this recognition from the Army.

OER

SIMMONS
ARMY AIRFIELD
FORT BRAGG,
NORTH
CAROLINA

IDENTIFICATION DATA (Read AFM 36-10 carefully before filling out any item.)

1. LAST NAME—FIRST NAME—MIDDLE INITIAL	2. AFSN	3. ACTIVE DUTY GRADE	4. PERMANENT GRADE
Fletcher, Robert M.	FR57874	Captain	Captain

5. ORGANIZATION, COMMAND AND LOCATION	6. AERO RATING	CODE	7. PERIOD OF REPORT
Detachment 3 16th Weather Squadron (MAC) Fort Bragg, N. C.	Nonrated		FROM: 8 Jun 68 THRU: 6 Feb 69

8. PERIOD OF SUPERVISION	9. REASON FOR REPORT
245	CRO

II. DUTIES—PAFSC E2524. DAFSC 2511. PRESENT DUTY: DET COMDR. Commands a weather detachment composed of four officers and 17 airmen which provides weather support to the XVIII Airborne Corps, the 82d Airborne Division, and other U. S. Army organizations at Fort Bragg, N.C., both in garrison and in the field. Provides operational weather service to organically assigned and transient aircraft operating from Simmons Army Airfield. Responsible for weather forecasts for large scale Army field training exercises including paradrop operations. Provides advice and assistance on weather matters to Army command staff personnel several grades his senior in rank.

III. RATING FACTORS (Consider how this officer is performing on his job.)

1. KNOWLEDGE OF DUTIES

NOT OBSERVED	SERIOUS GAPS IN HIS KNOWLEDGE OF FUNDAMENTALS OF HIS JOB.	SATISFACTORY KNOWLEDGE OF ROUTINE PHASES OF HIS JOB.	WELL INFORMED ON MOST PHASES OF HIS JOB.	EXCELLENT KNOWLEDGE OF ALL PHASES OF HIS JOB.	EXCEPTIONAL UNDERSTANDING OF HIS JOB. EXTREMELY WELL INFORMED ON ALL PHASES.
○	☐	☐	☐	☐	☒

2. PERFORMANCE OF DUTIES

NOT OBSERVED	QUALITY OR QUANTITY OF WORK OFTEN FAILS TO MEET JOB REQUIREMENTS.	PERFORMANCE MEETS ONLY MINIMUM JOB REQUIREMENTS.	QUANTITY AND QUALITY OF WORK ARE VERY SATISFACTORY.	PRODUCES VERY HIGH QUANTITY AND QUALITY OF WORK. MEETS ALL SUSPENSES.	QUALITY AND QUANTITY OF WORK ARE CLEARLY SUPERIOR AND TIMELY.
○	☐	☐	☐	☐	☒

3. EFFECTIVENESS IN WORKING WITH OTHERS

NOT OBSERVED	INEFFECTIVE IN WORKING WITH OTHERS. DOES NOT COOPERATE.	SOMETIMES HAS DIFFICULTY IN GETTING ALONG WITH OTHERS.	GETS ALONG WELL WITH PEOPLE UNDER NORMAL CIRCUMSTANCES.	WORKS IN HARMONY WITH OTHERS. A VERY GOOD TEAM WORKER.	EXTREMELY SUCCESSFUL IN WORKING WITH OTHERS. ACTIVELY PROMOTES HARMONY.
○	☐	☐	☐	☐	☒

4. LEADERSHIP CHARACTERISTICS

NOT OBSERVED	OFTEN WEAK. FAILS TO SHOW INITIATIVE AND ACCEPT RESPONSIBILITY.	INITIATIVE AND ACCEPTANCE OF RESPONSIBILITY ADEQUATE IN MOST SITUATIONS.	SATISFACTORILY DEMONSTRATES INITIATIVE AND ACCEPTS RESPONSIBILITY.	DEMONSTRATES A HIGH DEGREE OF INITIATIVE AND ACCEPTANCE OF RESPONSIBILITY.	ALWAYS DEMONSTRATES OUTSTANDING INITIATIVE AND ACCEPTANCE OF RESPONSIBILITY
○	☐	☐	☐	☐	☒

5. JUDGEMENT

NOT OBSERVED	DECISIONS AND RECOMMENDATIONS OFTEN WRONG OR INEFFECTIVE.	JUDGEMENT IS USUALLY SOUND BUT MAKES OCCASIONAL ERRORS.	SHOWS GOOD JUDGEMENT RESULTING FROM SOUND EVALUATION OF FACTORS.	SOUND, LOGICAL THINKER. CONSIDERS ALL FACTORS TO REACH ACCURATE DECISIONS.	CONSISTENTLY ARRIVES AT RIGHT DECISION EVEN ON HIGHLY COMPLEX MATTERS.
○	☐	☐	☐	☐	☒

6. ADAPTABILITY

NOT OBSERVED	UNABLE TO PERFORM ADEQUATELY IN OTHER THAN ROUTINE SITUATIONS	PERFORMANCE DECLINES UNDER STRESS OR IN OTHER THAN ROUTINE SITUATIONS.	PERFORMS WELL UNDER STRESS OR IN UNUSUAL SITUATIONS.	PERFORMANCE EXCELLENT EVEN UNDER PRESSURE OR IN DIFFICULT SITUATIONS.	OUTSTANDING PERFORMANCE UNDER EXTREME STRESS. MEETS THE CHALLENGE OF DIFFICULT SITUATIONS.
○	☐	☐	☐	☐	☒

7. USE OF RESOURCES

NOT OBSERVED	INEFFECTIVE IN CONSERVATION OF RESOURCES.	USES RESOURCES IN A BARELY SATISFACTORY MANNER	CONSERVES BY USING ROUTINE PROCEDURES.	EFFECTIVELY ACCOMPLISHES SAVINGS BY DEVELOPING IMPROVED PROCEDURES.	EXCEPTIONALLY EFFECTIVE IN USING RESOURCES.
Ⓜ Ⓟ	MATERIEL PERSONNEL	MATERIEL PERSONNEL	MATERIEL PERSONNEL	MATERIEL PERSONNEL	☒ MATERIEL ☒ PERSONNEL

8. WRITING ABILITY AND ORAL EXPRESSION

NOT OBSERVED	UNABLE TO EXPRESS THOUGHTS CLEARLY. LACKS ORGANIZATION.	EXPRESSES THOUGHTS SATISFACTORILY ON ROUTINE MATTERS.	USUALLY ORGANIZES AND EXPRESSES THOUGHTS CLEARLY AND CONCISELY.	CONSISTENTLY ABLE TO EXPRESS IDEAS CLEARLY.	OUTSTANDING ABILITY TO COMMUNICATE IDEAS TO OTHERS.
Ⓦ Ⓢ	WRITE SPEAK	WRITE SPEAK	WRITE SPEAK	WRITE SPEAK	☒ WRITE ☒ SPEAK

IV. MILITARY QUALITIES (Consider how this officer meets Air Force standards.)

NOT OBSERVED	BEARING OR BEHAVIOR INTERFERE SERIOUSLY WITH HIS EFFECTIVENESS.	CARELESS BEARING AND BEHAVIOR DETRACT FROM HIS EFFECTIVENESS.	BEARING AND BEHAVIOR CREATE A GOOD IMPRESSION.	ESPECIALLY GOOD BEHAVIOR AND BEARING. CREATES A VERY FAVORABLE IMPRESSION.	BEARING AND BEHAVIOR ARE OUTSTANDING. HE EXEMPLIFIES TOP MILITARY STANDARDS.
○	☐	☐	☐	☐	☒

AF FORM 77 NOV 66   PREVIOUS EDITION OF THIS FORM WILL BE USED UNTIL STOCK IS EXHAUSTED.   4 MAR 1969   COMPANY GRADE OFFICER EFFECTIVENESS REPORT

V. OVER-ALL EVALUATION (Compare this officer ONLY with officers of the same grade.)

SPECIFIC JUSTIFICATION REQUIRED FOR THESE SECTIONS								SPECIFIC JUSTIFICATION REQUIRED FOR THESE SECTIONS	
☐	☐	☐	☐	☐	☐	☐	☐	☐	☒
UNSATIS-FACTORY	MARGINAL	BELOW AVERAGE		EFFECTIVE AND COMPETENT		VERY FINE		EXCEPTIONALLY FINE	OUTSTANDING

VI. PROMOTION POTENTIAL

1. DOES NOT DEMONSTRATE A CAPABILITY FOR PROMOTION AT THIS TIME.	☐	
2. PERFORMING WELL IN PRESENT GRADE. SHOULD BE CONSIDERED FOR PROMOTION ALONG WITH CONTEMPORARIES.	☐	
3. DEMONSTRATES CAPABILITIES FOR INCREASED RESPONSIBILITY. CONSIDER FOR ADVANCEMENT AHEAD OF CONTEMPORARIES.	☐	
4. OUTSTANDING GROWTH POTENTIAL BASED ON DEMONSTRATED PERFORMANCE. PROMOTE WELL AHEAD OF CONTEMPORARIES.	☒	

VII. COMMENTS FACTS AND SPECIFIC ACHIEVEMENTS: During the reporting period Captain Fletcher performed his duties in an outstanding manner. He commands a 21-man detachment which furnishes weather support to the XVIII Airborne Corps, 82d Airborne Division, Simmons Army Airfield, and other subordinate Army units on Fort Bragg. He is also Staff Weather Officer (SWO) to the Fort Bragg post commander. (1) As a direct result of Capt Fletcher's initiative and efficient management of resources, the level of performance of his unit was raised from one of the worst to one of the best of 19 detachments in my squadron. (2) In the first two months after he assumed command, he solved a serious morale problem that had plagued detachment personnel since the unit was activated. His methods and approach to the problem now serve as a model for resolving similar enigmas throughout the squadron. (3) Capt Fletcher and his unit furnished a large portion of the weather support for the recent BRASS STRIKE III demonstration at Fort Bragg. In addition to making planning and operational forecasts for the demonstration, he performed SWO duties to the 82d Airborne Division for the assigned SWO who was absent on emergency leave. His performance of duty during the demonstration was so superior that I received several letters of appreciation from high ranking officers who were linked to or attended the display. (4) Capt Fletcher's unit was awarded the 5th Weather Wing Certificate of Achievement Award for unit training. (5) As a continuation of his objective to make his unit the best in the squadron he submitted the most constructive, comprehensive, and finest set of 1969 goals of any detachment in the squadron. STRENGTHS: Outstanding initiative and managerial ability combined with superior foresight. SUGGESTED ASSIGNMENTS: Due to his command and management ability, recommend he be given command of a larger weather unit. He is also highly qualified for duty as a squadron or wing operations officer. OTHER COMMENTS: Captain Fletcher has outstanding growth potential and I unequivocally recommend his promotion to Major as soon as possible.

VIII. REPORTING OFFICIAL

NAME, GRADE, AFSN, AND ORGANIZATION	DUTY TITLE	SIGNATURE	
LEWIS A. PITT, Col, FV794048 16th Weather Squadron (MAC) Fort Monroe, Virginia	Commander	*Lewis A Pitt*	
	AERO RATING	CODE	DATE
	Sr Nav	2	10 February 1969

IX. REVIEW BY INDORSING OFFICIAL I completely agree. I am personally acquainted with Capt Fletcher's outstanding performance. In addition to the letters of appreciation mentioned above, I have received one from the 7th Weather Wing Commander. It commended Capt Fletcher and his unit for support rendered to Exercise Linebacker. Typical of his superior management is his detachment's junior officer training program, which is one of the finest in over 40 weather units in this wing. Without reservation I strongly recommend his promotion to Major NOW.

NAME, GRADE, AFSN, AND ORGANIZATION	DUTY TITLE	SIGNATURE	
GEORGE E. RATH, Colonel FR5017, Hq 5 Wea Wg (MAC) Langley AFB, Va.	Commander	*George E. Rath*	
	AERO RATING	CODE	DATE
	Command Pilot	3	14 February 1969

U.S. GOVERNMENT PRINTING OFFICE : 1966 OF—258—529

LAST NAME-FIRST NAME-MIDDLE INITIAL	AFSN	ACTIVE DUTY GRADE
FLETCHER, Robert M.	FR57874	CAPTAIN

(CHECK APPROPRIATE BLOCK AND COMPLETE AS APPLICABLE)

☐ SUPPLEMENTAL SHEET TO RATING FORM WHICH COVERS THE FOLLOWING PERIOD OF REPORT	☒ LETTER OF EVALUATION COVERING THE FOLLOWING PERIOD OF OBSERVATION

FROM	THRU	FROM	THRU
		12 August 1968	27 January 1969

Precede comments by appropriate data, i.e. section continuation, indorsement continuation, additional indorsement, etc. Follow comments by the authentication to include: name, grade, AFSN, organization, duty title, date and signature.

FACTS AND SPECIFIC ACHIEVEMENTS: CPT Fletcher has performed in an outstanding manner during the period of this report. I have observed his duty performance and the operations of his detachment almost daily. Seldom have I seen a company grade officer possess such extensive knowledge in his field of work and such managerial ability in his command as does CPT Fletcher. Upon his assignment to Fort Bragg he immediately made himself known to all the members of my staff and began tackling weather support problems. On his own initiative he requested to be included in all my staff functions. He has contributed positive results and improved considerably the rapport between Detachment 3 and my Command. In the short while he has been here he has revised and rewritten all the Letters of Agreement between his Detachment and my Command. These difficult to write documents are now the most professional and effective I have known. Several large field exercises have taken place on Fort Bragg for which Detachment 3 was tasked for weather support. That CPT Fletcher was able to fully support these exercises and my Command simultaneously is a tribute to his ability as a Commander. After having been here only a short while, CPT Fletcher, through persistent personal effort, solved a serious morale problem in his Detachment. The overall morale and effectiveness of his Detachment have increased considerably since he took command. CPT Fletcher is the first weather officer I have known who is able to interpret and use the weather satellite pictures as an aid to forecasting. He is teaching his forecasters the use of this important tool, and he has taken the time to explain their use to me and my staff. STRENGTHS: Besides CPT Fletcher's extensive knowledge of forecasting, his sincerity and aggressiveness in helping us with our weather problems are his greatest strengths. SUGGESTED ASSIGNMENTS: After an appropriate amount of experience as a detachment commander on a U. S. Army Post, CPT Fletcher would make an outstanding staff weather officer at Corps or Army level. OTHER COMMENTS: CPT Fletcher has assimilated himself into U. S. Army functions with an enthusiastic spirit. His personal character, conduct and military bearing have enhanced the image of the Air Force officer on this Post. <u>I rate CPT Fletcher in the top 02% of all captains I have known.</u>

RAYMOND FOREHAND, LTC, ARTY
Commanding, Simmons Army Aviation Command
Fort Bragg, North Carolina

ADDITIONAL INDORSEMENT

The weather support provided by CPT Fletcher to this Post has been outstanding. We have placed many varied, demanding and exacting requirements upon him and his detachment, and they have never failed to exceed all our expectations. I commend CPT Fletcher for his performance during the period of this report.

CADER C. TERRELL, COL, INF
Deputy Post Commander
Fort Bragg, North Carolina

AF FORM 77a
FEB 65
PREVIOUS EDITION OF THIS FORM
WILL BE USED UNTIL STOCK IS EXHAUSTED
GPO : 1965 O—764-110
SUPPLEMENTAL SHEET TO AF FORMS 77, 707, 909, 910, 911 AND 475

U.S. ARMY COMMENDATION MEDAL

SIMMONS ARMY AIRFIELD

FORT BRAGG, NORTH CAROLINA

The Secretary of the Army has awarded the Army Commendation Medal to

CAPTAIN ROBERT M. FLETCHER
UNITED STATES AIR FORCE

for meritorious service:

Captain Robert M. Fletcher, United States Air Force, distinguished himself by meritorious service as Commander of the United States Air Force Weather Detachment, Simmons Army Airfield, Fort Bragg, North Carolina, during the period August 1968 to August 1969. During this period Captain Fletcher provided outstanding weather forecasting support to the XVIII Airborne Corps, 82d Airborne Division, Simmons Army Aviation Command, and other aviation units on Fort Bragg. Through personal initiative and effort Captain Fletcher acquired a thorough and comprehensive knowledge of Army aircraft, Army flight operations, and Army field exercises. He actively sought and found solutions to many weather support problems in the Simmons Army Airfield - Fort Bragg - Pope Air Force Base Complex. Captain Fletcher's efforts added immensely to the safety of Fort Bragg in the areas of severe weather warning procedures and flight safety, thus greatly reducing the number of weather caused accidents and incidents. Captain Fletcher developed the United States Air Force Weather Detachment at Simmons Army Airfield into an outstanding unit through his untiring devotion to mission accomplishment and his professional skill as a forecaster and supervisor. This was evidenced by the extremely high esprit de corps of his personnel, the rapport he and his airmen have with United States Army personnel with whom they work and, most important, the outstanding weather support he rendered to the Simmons Army Aviation Command and to units of the 82d Airborne Division and XVIII Airborne Corps in the field. Captain Fletcher's selfless and productive efforts were directed toward exceeding mission requirements of his unit and have contributed significantly to the accomplishment of the missions assigned Fort Bragg units involved in aircraft operations and field exercises. The outstanding manner in which Captain Fletcher performed his duties reflects great credit upon himself, his unit, and the military service.

18

FAYETTEVILE,
NORTH CAROLINA,
1970-1971

▶ POPE AIR FORCE BASE

PROMOTION TO
MAJOR POPE AFB

I became Commander of the weather detachment at Pope Air Force Base. It was a larger unit than the one at Simmons Army Base on Ft. Bragg.

We supported a C-119 cargo aircraft squadron, which was phasing out and being replaced by C-130's. Also, a C-130 squadron. These planes supported the airborne operations of Ft. Bragg. We flew the paratroopers everywhere. I was now in a new weather squadron and it was headquartered at Shaw AFB, S.C.

T.V. weather briefings were in their infancy at this time. We had cameras and a setup to give T.V. briefings to all the units. It was a headache! The equipment didn't work half the time.

We were involved in numerous exercises with the paratroopers. There were several large drop zones on Ft. Bragg. We were responsible for the weather support there. This was a headache to support too. Accidents out there were common. Many times in the middle of the night, I would get a call from my station "Sir, the troopers are in the trees again." I had a plan: get up, go to the weather station, find out what happened, check the weather at the time of incident, how we had forecasted, etc. About 7 A.M. the call would come. "General so and so wants you in his office immediately". There he would have the C-130 pilot, his navigator, the ground controllers, etc. Someone had to take the blame for the troopers landing in the trees instead of on the designated drop zone.

I was lucky. The wind forecasts were correct. Usually it was the navigator who put them over the wrong spot to jump and they wound up in the trees. On one mission, the troopers were supposed to land in a river. They would come in above the water, release their harnesses and drop into the water. It had been raining that night. A wet, shiny paved road was mistaken for the river. The troopers dropped on the road! There were a lot of casualties. Lots of broken legs and arms.

Not only were we responsible for the safety of the base and all flying operations and Army paratroop operations, Ft. Bragg and Pope AFB had a constant stream of worldwide military and government dignitaries visiting. Stands were erected on the runway near the weather station. For many of these events cannons were fired by the 82nd Airborne Division. The weather forecast for each even was critical. A military staff would be supervising our weather operations.

These were statements on my OER's from Commanders:

"During the recent Wing Operational Readiness Inspection Major Fletcher personally supervised the weather forecast section. He correctly forecasted a severe squall line situation and briefed me in sufficient time for me to make the decision to delay night operations for 24 hours. The squall line moved through the area as forcasted. Had the decision to delay not been made many aircraft and numerous Air Force and Army personnel might have been placed in an unsafe situation."

— Commander, 464th Tactical Airlift Wing, TAC

"In another instance the Italian Minister of Defense was due to land while many military and civilian dignitaries waited to present full military honors. Weather conditions for landing were marginal. When the aircraft was on final approach the field was placed below weather landing minimums by an unrepresentative visibility observation

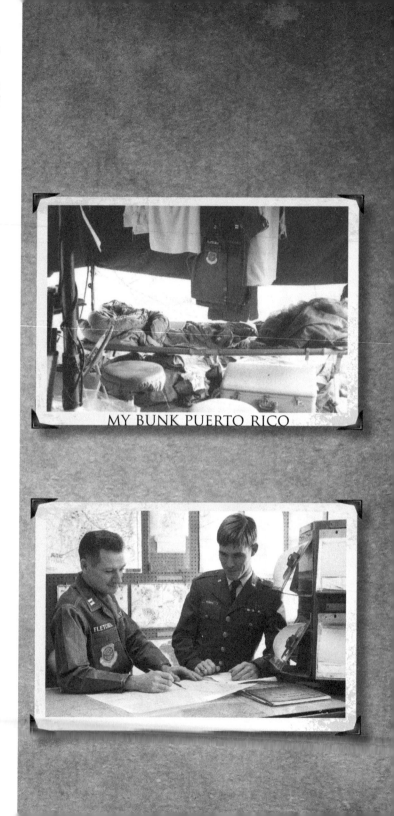

MY BUNK PUERTO RICO

232

Weather Units Observe 100th Year

DISCUSSES CHARTS - - Major Robert Fletcher, Detachment 20, 3rd Weather Squadron commander, (left), discusses a weather chart with First Lieutenant Edwin Marston (right), and Technical Sergeant Clifford Sanders (center). Both are weather forecasters with Det. 20.

recorded by the runway visibility recorder. Major Fletcher was notified of the critical situation. In less than three minutes he proceeded to the weather observation site, correctly diagnosed the visibility recorder problem, and made a personal official weather observation which placed the field above weather landing minimums. Due to Major Fletcher's prompt action the aircraft was permitted to land, and the ceremonies proceed on schedule."

— Commander, 839th Air Division, TAC

The astronauts were going to land on the moon. I bought our first color T.V. in Fayetteville so we could watch the landing.

One day just outside the weather station, an airman was leaning against the propeller of a C-130. Lightning hit the blade above him, traveled down the one he was leaning on and into the ground. He was knocked unconscious. But, he lived. They said the only thing that saved his life was that his flight suit had so many zippers they carried the charge into the ground. Unfortunately, he was permanently scarred with zipper marks on his body.

In another instance a soldier in a tank was riding halfway out of the turret. Lightning struck him and he was killed. No one else in the tank was injured. There was an investigation. We had out a thunderstorm warning so we weren't held responsible.

One day I gave a weather briefing to Neil Armstrong, one of the astronauts who landed on the moon.

I got two C-130 hops back to Europe. One was to Lakenheath Air Base near London. I had a good tour of London. I enjoyed the Soho area and Trafalgar Square. Lord Nelson's statue and monument was impressive. I also walked around the Parliment Building, listened to Big Ben boom out the hour. Saw the Crown Jewels in Old Bailey Museum. Such glitter! Most jewels I ever saw in one place. London Bridge wasn't there. It had been moved to Lake Havasu Arizona, USA. I have seen it there. The Imperial Museum was great. So much English Military History. Uniforms and armaments from every British War. In the churches it was interesting to read the plaques that covered the walls that told about fallen soldiers all over the globe. Strange seeing all the tombs under the floors of the churches.

In St. James Cathedral there is a huge book listing all the American servicemen stationed in England and then killed in Europe in WWII. Every day a priest turns a page, reads the names of those listed on the page, and says a prayer for them. I was shown the page with my brother's name on it. He was KIA in France July 23, 1944. He was only 19 at the time. So sad. So sad.

I had to visit the famous home of all the British Prime Ministers, #10 Downing Street. I stood there in front of the front door. I was engulfed with past historical events associated with this place. Winston Churchill had gone in and out of that door. I was surprised at how nondescript the place was. It was just a large section of a long line of regular looking apartment buildings. It has a beautiful wrought iron fence in front of it. I have seen this scene in many news reports over the years and the place still looks the same.

I had to try the famous London "fish and chips" I had heard and read about all my life. I went down

234

to the Thames River and found a small restaurant that specialized in "fish and chips". The plate just consisted of small pieces of fried fish and fried potato slices. I was disappointed. It was nothing special.

My other hop was to Rhein-Main Air Base in Frankfurt, Germany. My family and I had flown to and out of here several years earlier. I took a taxi out to Hedernheim where I had met Tommy and Phyllis. All the military housing was gone, replaced by upscale German homes. The stone wall and apple trees along the river were still there. So many memories of Phyllis. I saw no military around Frankfurt. Strange. Unrecognizable from the old days.

FIREPOWER DEMONSTRATIONS

Once a year, the Air Force and Army units on Ft. Bragg put on a huge show called "Firepower Demonstrations". Dignitaries and military from all over the world would attend this event. It was quite thrilling. You had a grandstand seat on a hill. There were old trucks, tanks, buildings, etc., set up on another hill about 1 mile away. Artillery shells would be screaming over your head and hitting trucks and tanks on the far hill. Machine guns and smaller artillery would be destroying targets closer in front. Fighter bombers would fly low and strafe and bomb the tank, trucks, etc. It was quite a show and went on for 3 days.

On the third day, there was inclement (bad) weather. Unfortunately, there was a bad accident. Two fighter bombers, F-4 and F-106, after the strafing runs, and heading back to their bases, collided with each other and crashed.

I was on the Pope AFB crash investigator team. I had to go immediately to the crash site and investigate what happened. The crash was about 40 miles South of Fayetteville on a small Indian reservation. In a wide turn, and at a very low elevation because of the weather, they had collided. The F-106 went straight in and the pilot died immediately. I saw the smoke, but didn't go to that site. The F-4 went through the top of a huge oak tree in an Indian farmer's yard. Several family members were on the front porch and they were traumatized. After going through the top of a tree, the F-4 hit the ground in a cotton field. It made a swath through the field, entered a stand of pines, disintegrated and the engine was the most forward piece. The pilot was killed. As I walked along the path of the plane through the pines, I heard flies buzzing and I knew what that meant. I saw the pilot's arm in the brush. I got out of there! It wasn't my job to pick up body pieces this time. The scene brought back memories of the crash site I went to when I was in the medics at Robins AFB, GA, in 1950.

There was a big investigation, of course. It took place on Seymore- Johnson AFB, Goldsboro, N.C. about 100 miles east of Fayetteville.

Weather appeared to be a major factor in the accident. The planes didn't have far to fly after participating in the demonstration. They were trying to fly VFR (Visual Flight Rules) which meant they were trying to stay in the clear under the clouds. They were too low above the ground. The planes had different types of controls. In a turn they collided.

I had to defend my unit's handling of the weather that day. Thank goodness the forecasts were correct. We took weather observations and the site of the demonstration. These were correct. Some observations showed that the weather at the demonstration site was below minimums for the type of flying demonstration. These were passed to the commander of the flight demonstrations, a 1-Star General. It was shown that he should have canceled the show. But, he chose not to. The conclusion of the accident investigation board was that he was negligent and this led to the crashes. He had a hearing and had to retire.

I spent several weeks TDY on that board. It was quite an experience!

Whew! My unit and I were absolved of any blame!!

The wing Commander on Pope liked me for some reason. During an ORI (Operation Readiness Inspection) the weather delayed the Operation for a couple of days. Our forecasts and observations were perfect. He was so appreciative of our work he requested a Commendation Medal for me. It was approved and awarded. I already had the Medal for my work in the Ramstien AB Forecast Center. So this was called "An Oakleaf Cluster". Any airman is proud to get one of these. And it helped to have this on your record.

Mae and "B" came up for a few days. We went on a tour of the outer banks of North Carolina and to Virginia Beach and Norfolk. We visited an older sister of mine, Hazel, in Norfolk. We visited the General Douglas MacArthur Museum there. He and his wife are entombed there in the rotunda of the building. All his gifts from foreign governments are on display, thousand of unusual objects, very beautiful and interesting. His staff car he used in Japan was there. It was a black Buick. I remembered his getting in and out of that car when I saw him in Japan in 1950 or 1951.

I was soon to get another transfer from Pope AFB to Vietnam.

Another exciting, unusual and interesting assignment.

Off to another adventure!

I. IDENTIFICATION DATA (Read AFM 36-10 carefully before filling out any item.)

1. LAST NAME—FIRST NAME—MIDDLE INITIAL	2. AFSN	3. ACTIVE DUTY GRADE	4. PERMANENT GRADE
Fletcher, Robert M	SSAN 253-38-3765FR	Major	Capt

5. ORGANIZATION AND COMMAND	6. AERO RATING	CODE	7. PERIOD OF REPORT
Detachment 20	Nonrated		FROM: 11 Aug 69 THRU: 10 Aug 70
3 Weather Squadron			

8. PERIOD OF SUPERVISION	9. REASON FOR REPORT
Pope AFB, NC (MAC)	
365	No report 1 yr

II. DUTIES—PAFSC A2516 **DAFSC** A2516 PRESENT DUTY: DET COMDR. Supervises all activities of a weather detachment which provides forecasting and observing service, 24 hrs a day, to the USAF Tac Airlift Center; 839 Air Div; 464 Troop Carrier Wing. As Staff weather officer to the Commander of the Airlift Center and 464 Troop Carrier Wing, presents formal and informal weather briefings, and interprets meteorological and climatological information in operational terms. Is directly responsible for the technical effectiveness of this detachment of 3 officers, 16 airmen, and 2 civilians, and its functioning as a part of the AWS world-wide meteorological network. Performs other functions and activities associated with or inherent in fulfilling responsibilities of command.

III. RATING FACTORS (Consider how this officer is performing on his job.)

1. JOB CAPABILITY
NOT OBSERVED ( ) | HAS GAPS IN FUNDAMENTAL KNOWLEDGE AND SKILLS OF HIS JOB | HAS A SATISFACTORY KNOWLEDGE AND SKILL FOR THE ROUTINE PHASES OF HIS JOB | HAS EXCELLENT KNOWLEDGE AND IS WELL SKILLED ON ALL PHASES OF HIS JOB | [X] HAS AN EXCEPTIONAL UNDERSTANDING AND SKILL ON ALL PHASES OF HIS JOB | HAS A FAR-REACHING GRASP OF HIS ENTIRE BROAD JOB AREA. AUTHORITY IN HIS FIELD.

2. PLANNING ABILITY
NOT OBSERVED ( ) | RELIES ON OTHERS TO BRING PROBLEMS TO HIS ATTENTION OFTEN FAILS TO SEE AHEAD. | PLANS AHEAD JUST ENOUGH TO GET BY IN HIS PRESENT JOB. | IS A CAREFUL EFFECTIVE PLANNER. ANTICIPATES AND TAKES ACTION TO SOLVE PROBLEMS. | CAPABLE OF PLANNING BEYOND REQUIREMENTS OF THE PRESENT JOB, SEES THE BIG PICTURE | [X] CAPABLE OF TOP LEVEL PLANNING; A HIGH CALIBER THINKER AND PLANNER

3. EXECUTIVE MANAGEMENT
NOT OBSERVED ( ) | IS A POOR ORGANIZER DOES NOT REALLY MAKE EFFECTIVE USE OF MATERIEL OR MANPOWER | MAINTAINS ORDINARY EFFICIENCY OF OPERATION. CONTROL COULD BE IMPROVED | GIVES ECONOMY OF OPERATION CAREFUL ATTENTION. MAKES WISE USE OF MANPOWER AND MATERIEL. | MAINTAINS EFFECTIVE ECONOMY. CAREFULLY WEIGHS COST AGAINST EXPECTED RESULTS | [X] HIGHLY SKILLED IN BALANCING COST AGAINST RESULTS TO OBTAIN OPTIMUM EFFECTIVENESS.

4. LEADERSHIP
NOT OBSERVED ( ) | OFTEN WEAK IN COMMAND SITUATIONS. AT TIMES UNABLE TO EXERT CONTROL | NORMALLY DEVELOPS FAIRLY ADEQUATE CONTROL AND TEAMWORK | CONSISTENTLY A GOOD LEADER COMMANDS RESPECT OF HIS SUBORDINATES. | EXCEPTIONAL SKILL IN DIRECTING OTHERS TO GREAT EFFORT. | [X] LEADERSHIP QUALITIES REFLECT POTENTIAL FOR HIGHEST LEVEL

5. EXECUTIVE JUDGMENT
NOT OBSERVED ( ) | DECISIONS AND RECOMMENDATIONS ARE SOMETIMES UNSOUND OR INEFFECTIVE. | HIS JUDGMENT IS USUALLY SOUND AND REASONABLE, WITH OCCASIONAL ERRORS. | DISPLAYS GOOD JUDGMENT, RESULTING FROM SOUND EVALUATION. HE IS EFFECTIVE. | AN EXCEPTIONALLY SOUND, LOGICAL THINKER IN SITUATIONS WHICH OCCUR ON HIS JOB | [X] HAS A KNACK FOR ARRIVING AT THE RIGHT DECISION, EVEN ON HIGHLY COMPLEX MATTERS.

6. HUMAN RELATIONS
NOT OBSERVED ( ) | DOES NOT GET ALONG WELL WITH PEOPLE, DEFINITELY HINDERS HIS EFFECTIVENESS. | HE HAS DIFFICULTY IN GETTING ALONG WITH HIS ASSOCIATES. | GETS ALONG WITH PEOPLE ADEQUATELY. HAS AVERAGE SKILL AT MAINTAINING GOOD HUMAN RELATIONS. | HIS ABOVE AVERAGE SKILLS IN HUMAN RELATIONS ARE AN ASSET. | [X] OUTSTANDING SKILLS IN HUMAN RELATIONS. INCREASES HIS EFFECTIVENESS.

7. WRITING ABILITY AND ORAL EXPRESSION
NOT OBSERVED (W) (S) | UNABLE TO EXPRESS THOUGHTS CLEARLY LACKS ORGANIZATION. WRITE / SPEAK | EXPRESSES THOUGHTS SATISFACTORILY ON ROUTINE MATTERS. WRITE / SPEAK | USUALLY ORGANIZES AND EXPRESSES THOUGHTS CLEARLY AND CONCISELY. WRITE / SPEAK | CONSISTENTLY ABLE TO EXPRESS IDEAS CLEARLY. WRITE / SPEAK | OUTSTANDING ABILITY TO COMMUNICATE IDEAS TO OTHERS. [X] WRITE [X] SPEAK

8. JOB ACCOMPLISHMENT
NOT OBSERVED ( ) | QUALITY OR QUANTITY OF HIS WORK DOES NOT ALWAYS MEET JOB REQUIREMENTS. | PERFORMANCE IS BARELY ADEQUATE TO MEET JOB REQUIREMENTS. | QUALITY AND QUANTITY OF HIS WORK ARE VERY SATISFACTORY. | [X] PERFORMANCE IS ABOVE NORMAL EXPECTATIONS FOR MEETING JOB REQUIREMENTS. | QUALITY AND QUANTITY OF HIS WORK ARE CLEARLY SUPERIOR.

IV. MILITARY QUALITIES (Consider how this officer meets Air Force standards.)
NOT OBSERVED ( ) | BEARING OR BEHAVIOR INTERFERE SERIOUSLY WITH HIS EFFECTIVENESS. | CARELESS BEARING AND BEHAVIOR DETRACT FROM HIS EFFECTIVENESS. | BEARING AND BEHAVIOR CREATE A GOOD IMPRESSION. | ESPECIALLY GOOD BEHAVIOR AND BEARING. CREATES A VERY FAVORABLE IMPRESSION. | [X] BEARING AND BEHAVIOR ARE OUTSTANDING. HE EXEMPLIFIES TOP MILITARY STANDARDS.

AF FORM 707 FEB 69   PREVIOUS EDITION OF THIS FORM WILL BE USED UNTIL 30 JUN 69. AFTER THIS DATE, PREVIOUS EDITIONS WILL BE OBSOLETE.   **FIELD GRADE OFFICER EFFECTIVENESS REPORT**

V. OVER-ALL EVALUATION (Compare this officer ONLY with officers of the same grade)

Specific justification required for these sections ... *Specific justification required for these sections*

UNSATIS-FACTORY	MARGINAL	BELOW AVER AGE	SLIGHTLY BE LOW AVERAGE	EFFECTIVE AND COMPETENT	EFFECTIVE-NESS WELL ABOVE MOST	EXCELLENT, SELDOM EQUALED	OUTSTANDING, ALMOST NEVER EQUALED	ABSOLUTELY SUPERIOR
☐	☐	☐	☐	☐	☐	☐	☒	☐

VI. PROMOTION POTENTIAL

1. DOES NOT DEMONSTRATE A CAPABILITY FOR PROMOTION AT THIS TIME. ☐	2. PERFORMING WELL IN PRESENT GRADE. SHOULD BE CONSIDERED FOR PROMOTION ALONG WITH CONTEMPORARIES. ☐
3. DEMONSTRATES CAPABILITY FOR INCREASED RESPONSIBILITY. CONSIDER FOR ADVANCEMENT AHEAD OF CONTEMPORARIES. ☐	4. OUTSTANDING GROWTH POTENTIAL BASED ON DEMONSTRATED PERFORMANCE. PROMOTE WELL AHEAD OF CONTEMPORARIES. ☒

VII. COMMENTS

FACTS AND SPECIFIC ACHIEVEMENTS: Major Fletcher is commander of one of our more active weather detachments and he has completely fulfilled his command and technical supervisory responsibilities in an outstanding manner. He provides complete weather support to every facet of a very busy air base and for a "one of a kind" USAF Tactical Airlift Center. (1) Letters of Evaluation from Commanders of 839th Air Division, 464th Tactical Airlift Wing and 464th Combat Support Group list several specifics regarding his activities in support of Special Exercises, Airdrop tests, total functions of a Tactical Wing and staff work at base level. (2) His detachment won the Pope AFB Ground Safety Award for 1969 and has maintained this fine record thus far in 1970. (3) He represented Air Weather Service and the Air Force in a very professional manner while on TDY as a member of a board investigating a serious air craft accident. His recommendations (one which touched on matters other than meteorology) have been adopted. (4) Physical appearance and working arrangements of the weather station have been improved. An expanded and improved maintenance work shop, which was started prior to this period was completed by self help. (5) Administra tive activities and all routine or controlled reports are always timely and accurate. STRENGTHS: Demonstrates good judgement with a high degree of technical competence. A completely dedicated and reliable unit commander. Wants more responsibility. Works diligently, unlimited initiative, very resourceful. SUGGESTED ASSIGNMENTS: Armed Forces Staff College would be very appropriate prior to an assignment on a squadron or wing staff for career broadening. OTHER COMMENTS: The Fletchers are highly respected members of the Army/Air Force community. He is on his third term as a member of a Ft Bragg School PTA Council; and is active as a Coach of Little League Baseball and Football. He is a professional member of American Meteorological Society. 5 Atchs. Letters of Evaluation.

VIII. REPORTING OFFICIAL

NAME, GRADE, AFSN, AND ORGANIZATION	DUTY TITLE		SIGNATURE
WALTON L. HOGAN, SR., Colonel 229-52 4776FR, 3 WSq Shaw AFB, South Carolina (MAC)	Commander		*Walton L Hogan Sr*
	AERO RATING Senior Pilot	CODE 2	DATE 10 August 1970

IX. REVIEW BY INDORSING OFFICIAL

I agree. Major Fletcher was selected for command of this detachment even though he was quite junior to others available for the assignment. He has produced outstanding results in satisfying supervisory, technical, and staff requirements of a complex operation. Recommend Armed Forces Staff College or Command and Staff College for increased formal training.

NAME, GRADE, AFSN, AND ORGANIZATION	DUTY TITLE		SIGNATURE
WALTER A. KEILS, Colonel 288-14-7937 FR, Hq 5 WWg (MAC), Langley AFB, Va.	Commander		*Walter A. Keils*
	AERO RATING Command Pilot	CODE 3	DATE 24 August 1970

¤ U.S. GOVERNMENT PRINTING OFFICE : 1969 OF — 332-940

LAST NAME–FIRST NAME–MIDDLE INITIAL	AFSN/SSAN	ACTIVE DUTY GRADE
FLETCHER, ROBERT M.	253-38-3765FR	Major

(CHECK APPROPRIATE BLOCK AND COMPLETE AS APPLICABLE)

☐ SUPPLEMENTAL SHEET TO RATING FORM WHICH COVERS THE FOLLOWING PERIOD OF REPORT

☒ LETTER OF EVALUATION COVERING THE FOLLOWING PERIOD OF OBSERVATION

FROM	THRU	FROM	THRU
		11 Aug 1969	10 Aug 1970

Precede comments by appropriate data, i.e. section continuation, indorsement continuation, additional indorsement, etc. Follow comments by the authentication to include: name, grade, AFSN, organization, duty title, date and signature.

FACTS AND SPECIFIC ACHIEVEMENTS: Major Fletcher has performed in an outstanding manner. As Staff Weather Officer to the Commander, 464th Tactical Airlift Wing, he has provided outstanding weather support. The 464th Tactical Airlift Wing is one of the busiest in the Tactical Airlift Command. The wing is involved almost continuously in a tactical exercise or contingency of local, national, or international importance. Also, because of the availability of paratroops and drop zones at Fort Bragg, other tactical airlift wings use the Pope Air Force Base facilities. These operational requirements impose extremely heavy demands upon the weather detachment and its resources. Major Fletcher and his detachment have never failed to meet these demands in a highly professional manner, nor fallen short of outstanding support for them. Major Fletcher's abilities encompass many areas. He is equally proficient at presenting briefings to the commanders, staffs, and squadron formations; participating in command functions as a unit commander; or analyzing weather charts and preparing weather forecasts in the weather station. During the recent Wing Operational Readiness Inspection Major Fletcher personally supervised the weather forecast section. He correctly forecasted a severe squall line situation and briefed me in sufficient time for me to make the decision to delay night operations for 24 hours. The squall line moved through the area as forecasted. Had the decision to delay not been made many aircraft and numerous Air Force and Army personnel might have been placed in an unsafe situation. STRENGTHS: Major Fletcher is operationally oriented. He fully understands the impact of weather forecasts upon the Wing Commander's operational decisions. This strength makes him a most effective Staff Weather Officer for a tactical airlift wing. SUGGESTED ASSIGNMENTS: Major Fletcher has demonstrated his ability to manage his resources and accomplish his demanding mission under the most trying and complex circumstances. He is capable of commanding a larger unit or acting as Staff Weather Officer to commanders of higher than wing level. OTHER COMMENTS: Major Fletcher possesses the desirable traits for a staff officer. It would be a pleasure to have him as a member of my command.

N. T. Lawrence

N. T. LAWRENCE, Colonel, 164-18-8036FR, 464th Tactical Airlift Wing (TAC), Commander, 11 August 1970

AF FORM 77a SEP 68 — PREVIOUS EDITION OF THIS FORM WILL BE USED UNTIL 30 JUN 69. AFTER THIS DATE, PREVIOUS EDITIONS WILL BE OBSOLETE.

SUPPLEMENTAL SHEET TO AF FORMS 77, 707, 909, 910, 911 AND 475

* U.S. GOVERNMENT PRINTING OFFICE : 1968 O—320-737

LAST NAME-FIRST NAME-MIDDLE INITIAL	SSAN	ACTIVE DUTY GRADE
FLETCHER, ROBERT M.	253-38-3765FR	MAJOR

(CHECK APPROPRIATE BLOCK AND COMPLETE AS APPLICABLE)

☐ SUPPLEMENTAL SHEET TO RATING FORM WHICH COVERS THE FOLLOWING PERIOD OF REPORT	☒ LETTER OF EVALUATION COVERING THE FOLLOWING PERIOD OF OBSERVATION

FROM	THRU	FROM	THRU
		11 August 1970	4 March 1971

Precede comments by appropriate data, i.e. section continuation, indorsement continuation, additional indorsement, etc. Follow comments by the authentication to include: name, grade, AFSN, organization, duty title, date and signature.

FACTS AND SPECIFIC ACHIEVEMENTS: As Staff Weather Officer to the Commander, 839th Air Division, TAC, and the USAF Tactical Airlift Center, Major Fletcher has provided outstanding weather support. The very nature of airlift and airdrop operations demands prompt, accurate weather forecasts and information upon which the Air Division and Airlift Center Staffs must base their planning and decisions. Major Fletcher has shown that he is capable of optimum performance under extreme pressure. During a recent Operational Readiness Inspection (ORI) of a tactical airlift wing of the Division, strong surface winds adversely affected the night airdrop performance. It appeared the entire operation would have to delayed at least 48 hours until the winds subsided. On very short notice Major Fletcher was called upon to forecast when optimum wind conditions would prevail. The decision to airdrop again in less than 24 hours was based upon his forecast. The weather and winds occurred exactly as forecasted, and the operation proceeded to completion on schedule. In another instance the Italian Minister of Defense was due to land while many military and civilian dignitaries waited to present full military honors. Weather conditions for landing were marginal. When the aircraft was on final approach the field was placed below weather landing minimums by an unrepresentative visibility observation recorded by the runway visibility recorder. Major Fletcher was notified of the critical situation. In less than three minutes he proceeded to the weather observation site, correctly diagnosed the visibility recorder problem, and made a personal official weather observation which placed the field above weather landing minimums. Due to Major Fletcher's prompt action the aircraft was permitted to land, and the ceremonies proceeded on schedule. Major Fletcher is often called upon to provide, or make a technical evaluation of, a weather input into an Airlift Center test or study. He was highly commended by the Airlift Center Staff for the assistance and information he provided for the Verification of Airdrop Data Test. STRENGTHS: Major Fletcher possesses the faculty for knowing the long- and short-term consequences of his decisions. He considers the alternatives carefully; yet, he is able to make his decisions quickly and correctly. This is a most desirable strength in a weather officer. RECOMMENDED ASSIGNMENTS: This officer would perform effectively as a Staff Weather Officer to any level of command. OTHER COMMENTS: Major Fletcher and his detachment support a very active Tactical Airlift Wing and Air Base. The fact that he has done this effectively while providing support to this Command is a tribute to his command and managerial ability.

WILLIAM A. DIETRICH, Brigadier General, 445-14-4963FR, 839th Air Division, TAC, Commander, 4 March 1971

AF JUL 69 77a BE USES UNTIL BLOCK IS EXHAUSTED

SUPPLEMENTAL SHEET TO AF FORMS 77, 77a, 77a, 77b, 77a AND 475

CITATION TO ACCOMPANY THE AWARD OF

THE AIR FORCE COMMENDATION MEDAL

(FIRST OAK LEAF CLUSTER)

TO

ROBERT M. FLETCHER

Major Robert M. Fletcher distinguished himself by meritorious service as Commander, Detachment 20, 3d Weather Squadron, and as Staff Weather Officer to the Commander, 464th Tactical Airlift Wing (TAC) and to the Commander, 464th Combat Support Group (TAC), Pope Air Force Base, North Carolina, from 1 September 1969 to 15 February 1971. During This period Major Fletcher provided outstanding weather and weather Warning support to the 464th Tactical Airlift Wing and Pope Air Force Base. Major Fletcher's efforts added immensely to the outstanding flight Safety records of the 464th Tactical Airlift Wing and Pope Air Force Base. Major Fletcher's selfless and productive efforts were directed toward Exceeding mission requirements of his unit and contributed significantly To the accomplishments of the missions assigned to the 464th Tactical Airlift Wing and Pope Air Force Base. The distinctive accomplishments of Major Fletcher reflect credit upon himself and the United States Air Force.

THE AIRFORCE
COMMENDATION
MEDAL

POPE AIR FORCE
BASE

1971-1972

▶ TAN SON KNUT AIR BASE
   VIETNAM

▶ EGLIN AIR FORCE BASE
   FLORIDA

MY "HOOCH"

Lambro550

MY "HOOCH"

After 3 years in the Ft. Bragg, Pope AFB assignments, I knew I was due for another transfer and it would probably be overseas again.

Pat and I discussed my volunteering for an assignment to Alaska. She could make good money teaching, and the living allowances were so liberal, we could make and save a lot of money. We even planned on buying a Volkswagon camper and driving it to Alaska. So an assignment came in for me to be the commander of the weather detachment at Eilson AFB, Fairbanks, Alaska. Another cold weather assignment! Fairbanks area was just like North Dakota.

Well, I received news that the DETCO (Detachment Commander) at Eilson extended his tour for a year. Then in a short while I was alerted for an assignment to Okinawa.

Pat and I both did not want to go back to Okinawa! We decided I would volunteer for a one year tour in Vietnam. It just so happened that my squadron commander at Ramstein Air Base in Germany was now in charge of all personnel at HQ, Air Weather Service. I called him with my proposal. He fixed it. My assignment to Okinawa was cancelled and I was assigned to Tan Son Knut Air Base, Saigon, S. Vietnam.

Pat would keep the boys and stay in Fayetteville. She loved her job and many friends, and the boys were happy in school and with their friends. It was a sad farewell at the Greyhound bus station in Fayetteville. I had to take a bus to Atlanta and catch a plane to San Francisco.

I had a day or two to kill in San Francisco and decided to take a day's city bus tour of San Francisco.

While waiting for a tour bus at a bus stop, I struck up a conversation with a young woman. She was waiting for the same bus. Turned out she worked at the University of Georgia, and she was in San Francisco on some sort of conference. We had a lot in common and really enjoyed the tour together.

Took a bus out to the Travis Air Force Base. Same place as when I went to Okinawa in 1959. Lots of memories.

Flew to Tachikawa Air Base in Japan. Lots of memories here. I had flown in and out of here several times to Korea in 1951.

From Tachikawa to Kadena Air Base in Okinawa. Lots of memories here from 1960 – 1963.

From Kadena to Tan Son Knut Air Base in Saigon. First thing I noticed on deplaning was the oppressive humidity and heat.

I reported to in-processing and was assigned a small room in a barracks type building. I was a Major now and this rank is known as "Field Grade". Lt's and Captains were called "Company Grade". It was soon obvious to me that this was a "Company Grade" billet. I complained and was assigned a room in the "Field Grade" area. Only Majors and Lt. Colonels were billeted here. Full Colonels had their own area.

My quarters were really comfortable. A low single story building. A very large room. Not air conditioned, but cool enough. There were no windows. Just screen covered slats. Fresh air always. You looked out at thick banana trees. The banana trees lined the entire length of the building and they were full of bananas.

We had a full time maid and cleaning lady. She kept the room clean, changed the linens and washed our clothes. Our uniforms were done elsewhere. She kept fresh bananas on the table all the time. More about her later.

Our showers were in a separate building next door. We had barbeque pits out back and some of the guys cooked up some great meals.

One of my weather school buddies was stationed in the Azores. There they had access to the BX network in Germany. I got him to order me a Feinwerkbrau pellet pistol from Germany. This was the finest made in the world at that time. I spent hours target practicing out back of my "hooch" (this was what quarters were called). I could hit a thumbtack at 20 feet!

Food, food, food! The most elaborate and best in the world! The amount of food available to us was unbelievable! In our dining hall, all the cooks were Vietnamese. Every meal was like an elaborate buffet. Same at the officers club. Food and drinks were cheap. There was a large army compound on the base. They had a large swimming pool and their officer's dining hall was out of this world! Food, food, food! They also had a couple of hundred civil service American girls working there and the pool was always full of bikini-clad girls. That area made you forget there was a war going on!

I was eating so much I had to walk it off!! Every chance I got I would walk miles and miles. It was a huge base. The Vietnamese Air Force had a large section. Their families lived in huts. I walked through their area a lot because it was so interesting. Also, there was a large area where there were remnants of buildings and tent sites where the soldiers stayed during the half million man build up in the late 60's. I did a lot of walking and sight seeing.

I never went into Saigon. It was dangerous. At least one airman a week was killed there. The Viet Cong on motorcycles would throw hand grenades into bars and restaurants if there were Americans there.

We had a fabulous Officers Club. It was known as the largest one in the Vietnam. We had USO shows every week. We all would sing along with the entertainers. Once we had Miss America and her entourage put on a show! Beautiful! Beautiful!

Everyone of the shows knew our favorite songs. There were two of them. One was "We Gotta Get Out Of This Place" by the Animals. The other was "Hang on Sloopy" by the McCoys. (I always thought it was "Snoopy".) Everyone would sing them out loudly. Three or four hundred men singing. These were really fun.

In the toilets graffiti covered every stall. Men wrote about their thoughts of the war. These expressions were great. Overall, we had no confidence in the South Vietnamese and we knew the Viet Cong would take over eventually no matter what we did. Playboy Magazine did an article about this graffiti. I wish I had a section of those stalls.

There is something in any war zone that you won't find anywhere else. There is a camaraderie, a spirit, among all the military. It is hard to describe. You are all like brothers, all working for the same goal – to win the war.

I have never seen such tropical downpours of rain. It was as though it was poured out of buckets. There were huge drainage ditches all over the base about 10 feet wide and 6 feet deep. They would completely fill and spill over the roads. They would be full of fish from the Mekong River a few miles away. In just a few hours, they would be drained dry and the fish would be gone.

There was one of these ditches in front of the officers club. At times, we would stand in front of the club and watch some army guys in jeeps, who had never seen our base, come sloshing down the street and think the covered ditch was a parking area. Plop! The jeep went totally covered in the ditch! It was so funny seeing their facial expressions as they came up and splashed about!

MY JOBS

I was supposed to be the operations officer of a weather squadron. But, the American forces were being reduced, winding down and the Vietnamese were taking over more of our military operations. The squadron was being disbanded.

So, I was assigned as the Staff Weather Officer to a 2-Star General who handled all the transport planes in Vietnam. We had typhoons in Vietnam. Had two big ones while I was there. One of them wiped out one of the Army bases up near the DMZ (Demilitarized Zone) (Front Line) (Border between N. Vietnam and S. Vietnam)

A spine of high hills (small mountains) runs North-South through S. Vietnam, ending at the Mekong delta, just north of Saigon. There was no such thing as a cold or warm front. A wind direction is known as a "monsoon". You can have a "wet" monsoon or a "dry" monsoon. The "wet" monsoons of India are the most famous.

When the wind blew in from the East from the South China Sea, the area East of the hills would be "socked in" and the area West of the hills would be partly cloudy or clear. This meant very few military operations could be done along the sea coasts and the Eastern half of Vietnam. There could be very little flying. The Viet Cong would operate under the cloud cover and hide in the clear areas. When the wind blew from the West out of Cambodia, the West half of Vietnam would be "socked in". The Viet Cong would use the cloud cover to move supplies down the "Ho Chi Minh Trail".

So my job was determining when we could fly the transports. Sometimes the supplies would be air dropped. Visibility was critical. Sometimes our troops would need supplies while they were "socked in". The General would be on my butt about when the clouds would end so supplies could be dropped to our troops. He had a habit of pointing his finger at me and saying, "You better be right!" I knew hundreds of planes would be launched on what I said. That was pressure! I did a lot of praying! But, I was good and I was lucky. Never got into any serious trouble.

I also had to be good on another operation. The C-130's would fly low and drop a huge bomb on a parachute. The bomb was designed to explode at the surface so as to create an instant landing pad for Army helicopters. These were called "Daisy Cutters". The surface wind and direction were extremely critical. Again, a lot of pressure on me! But, I did O.K., for I never got any reprimands or trouble.

My office was in a "blockhouse" similar to the one on Okinawa. Huge screens showed the positions of all the cargo planes at any one time. Very interesting to see what was going on.

Right next to the blockhouse was a parking apron for C-130's. They were always unloading Vietnamese refugees there. They would just pile out the back of the plane. One day, an old lady walked into a turning propeller. She was killed in a gruesome manner. I saw the place right after it happened.

I talked to Pat weekly on the phone. I knew how to use the military phone system. I would call Ft.

Bragg or Pope Air Force Base and they would patch me into her home phone. The 12 hour difference in hours created a few problems. We also sent recorded tapes back and forth. Later the boys erased those tapes and used them. I'd give anything to be able to hear them now.

We were granted leave for R&R to the states. The Air Force flew me free to Travis AFB in San Francisco. I flew to Atlanta and then I took a bus to Fayetteville. It was a great trip. On the way back, I flew Atlanta to Dallas then non-stop to Hawaii. There I had a 6 hour layover. My brother, Louie, lived there. Had a nice visit with him and his wife and he took me to all the famous hotels and beaches. From Hawaii to Guam. From Guam to Clark Air Base, Philippines. From Clark Air Base to Tan Son Knut, Saigon. Quite a trip!

My maid wanted me to buy her a toaster oven in the States. I did and I hand carried that thing all the way. She was so happy to receive it. She was a wonderful lady. I often wonder what happened to her after the Viet Cong took over.

We had a large area on the base filled with Vietnamese vendors. It was interesting to stroll through to see all the beautiful unusual things. Can you imagine every piece of furniture in a house made of rosewood? I would love to have bought it all. I had a weight limit on shipping my things home. I did buy a large chest that holds silverware. It is still in the family. A beautiful piece.

For some reason my commander kept sending me on TDY trips all over Vietnam. I had to make an official investigation into regulation infractions by our airmen. Fights, drunkenness, drugs, dereliction of duty, etc. This was scary, for I had to hitchhike to the locations and back to Tan Son Knut. I must have ridden every type of army helicopter and plane, plus Air Force helicopters and planes. At times flying along low in a helicopter, I couldn't help but think, "There are Viet Cong down there. If we get shot down I'm in deep trouble." We never got fired on, thank goodness. On a couple of the bases out in the boondocks there were mortar rounds fired by the Viet Cong to the edge of the base. They were just muffled far off explosions, but they made me nervous. I spent a few nights under my bed with my flak jacket over my privates.

About nine months into my tour, the transport business fell off and the Vietnamese Air Force started supplying their own troops. Since I didn't have much to do it appeared I would take on the job of teaching Vietnamese weather forecasters. I really didn't want to do that. Out of the blue and to everyone's surprise, two Captain weather officers got off the plane and were assigned to us. Somebody back at Air Weather Service HQS really screwed up for we were reducing our staff drastically. I went to my commander. "Sir, those two captains have nothing to do. Let them teach the Vietnamese forecasters. I'm past 9 months in the country and can get credit for a full tour. Also, I have put in my retirement papers, and I'm going back to retire. Let them teach the Vietnamese."

He agreed and I was set up for rotation.

While at Tan Sun Knut Air Base, I got to thinking: I have over 22 years of active duty. I am 42 years old. If I am to start another career, I need to get started on it. I had a Masters Degree in Education. I had more than enough of everything to qualify for a state teaching certificate. So, I decided to retire from the Air Force and go into teaching.

I put in my papers. Everything was approved. I would be sent to Eglin AFB FL to retire.

I was eligible for a Bronze Star for just being in Vietnam. I turned it down for I didn't think I deserved it. But it was awarded to me anyway.

Flew back to Fayetteville on leave. Then down to Eglin AFB, Ft. Walton Beach, FL. Pat stayed in Fayetteville so she and the boys could finish their school terms.

I had a couple of months to pull duty at Eglin weather station. Because of my status, I was given a lot of odd jobs. I took on all the weather briefings out of station. The "Air Rescue Service" was headquartered at Eglin. They had rescues going on all over North America. I would brief the Commander on the weather at the rescue sites. The 33rd Fighter Wing was very active. They deployed a lot to Alaska. I briefed the Commander and staff daily.

I had a lot of time on my hands and started clearing the lots in Piquito Bayou. It was hard work, but I enjoyed it.

In Vietnam, I had drawn a set of house plans. Pat liked them. So, I set about finding a builder.

This was 1972. Ft. Walton Beach had exploded! Suddenly discovered! Thousands of houses going up everywhere! I couldn't find a builder! Finally, a lady I met in the construction business sort of liked me, and she said her husband's business would build my house.

Then, I set about finding a teaching position. I was well armed. I was certified to teach Physics, Natural Science, Earth Science, Physical Science, and Math in Junior High and Senior High.

So, I took my resume to all the high school principals in the area. Mister Reynolds, principal of Ft. Walton Beach High School, took a liking to me and offered

247

me a job teaching Physics. They only had one class. It was taught by a Chemistry teacher, and he was leaving. I eventually built the Physics section into 6 to 8 classes.

BACK TO THE AIR FORCE

I had accumulated over 90 days of leave time. My retirement was scheduled for October 1st, 1972. School started in late August. So, I was authorized to take "Terminal Leave". In other words, I could be absent on leave till my retirement date. So, I did this and joined the staff at Ft. Walton Beach High School.

My Commander wanted to know if I wanted an official retirement ceremony. I said, "No". I'll just salute for the last time and walk out the door. My retirement orders were mailed to me.

I. IDENTIFICATION DATA (Read AFM __-10 carefully before filling out any item.)

1. LAST NAME—FIRST NAME—MIDDLE INITIAL	2. AFSN	3. ACTIVE DUTY GRADE	4. PERMANENT GRADE
Fletcher, Robert M.	SSAN 253-38-3765FR	Major	Major
5. ORGANIZATION AND COMMAND	6. AERO RATING CODE	7. PERIOD OF REPORT	
1 Weather Group	Nonrated	FROM: 5 Mar 71	THRU: 25 Nov 71
Tan Son Nhut Afld, Vietnam (MAC)	8. PERIOD OF SUPERVISION	9. REASON FOR REPORT	
	218	CRO	

II. DUTIES—PAFSC A2516 . DAFSC 2516 . PRESENT DUTY: DIV STAFF WEATHER OFFICER. Performs

duty as Staff Weather Officer to the Commander, Hq Staff, and Airlift Control Center
(ALCC) of the 834th Air Division (PACAF). Presents daily weather briefings to the
Commander and Staff. Furnishes observations, forecasts, and climatological data for
plans which are used in the direction and control of the entire airlift effort in the
Republic of Vietnam (RVN). Performs liaison between the activities of the 834th AD
and the 1st Wea Gp. Acts as OIC of the ALCC Weather Section and supervises two officer forecasters.

III. RATING FACTORS (Consider how this officer is performing on his job.)

1. JOB CAPABILITY

NOT OBSERVED	HAS GAPS IN FUNDAMENTAL KNOWLEDGE AND SKILLS OF HIS JOB.	HAS A SATISFACTORY KNOWLEDGE AND SKILL FOR THE ROUTINE PHASES OF HIS JOB.	HAS EXCELLENT KNOWLEDGE AND IS WELL SKILLED ON ALL PHASES OF HIS JOB.	HAS AN EXCEPTIONAL UNDERSTANDING AND SKILL ON ALL PHASES OF HIS JOB.	☒ HAS A FAR-REACHING GRASP OF HIS ENTIRE BROAD JOB AREA AUTHORITY IN HIS FIELD

2. PLANNING ABILITY

NOT OBSERVED	RELIES ON OTHERS TO BRING PROBLEMS TO HIS ATTENTION. OFTEN FAILS TO SEE AHEAD.	PLANS AHEAD JUST ENOUGH TO GET BY IN HIS PRESENT JOB.	IS A CAREFUL EFFECTIVE PLANNER. ANTICIPATES AND TAKES ACTION TO SOLVE PROBLEMS.	CAPABLE OF PLANNING BEYOND REQUIREMENTS OF THE PRESENT JOB, SEES THE BIG PICTURE	☒ CAPABLE OF TOP LEVEL PLANNING, A HIGH CALIBER THINKER AND PLANNER.

3. EXECUTIVE MANAGEMENT

NOT OBSERVED	IS A POOR ORGANIZER. DOES NOT REALLY MAKE EFFECTIVE USE OF MATERIEL OR MANPOWER.	MAINTAINS ORDINARY EFFICIENCY OF OPERATION. CONTROL COULD BE IMPROVED	GIVES ECONOMY OF OPERATION. CAREFUL ATTENTION. MAKES WISE USE OF MANPOWER AND MATERIEL	MAINTAINS EFFECTIVE ECONOMY. CAREFULLY WEIGHS COST AGAINST EXPECTED RESULTS.	☒ HIGHLY SKILLED IN BALANCING COST AGAINST RESULTS TO OBTAIN OPTIMUM EFFECTIVENESS.

4. LEADERSHIP

NOT OBSERVED	OFTEN WEAK IN COMMAND SITUATIONS. AT TIMES UNABLE TO EXERT CONTROL.	NORMALLY DEVELOPS FAIRLY ADEQUATE CONTROL AND TEAMWORK.	CONSISTENTLY A GOOD LEADER. COMMANDS RESPECT OF HIS SUBORDINATES	☒ EXCEPTIONAL SKILL IN DIRECTING OTHERS TO GREAT EFFORT.	LEADERSHIP QUALITIES REFLECT POTENTIAL FOR HIGHEST LEVEL.

5. EXECUTIVE JUDGMENT

NOT OBSERVED	DECISIONS AND RECOMMENDATIONS ARE SOMETIMES UNSOUND OR INEFFECTIVE.	HIS JUDGMENT IS USUALLY SOUND AND REASONABLE, WITH OCCASIONAL ERRORS.	DISPLAYS GOOD JUDGMENT, RESULTING FROM SOUND EVALUATION. HE IS EFFECTIVE.	☒ AN EXCEPTIONALLY SOUND, LOGICAL THINKER IN SITUATIONS WHICH OCCUR ON HIS JOB.	HAS A KNACK FOR ARRIVING AT THE RIGHT DECISION, EVEN ON HIGHLY COMPLEX MATTERS.

6. HUMAN RELATIONS

NOT OBSERVED	DOES NOT GET ALONG WELL WITH PEOPLE. DEFINITELY HINDERS HIS EFFECTIVENESS.	HE HAS DIFFICULTY IN GETTING ALONG WITH HIS ASSOCIATES.	GETS ALONG WITH PEOPLE ADEQUATELY. HAS AVERAGE SKILL AT MAINTAINING GOOD HUMAN RELATIONS.	HIS ABOVE AVERAGE SKILLS IN HUMAN RELATIONS ARE AN ASSET.	☒ OUTSTANDING SKILLS IN HUMAN RELATIONS. INCREASES HIS EFFECTIVENESS.

7. WRITING ABILITY AND ORAL EXPRESSION

NOT (W) (S) OBSERVED	UNABLE TO EXPRESS THOUGHTS CLEARLY. LACKS ORGANIZATION. WRITE / SPEAK	EXPRESSES THOUGHTS SATISFACTORILY ON ROUTINE MATTERS. WRITE / SPEAK	USUALLY ORGANIZES AND EXPRESSES THOUGHTS CLEARLY AND CONCISELY. WRITE / SPEAK	CONSISTENTLY ABLE TO EXPRESS IDEAS CLEARLY. WRITE / SPEAK	OUTSTANDING ABILITY TO COMMUNICATE IDEAS TO OTHERS. ☒ WRITE / ☒ SPEAK

8. JOB ACCOMPLISHMENT

NOT OBSERVED	QUALITY OR QUANTITY OF HIS WORK DOES NOT ALWAYS MEET JOB REQUIREMENTS.	PERFORMANCE IS BARELY ADEQUATE TO MEET JOB REQUIREMENTS.	QUALITY AND QUANTITY OF HIS WORK ARE VERY SATISFACTORY	PERFORMANCE IS ABOVE NORMAL EXPECTATIONS FOR MEETING JOB REQUIREMENTS.	☒ QUALITY AND QUANTITY OF HIS WORK ARE CLEARLY SUPERIOR.

IV. MILITARY QUALITIES (Consider how this officer meets Air Force standards.)

NOT OBSERVED	BEARING OR BEHAVIOR INTERFERE SERIOUSLY WITH HIS EFFECTIVENESS.	CARELESS BEARING AND BEHAVIOR DETRACT FROM HIS EFFECTIVENESS.	BEARING AND BEHAVIOR CREATE A GOOD IMPRESSION.	ESPECIALLY GOOD BEHAVIOR AND BEARING. CREATES A VERY FAVORABLE IMPRESSION	☒ BEARING AND BEHAVIOR ARE OUTSTANDING. HE EXEMPLIFIES TOP MILITARY STANDARDS.

AF FORM 707 FEB 69   PREVIOUS EDITION OF THIS FORM WILL BE USED UNTIL 30 JUN 69. AFTER THIS DATE, PREVIOUS EDITIONS WILL BE OBSOLETE.   2 2 DEC 1971   **FIELD GRADE OFFICER EFFECTIVENESS REPORT**

V. OVER-ALL EVALUATION (Compare this officer ONLY with officers of the same grade)

☐	☐	☐	☐	☐	☐	☐	☐	☒
UNSATIS-FACTORY	MARGINAL	BELOW AVER-AGE	SLIGHTLY BE-LOW AVERAGE	EFFECTIVE AND COMPETENT	EFFECTIVE-NESS WELL ABOVE MOST	EXCELLENT, SELDOM EQUALED	OUTSTANDING, ALMOST NEVER EQUALED	ABSOLUTELY SUPERIOR

Specific justification required for these sections (leftmost group) ... *Specific justification required for these sections* (rightmost group)

VI. PROMOTION POTENTIAL

1. DOES NOT DEMONSTRATE A CAPABILITY FOR PROMOTION AT THIS TIME. ☐

2. PERFORMING WELL IN PRESENT GRADE. SHOULD BE CONSIDERED FOR PROMOTION ALONG WITH CONTEMPORARIES. ☐

3. DEMONSTRATES CAPABILITY FOR INCREASED RESPONSIBILITY. CONSIDER FOR ADVANCEMENT AHEAD OF CONTEMPORARIES. ☐

4. OUTSTANDING GROWTH POTENTIAL BASED ON DEMONSTRATED PERFORMANCE. PROMOTE WELL AHEAD OF CONTEMPORARIES. ☒

VII. COMMENTS FACTS AND SPECIFIC ACHIEVEMENTS:

Major Fletcher has performed in a superior manner. Letters of Evaluation from the Commanders, 834 AD, attest to the fact that he has performed his duties in an extremely efficient and proficient manner. The 834th AD, in its role of supplying all the combat airlift capability in RVN, is involved in nearly every combat action that takes place in RVN. Planning and execution of the mission requires the utmost from all the personnel involved. As the Staff Weather Officer, Major Fletcher was intimately involved in all the planning and direction phases of the airlift mission. He was able to solve every weather problem that arose. Examples of his superior performance were demonstrated during the past year when several typhoons swept the northern coastline of the Republic. The timeliness and accuracy of his forecasts permitted the airlift to be accomplished with no mission degradation and no damage or injuries to airlift personnel or equipment. The 1st Wea Gp has never received a complaint of any kind about the weather support furnished the vast organizational structure of the 834th AD; but it has, time and time again, received praise about the weather support provided by Major Fletcher. Through superior management and organizational ability, Major Fletcher reorganized the ALCC Weather Section in such a manner as to eliminate two officer spaces with no loss of mission support. STRENGTHS: Superior knowledge of his job and its requirements and the initiative and ability to perform this job in a superior manner. SUGGESTED ASSIGNMENTS: Major Fletcher has voluntarily requested retirement and is returning to the CONUS to a terminal assignment. Should he elect to remain on active duty, he is highly recommended for duty in any of the operational areas of the Weather Wings or at Hq Air Weather Service. SELF-IMPROVEMENT EFFORTS: Major Fletcher has completed 3/4 of the Armed Forces Staff College by correspondence. His grades so far have been with distinction. OTHER COMMENTS: The USAF and Air Weather Service need this type of officer. Every effort should be made to keep Major Fletcher on active duty. Recommend promotion well ahead of contemporaries.

VIII. REPORTING OFFICIAL

NAME, GRADE, AFSN, AND ORGANIZATION	DUTY TITLE		SIGNATURE
BOYCE M. SMITH, Colonel 432-20-4128FR, 1 Weather Group Tan Son Nhut Afld, Vietnam(MAC)	Commander		Signed
	AERO RATING: Master Navigator	CODE: 3	DATE: 7 Dec 1971

IX. REVIEW BY INDORSING OFFICIAL

I concur. During my visit to the 1st Weather Group, it was evident to me that the weather support being provided to the 834 Air Div was superior. Members of my staff who have visited Southeast Asia confirm that this is largely due to Major Fletcher's management and direction of the weather support for the division. I fully concur with the promotion recommendation.

NAME, GRADE, AFSN, AND ORGANIZATION	DUTY TITLE		SIGNATURE
MORRIS H. NEWHOUSE, Colonel 302-26-6945FR, 1 Weather Wing	Commander		Signed
	AERO RATING: Senior Navigator	CODE: 3	DATE: 17 December 1971

LAST NAME-FIRST NAME-MIDDLE INITIAL	SSAN	ACTIVE DUTY GRADE
Fletcher, Robert M.	253-38-3765FR	Major

(CHECK APPROPRIATE BLOCK AND COMPLETE AS APPLICABLE)

☐ SUPPLEMENTAL SHEET TO RATING FORM WHICH COVERS THE FOLLOWING PERIOD OF REPORT	☒ LETTER OF EVALUATION COVERING THE FOLLOWING PERIOD OF OBSERVATION

FROM	THRU	FROM	THRU
		25 March 1971	3 June 1971

Precede comments by appropriate data, i.e. section continuation, indorsement continuation, additional indorsement, etc. Follow comments by the authentication to include: name, grade, AFSN, organization, duty title, date and signature.

FACTS AND SPECIFIC ACHIEVEMENTS: Major Fletcher has performed as the Staff Weather Officer to the Commander and Staff, Headquarters, 834th Air Division, in an outstanding manner. Major Fletcher briefs the Commander and Staff daily. These briefings are professionally presented and pertinent to the weather support problems associated with the total airlift effort in the Republic of Vietnam. The mission of the 834th Air Division is to provide sustained tactical airlift and to maintain the air line of communications for all the Free World Forces in the Republic of Vietnam. To fulfill this mission rigid controls must be maintained by the Commander and the Airlift Control Center personnel on all airlift resources and missions. Major Fletcher and the Airlift Control Center Weather Section play an important role in this control by providing weather information that affects the scheduling and execution of operations. Major Fletcher's supervision of the Airlift Control Center Weather Section has insured the highest caliber of weather support, and the Weather Section has become an indispensable part of the Airlift Team. During the recent passage of Typhoon Wanda along the coast, Major Fletcher and his forecasters worked many extra hours keeping all airlift elements informed of the typhoon's progress. As a result very few airlift elements had to stand down and very few airlift sorties were lost due to the adverse winds and weather generated by the typhoon. STRENGTHS: Major Fletcher's background and experience with tactical airlift are evident in the manner he performs his duties and in his personal association with airlift personnel. He is a definite asset in the weather support role for airlift forces. SUGGESTED ASSIGNMENTS: Major Fletcher would perform well as a Staff Weather Officer to any level of command concerned with tactical airlift.

JOHN H. HERRING, JR., Major General, 137-12-3227FR, 834th Air Div (PACAF)
Commander, 3 June 1971

AF FORM 77a JUL 69   PREVIOUS EDITION OF THIS FORM WILL BE USED UNTIL STOCK IS EXHAUSTED.

* GPO : 1969 O—355-593

SUPPLEMENTAL SHEET TO AF FORMS 77, 707, 909, 910, 911 AND 475

LAST NAME-FIRST NAME-MIDDLE INITIAL	SSAN	ACTIVE DUTY GRADE
Fletcher, Robert M.	253-38-3765FR	Major

(CHECK APPROPRIATE BLOCK AND COMPLETE AS APPLICABLE)

☐ SUPPLEMENTAL SHEET TO RATING FORM WHICH COVERS THE FOLLOWING PERIOD OF REPORT	☒ LETTER OF EVALUATION COVERING THE FOLLOWING PERIOD OF OBSERVATION

FROM	THRU	FROM	THRU
		9 June 1971	8 November 1971

Precede comments by appropriate data, i.e. section continuation, indorsement continuation, additional indorsement, etc. Follow comments by the authentication to include: name, grade, AFSN, organization, duty title, date and signature.

FACTS AND SPECIFIC ACHIEVEMENTS: Major Fletcher has performed in a superior manner as the Staff Weather Officer to the Commander, Headquarters Staff, and the Airlift Control Center of the 834th Air Division. He provided weather forecasts and climatological information which was used daily in the overall planning and execution of the total combat airlift effort in the Republic of Vietnam. This was a difficult task in that there are vast areas from which no weather information whatsoever is available. Major Fletcher displayed superior skill and knowledge in forecasting for these "blind" areas. In one instance ground combat operations in the Tay Ninh City area were reaching a critical stage due to depletion of munitions and supplies. Adverse weather conditions prohibited resupply by air for several days. Major Fletcher forecasted a first break in the weather 24 hours in advance of its actual occurrence. Airlift resupply operations were based on his forecast. The weather improved as forecasted and the airlift resupply missions were completed on schedule. Several typhoons such as Harriet, Kim, and Hester swept the northern portions of the Republic and adversely affected flight conditions. During these periods Major Fletcher worked many extra long and arduous hours. Based on his forecasts, advance planning for airlift operations during actual typhoon conditions resulted in no adverse effects to mission accomplishment and no damage or injuries to airlift personnel or equipment. STRENGTHS: Profound understanding of airlift operations and how these operations are affected by weather conditions. Ability to make the right decisions quickly and instill confidence while under pressure. Technical competence in forecasting skill and superior ability as a briefing officer. SUGGESTED ASSIGNMENTS: Major Fletcher would perform well as a Staff Weather Officer or Weather Liaison Officer to any level of command. OTHER COMMENTS: Major Fletcher entered into the activities and functions of the 834th Air Division in an enthusiastic spirit. He was regarded by everyone as an actual member of the Division and was accepted as such. This total acceptance made him a most effective Staff Weather Officer. It would be a pleasure to have Major Fletcher as a member of my command. This duty was performed in Southeast Asia.

John H. Germeraad

JOHN H. GERMERAAD, Brigadier General, 517-18-4761FR, 834 Air Div (PACAF), Commander, 8 November 1971

PAGE 4 OF 4

AF FORM 77a PREVIOUS EDITION OF THIS FORM WILL BE USED UNTIL STOCK IS EXHAUSTED.

SUPPLEMENTAL SHEET TO AF FORMS 77, 707, 909, 910, 911 AND 475

CITATION TO ACCOMPANY THE AWARD OF

THE BRONZE STAR MEDAL

TO

ROBERT M. FLETCHER

Major Robert M. Fletcher distinguished himself by meritorious service as Staff Weather Officer, 834th Air Division, and as Officer In Charge, 834th Air Division Airlift Control Center Weather Section, Tan Son Nhut Air Base, Republic of Vietnam, while engaged in ground operations against an opposing armed force from 25 March 1971 to 17 December 1971. During this period, Major Fletcher performed in an outstanding manner while providing weather forecasts, observations and climatological information to the Commanding General, Headquarters Staff, and Airlift Control Center personnel of the 834th Air Division in their planning and execution of the entire combat airlift effort in the Republic of Vietnam. His professional competence, knowledge of airlift operations, and outstanding managerial ability contributed immeasurably to the overall success and effectiveness of the weather support mission in Southeast Asia. The exemplary leadership, personal endeavor and devotion to duty displayed by Major Fletcher in these responsible positions reflect great credit upon himself and the United States Air Force.

BRONZE STAR
MEDAL

VIETNAM

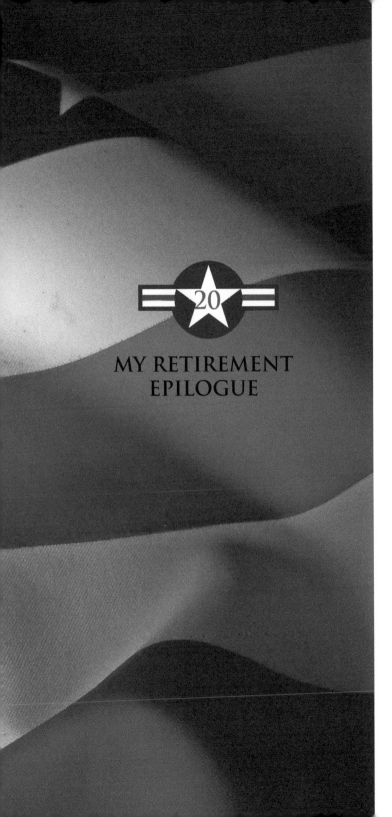

20

MY RETIREMENT
EPILOGUE

It had been a great 25 years in the United States Air Force. I have to say that I loved it. Now the journey was over. I had to start a new life.

…How can you describe your emotions?

I gave my last weather briefing to the 33rd FIS (Fighter Interceptor Squadron) at Eglin Air Force Base in August 1972. How many thousands had I given in the past!

I saluted my Commander for my last salute.

You hang up your uniform and think about how long you wore it and how it was a part of you.

I took the dog tags from around my neck where they had been for twenty-two years. They were a part of me. Thank God they never had to be used.

In my closet hung my fatigues, and on the floor my combat boots.

In a box went my medals. None for valor or combat I have to admit. I never fired at anyone and no one ever fired at me. There was a good conduct medal with second clasp (given only to enlisted). The commendation medals from the 82nd Airborne Division and 18th Airborne Corps, the forecast center in Ramstein and the Pope AFB commander, my Japanese Occupation medal with clasp for the occupation of Germany the United Nations service medal for Korean duty, the presidential unit citation from President Truman for my unit's work in Korea, the Sigman Rhee presidential citation for my unit's work in Korea, the Korean service medal with 5 battle stars. I was never in battle. You were awarded a star if you were "in country" during major battle

255

period. 1951 saw many major battles. The Vietnam service medal for "in country" service in Vietnam.

Well, that's the story of on airman's journey in the Air Force of the United States. I am proud of my military service. I feel in a small way I contributed to the defense of my country. The Air Force was very good to me and my family. Along the way I saw so much of the world. I now have a global view of everything that goes on in the world.

I live in an area with two large Air Force bases. I see many airmen in groups on base and in town. Sometimes I feel I am one of them and should join them. I guess I will always be an airman at heart. It's something you never get over.

EPILOGUE

This book was written for my sons and their families. I feel it may be of interest to many veterans of the time periods involved.

As of this writing I am 87 years old. I'm healthy and enjoying life. I have been very fortunate. I have two successful sons with great families. I am now the oldest in my family of thirteen brothers and sisters. There are only three of us left. The cycle of life.

After retiring from the Air Force, I taught at Fort Walton High School for 23 years. I taught mostly Physics. Also, Math, Earth Science, Physical Science and Meteorology. I was always involved with Pat's teaching and my sons' education. I think this is why I wanted to teach some day. I had the best students in school and really enjoyed being part of their lives. I still run into two or three a month, and it makes me feel good to hear that they enjoyed my class and how much effect I had on their lives. I still miss

them very much. I was 42 years old when I started teaching. I retired at 65. I think a teacher who has been "out in the world" makes a better teacher than one who has done nothing but teach.

Since I retired from teaching, I have worked for my youngest son, Brad. I enjoy the work and am glad I have a reason to get up early every morning. You have to be tired to enjoy resting.

Pat was head of the Math department at Pryor Junior High School, Ft. Walton Beach. She was an outstanding Math teacher. She developed breast cancer at the age of 40. She had a radical mastectomy which removed her left breast. She took a lot of radiation, but never lost her hair. The cancer seemed to be in remission, but reappeared in her ribs in the area of the removed breast. She slowly got worse. She was teaching at the end in a wheel chair. I had to take her often to the cancer center at the base hospital at Keesler AFB, Biloxi, Mississippi. As she got worse, she was taken to the cancer center at Lackland AFB, San Antonio, Texas. This is the base where I took basic training.

She got worse. Finally, she was transferred to Eglin AFB in Ft. Walton. There she got worse and went into a coma. Her Mom and I took turns staying with her in 12 hour shifts. I was with her when she died about 5A.M., July 30th, 1982. She just gasped for breath a few times and passed away. She was 45 years old.

Of course this was traumatic on all of us. I sold the house and bought a condo at the Breakers on Okaloosa Island, Ft. Walton Beach. I really loved it there.

I thought I would enjoy the bachelor life, but I didn't. I met Pam and we got married in 1984. She turned out to be a wonderful person. We have been married 30 years.

Pam wanted a house instead of a condo, so we bought a lot on East Bay in Navarre, Florida. It is a beautiful waterfront setting. We catch all the fish and crabs we can eat right off our dock. I never tire of the view.

We have a nice motor home. We have been to San Antonio several times. We've been all over the Northeastern and Midwest United States. We have toured the Northwest and Western U.S. We have been to Las Vegas several times. My brother, Monte, still lives there.

I am in the late December of my life. I can anticipate the future where I won't be able to travel anymore. The only real regrets I have had in my life are the deaths of Pat and my family members. Such is the cycle of life. I believe I was saved as a teenager. Wherever I traveled, religious services were part of my life. I worshipped in some strange places. I have strived to be a good Christian all my life. I expect to meet all my family members some day.

Goodbye for now. Thanks for reading this and thinking of me. I love you all. God bless and keep you.

As Frank Sinatra once sang, "I Did It My Way" and another: "Somewhere Along The Way, Love's Been Good to Me".

One more thing!

From the WWII 8th Air Force movie "12 O'clock High" and a hit song, "The Wiffenpoof Song" by Bing Crosby...

"...*We will seranade our Louie while life and voice shall last, then we'll pass and be forgotten with the rest...*"

How true...

I wish to thank Robert M. Fletcher, Jr,, and Leslie Williams. It is only through their hard work and dedication that this book was ever published. Thanks again, you two. I love you both.

Love always,

Dad

Robert

Papa Bob

Robert M. Fletcher
Major USAF (ret.)

Robert M. Fletcher